Sikh Philosophy
and Religion

Sikh Philosophy and Religion

11th GURU NANAK MEMORIAL LECTURES

Nirmal Kumar

NEW DAWN PRESS, INC.
USA• UK• INDIA

NEW DAWN PRESS GROUP

Published by New Dawn Press Group
New Dawn Press, Inc., 244 South Randall Rd # 90, Elgin, IL 60123
e-mail: sales@newdawnpress.com

New Dawn Press, 2 Tintern Close, Slough, Berkshire, SL1-2TB, UK
e-mail: sterlingdis@yahoo.co.uk

New Dawn Press (An Imprint of Sterling Publishers (P) Ltd.)
A-59, Okhla Industrial Area, Phase-II, New Delhi-110020
e-mail: sterlingpublishers@airtelbroadband.in
www.sterlingpublishers.com

First published in 1979 by Sterling Publishers, India

Sikh Philosophy and Religion
© 2006, Nirmal Kumar
ISBN 1 932705 68 6

PRINTED IN INDIA

Dedicated to

My mother-in-law
Shrimati. Malti Devi Chauhan1

The peaks are naked, frozen and white
Fresh snow sparkles laden bright
Himalayas from your kitchen window!
The moon shines terrible tonight

Angels bemused walk on tiptoes
Around the willow and the red rose
They know not fear they know not death
They keep no track of mortal dread

You said love is what humans make it
Zenith, mysterious to Angel and Cherub
Or misty cavern of a wizard demon
Where even witches fear enchantment

Love can be the rapid way to lose the soul
Or the high tide to drive the soul to afar Soul
Or audacity that dares insanity and reaches the goal
A bed of roses or thorns, whatever one reckons
Destiny or dice play with uncertainty
What a wonder love is - stales not; it is immortality

Has death taught you what life knew not?
The hidden half-truth or some unravelled knot
Revealing which Queen Death qualms not
Prudence, sanity and shame mute it not

I thought love was a beacon of God, the ray of joy
Blessing of Mother, human heart's little treasure
That world robs by obscenity, pain and ploy
Only stable love attains victory and eternal joy
Life wastes tied in worries, withers in tether
Love waits to awaken the heart with a feather

Hark! Is it mind's play or Divine vision?
Was it you, or waning shadow of rainy season?
A love struck fairy's dance by moon's glow?
Or magic pattern that moonbeams wove on snow?

A whisper in beats of heart I hear all the same
"Wisdom is love when it transcends form and name
Now talk not of minors, like pleasure and pain
Eternal joy and incessant wonder are love's gain."

Preface to the Second Edition

This book has been out of print for several years. The pressure of demand is perhaps the cause behind the second edition. I am grateful to the readers who wrote me about this book. The insight shown by some of the readers has strengthened my belief that when God inspires some body to write something he also gifts the inspiration to many readers to receive it. Such readers will receive this revised book not much as a gift from the author as by then it will have already appeared in their hearts in musical notes.

The wise say truth is the most common thing available. It is all around us. Yet truth is called a rare thing, since we see it and do not receive it. It is so mixed with worldly noise that we cannot separate and contain it exclusively. It comes and goes with the changing din of daily chore. It is only when the faculties of the heart and the mind and their powers—intuitions, thoughts, emotions and visions—get strung properly, like the players and the musical instruments in an orchestra, that the Divine, sometimes, plays the note that revives the lost memory in the soul of its existence in God, before creation. Then its sleeping ability to separate the milk of truth from the water of worldly noise awakens. The worldly noise is with us much more now than it was with Wordsworth when he had lamented: "the world is too much with us."

We pine for miracles. Isn't it a miracle that in certain hearts the milk of truth does not spill in the water of worldly noise? Perhaps political theories and social formulas cannot do what this little miracle can. It is as much a miracle as would be the staying of the scent of a rose in the surrounding air long after it had withered.

Amidst the many great achievements of the ten Gurus, this often ignored little achievement of theirs—to have awakened with their music the lost memory of the childhood that we all had spent before creation in Him— is to me the greatest. It was nothing short of a miracle that they could help ignorant people, thousands at a time, to keep their hearts and minds strung to listen to the Divine whisper of love so well that they could keep the noise of daily life away from it. It was this whisper of love that ultimately proved stronger than the armed might of those who ruled over the waves of medieval times. It was a miracle that the Gurus could impart 'this soundless melody' (*nad anahad)* to the hearts and minds of millions. Another miracle is that those millions could stay strung for years without tension and fatigue.

Wisdom was never so widely published as nowadays. What is lacking is the soundless melody that alone has the ability to grasp and retain it, and keep the water of worldliness away from the milk of truth, in spite of being served in the same beverage. The soundless melody (*nad anahad*) is like the rebellious dance of a fragile wave of a river in a tumultuous ocean, even after the river had merged in it. I pray that modern people may hear it, for then no matter how loud the worldly noise, they will not miss this whisper of God's love that has ever been and that shall ever be in every heart.

In translating the Divine songs of the Gurus I have tried to catch their noble emotions, the divine music and the sublime spirit behind the words far more than translating their words verbatim.

I am thankful to Pragye Kisslay for proofreading, and giving me the joy of seeing the radiance that the Gurus' ideas might have imparted to youthful faces in their days.

I wanted to add a couple of chapters to the second edition, but circumstances would not let it. The text has been revised and updated to incorporate current research and suit modern needs. If God wills, even this little book should be able to convey all that needs to be known, because wisdom is not locked in books. The best books only knock at the heart of the reader to awaken the treasure already hidden there by God. Keats said: "Beauty is truth,

truth beauty, —that is all ye know on earth, and all ye need to know." To know the oneness of truth and beauty is enough. I hope this little piece of knowledge has the key that will unlock the wisdom that is already hidden in every heart.

24.4.06

Nirmal Kumar
266, Vasant Vihar, Phase-2
Dehradun-248006

Preface

*A*fter the advent of Shankaracharya, the refined and sensitive Hindu mind had started withdrawing from *'the sturm und drang'* of political life. Tulsi Das, who restored order to disintegrating social life, completely ignored the political life. It was so full of cruelty and macaberesque horror that poetry fled from it while sensitivity got stunned. It was therefore no small task that the Sikh Gurus attempted when they drew the attention of saints and *siddhas*, noblemen and laymen alike to the political obligations of man, and to the hard fact that without repairing the political ruins it was not possible to build a coherent and integrated society. The cleaning of the tank at the Golden Temple of Amritsar by the Sikhs of all ranks, with a religious zeal and fervour, is a symbolic activity, very much reminiscent of the medieval vow that the Gurus took to cleanse the political tanks and pools of those days.

The Gurus had seen the shattered dreams of the Indians who had cultivated human virtues, because they did not want to cultivate spiritual pride to hide the lack of virtues. People who had learnt to be spiritually proud and who thought they had no use for human virtues had trampled the Indians. They had been given second-class citizenship in their homeland. They had been denied all human freedoms. Innumerable humiliations had been piled on them. A tired, regressed collective spirit—this was the heritage that the Gurus had. They re-shaped it into a determined and inspired spirit, aimed at wrenching political and social freedom on the very road to spiritual freedom. The cruelty of constant royal suspicion hung over them like an ominous cloud. The cruelty of irrational royal anger wrapped them on all sides. The cruelty of prejudicial enquiries of all their acts for human upliftment oppressed the very breath they inhaled. And the cruelty of illicit pleasures of the immoral nobility, blind to the poverty and despair of women, was there constantly to provoke their sensitive and pious souls. The atmosphere surcharged all around with cruelty in different forms was petrifying the hearts of the Indians. The learned were taking recourse to renunciation. Many of them had fled to forests and the Himalayas where, through penance and isolated upward-search, they were intensifying their spiritual powers. The Gurus denounced it. They preached that the course of a true life was not only vertical but horizontal too. To ignore the distress of the people and to cultivate spiritual isolation was to run away from reality. They said man couldn't find happiness in Nirvana, Shangri-La or Eldora-do if he looked away from the tragedy of his Motherland.

Love remained the central string of their lyre. Knowledge was its firstborn. Thus far the road was common with other medieval saints. The bifurcation lay here. Beyond this, the Gurus emphasised on the necessity of a life of action. One has no right to keep his knowledge to himself and to retire and live a life of meditation. Knowledge is vain if not interpreted into action. The fabric of life of all human beings is one seamless whole. It should get the imprints of great humans' spiritual, moral or intellectual gains. Then alone what gifted individuals attain becomes the property of all. This helps the entire humanity of a nation to march toward light. It ennobles social institutions and rids politics of lust and greed. They said disinterested spiritual command to temporal power was a precious lesson taught by the ancient seers and should not be forgotten in any case.

One significant thing about Sikhism is its ardent effort to reduce the 'pathos of distance'. Not only among the rich and the poor, even the distance between an awakened and a layman has to be reduced. Distance breeds distrust. It leads to privacy and isolation, which are sure ways to social disintegration. The art of meditation, they said, was not a magic known to only a few yogis. It was as simple as remembering the name of God while doing our ordinary daily jobs and duties. A soldier, a farmer, a grocer, or a weaver could meditate while busy with his daily routine, for no special training or yogic posture was required for it. The constant repetition of God's name controls the space, i.e., *aakash*. Space is the gross form of word, and God's name is the subtlest form of word. Word is the essence from which all matter springs. It impregnates space and converts a part of this root of all matter into illuminated life force. Control over the word gradually enables us to control all the five elements. One who attains this becomes fearless of death.

The message of Sikhism was a discovery of the same perennial stream of wisdom that had been shrouded by the moss and twigs of time, and human ignorance. It was a good opportunity for me to pay my homage to this brilliant medieval awakening when the Punjabi University, Patiala, called me in 1977 to deliver the 11th Guru Nanak Memorial Lectures. This great flame of knowledge and activity had pierced, like lightning, the frustration and surrender of our medieval ancestors. It is a pious heritage of all Indians. I had tried to show the place of Sikhism in the context of Indian and Western thought, and I am thankful to the learned and sensitive audience for their encouraging response. I am thankful to the Vice-Chancellor Mrs I.K. Sandhu for her sincere hospitality. This book is a further development on the full text of the lectures I had prepared. The lectures I delivered were shorter but friends had advised me to publish the full text in the first edition, for subtraction had taken away much of it.

I am also thankful to Bimla, Nirmala, Sushma, Alka and Pradeep who graced the occasion by their presence.

Nirmal Kumar

Contents

Approach to Heritage

There have been enthusiasts who have tried to prove that Sikhism discarded and condemned the Hindu heritage. They maintain that it was entirely original in inspiration, original in philosophy and original in practice. They are as mistaken as those who think Sikhism to be an offshoot of Hinduism. Like every original religion, it is born of intimacy with God. It is not based on any scripture. As it does not derive from any established creed, it does not fight any preceding one. Sikh philosophy and religion are enlightened growths from within the Indian heritage. Far from dissociating it completely from Hinduism, they have accepted the Hindu pantheon of Gods without any dispute. Lakshmi, Durga, Brahma, Shiva and Vishnu are celebrated deities in the songs of the Gurus. There is no attempt to deny their existence or divinity. The effort is only to put them as lesser deities, serving the Supreme Lord. The Vedic rishis had seen and personified the many forms of God to suit people of varying sensibilities and Divine intimations. The rishis (seers) of Upanishads had discovered the one single Brahm behind the pantheon of gods that were there to satisfy the emotional needs of people with different natures. Later, in the epic age, the pantheon again appeared and the unity discovered got lost. This gave rise to religious arguments and confusions, as well as to superstitions and ignorance. The Gurus did only what the rishis of Upanishads had done earlier. But they did it differently, and in a new way that suited their times and people.

It would not be far from truth to call them original. Originality, as Goethe said, is not in having nothing from others. It is in the use to which we put those gifts.

The social institutions of Hindus were direct targets of attack for the Gurus who never compromised with these mossy growths. The higher caste ideology, the suttee custom and the various rituals in the name of religion never appealed to the Gurus. They lashed out bitterly at them.

> Pride of Caste is the root of error
> Nothing but error comes out of error
>
> Guru III, *Bhairo Rag*

> Pride of high caste parentage is vain
> Pedigree is not the distinction of men
>
> Guru I, *Sri Rag*

> Karma reveals the caste of man
> Neither pedigree, caste nor clan.
>
> Guru I, *Prabhati Rag*

This is the same that the Upanishads, Mahavir and Buddha had taught. The ignorant and the vain seek distinctions. The wise see the same light in everyone. Wisdom is not confined to a born Brahman. It can grow in any soul that is on the fire of love, for all knowledge, otherwise, is mere information, or a confounding attack of words. It is love, again, that turns a deed good. Without it, however good a deed may be, it is rendered useless as it serves pride.

Quite a few of the holy saints who have been honoured by inclusion of their hymns in the *Granth Sahib* (the holy book of the Sikhs) belonged to lesser castes. Namadev was a washerman and Kabir a weaver. Dhanna was a *jat* and Trilochan a *vaisya*. No distinction is observed between them.

> 'Surely shall I go with the lowest and the low
> I shall go with them.'
>
> Nanak, *Bhairo Rag*

In order to explain the approach of the Sikh Gurus to heritage, it would be better to take up certain important items of this heritage. I have taken the concepts of trinity and *nama-yoga*. I shall strive to show that instead of revolting against the rich heritage of the Hindus, the Sikh Gurus have accepted and rationalised it. They removed the dark mystical webs of ritualism and simplified the doctrines in the light of reason. In this context of heritage, I shall also discuss the age-old Hindu concept of beyond good and evil and the Gurus' approach to it. Still another point discussed in this reference is of 'archetypes' which is a 20th century concept. I have taken it, for it will help to show the relation of the Gurus to human heritage.

The Balance of Trinity

Certain foreign priests and scholars, commissioned by the then British Government of India for this very purpose, have tried to create schism between the Hindu heritage and Sikhism. Some of the Sikhs seem to have missed the political motive behind their scholarship. They have ignored the message of the Gurus that disinterested quest of truth is the soul of true scholarship. As a result, they have developed a sense of pride in the distorted idea of 'originality' that motivated scholarship had created. It will be unfair to the spirit of the *Granth Sahib* if the sinister web of motivated scholarship is not dispelled.

The Gurus talked of one God, the '*Waheguru*,' who transcends all deities. They found people in their time lost in splitting the same faith into sects, like the devotees who called Shiva the Absolute and the devotees who called Vishnu the Absolute. The Gurus also found that in their zealous idolatry, the people had forgotten to install the highest Truth conceived by reason as 'God'. They knew that a faith that contradicted the findings of free reason could not sustain itself. Therefore they strove to give people a faith that their minds and hearts might accept after open and free enquiry. Their prime objective was to integrate the badly shattered personalities of the men and women of their times. To integrate a shattered personality, the first thing needed was to make its parts agree with each other. Blind faith cannot silence intellect and arrogant intellect cannot let faith grow.

The *Japji* is full of numerous references to show that the Gurus believed in the pantheon of Hindu gods and goddesses. They never denied their existence. However, they recognised them only as elemental forces or presiding deities of various functions. They were not God but his appointed angels.

They all have their rightful place in the creation of God. They serve God. One who realizes this knows the way to transcend the confusion caused by the sectarian spirit that elevates one of them as God to the chagrin of others. Chitragupta, Indra, and several goddesses, too, have been acknowledged in the *Japji*. It assigns the *Gopis*, Krishna and even Buddha noble places. The spirit behind the Sikh hymns is not to question the nobleness and worthiness of the Hindu gods and goddesses. The aim of the Gurus is different. They seem to be emphasising the eternal light behind all divinities that were worshipped by the people in their times. Instead of denouncing, the spirit was to integrate the faith of the people into a hierarchy topped by the *Waheguru*. The aim was to unite the people by showing them the one God, who had been only differently interpreted in their respective faiths. Still the Trinity has been accorded the highest place. At different places, the *Japji* says: "The Guru is Shiva; the Guru is Vishnu; the Guru is Brahma; the Guru is Parvati; the Guru is Laxmi; the Guru is Saraswati."

Emphasis on Brahma

My Lord became *Maya*
And yet remained himself
A word 'Om' spoke *Maya*
And came forth Brahma
He created gods and man
And this colourful vista
Of birds, beasts, mountains.

Japji

One very important feature in Sikh scriptures is the repeated mention of Brahma. It is not just by chance that the Gurus have emphasised this face of the Hindu Trinity. Already in their time the worship of Brahma had faded. Today we have only one temple of Brahma in the whole of India, while his worship is galore in Thailand, Burma, Indonesia, Cambodia and other lands. It is a strange phenomenon. Why did the worship of Brahma die out in this country? He is as important in the trinity as the remaining two, Vishnu and Shiva. Both of them have ardent worshippers, who have built thousands of temples to them. Brahma has only one, in Pushkar.

The Gurus in their meditation and *pragya* (higher immediacy) realized the deeper meaning behind this phenomenon and tried to remind the people of their error by repeatedly mentioning the name of Brahma. The practice of worshipping Brahma had been dropped suddenly, as a result of some pernicious manipulation in the faith of the Hindus. It was far-reaching as it misbalanced their lives. The Gurus had detected it. They had been warning the Hindus against it by repeatedly giving the same elevated position to Brahma in their prayers.

Explaining deities in intellectual terms, Vishnu is the personification of Truth (*Satyam*), Shiva the personification of Good (*Shivam*), and Brahma the personification of Beauty (*Sunderam*). The Hindus have been attributing these three virtues to God. Beauty has been recognized as a virtue of God by their collective unconscious, since the beginning.

A remarkable thing about these three is that if intellectually you miss one of them, you cannot comprehend God as he appeared to the Indian intellect. The three can represent God only collectively, not individually. God cannot be realized even by any two of them if the third is excluded. The invaders had known the intellectual might of the Indian people apart from their spiritual might. One of the main strategies they had adopted was to isolate the Indian intellect from his God and then confuse it.

Beauty is always a victim of the invader. People who had beautiful daughters and wives had cause to curse themselves for their fatal gift of beauty. A general atmosphere had been created by the obscenity of the rulers in which beauty had turned into a source of dishonour and misery. This was the dark night of the history of India. The low culture of the new rulers, especially with regard to women, was forcing the Indians to give up their age-old practice of free and fearless socialization between men and women. Theirs had been an open society in which people respected each other's family life. The foreign rulers' indiscreet behaviour was forcing them now to abandon openness with regard to women, and to develop a clumsily lusty and frightened approach to beauty. The invaders, due to their irreverence of beauty, had crippled the free and worshipful attitude of the Indians toward beauty. The invaders did not recognize feminine beauty as an aspect of God, since God was abstract to them. They did not know that beauty was an object of reverence as it was the daily visible face of God. It was not a thing to be ravished wherever possible.

This new attitude to beauty baffled and stunted the Indian genius. Whirlpools started confounding its spontaneous and uniform flow in three currents. Beauty was no longer the radiant, pious face of God that was no different than a virgin's. Beauty became a thing of shame that brought shame. Truth, Beauty and Good are a dangerous trinity. They help in our development only if all the three are uniformly present, balancing each other. You remove Beauty out of the three, and Truth and Good start turning abstract. Beauty is what prevents Truth and Good from running to abstraction. Beauty is the principle of concretization that compels man to express himself in sound, colours, lines or words or anything material. Beauty, as the virtue of God, is the dynamics of spirituality that impels God to shed some of his mystery and secrecy and reveal to mortals a bit of the Wonder that he is. Beauty draws the Divine to earth and to material manifestation.

Another unique characteristic of Beauty is that it cannot be imagined as pure abstraction. Beauty can be imagined only in some form or figure, not in void. The abstract painters have not been able to paint beauty, even if they have been able to give some idea of truth. That is why some religions have talked of God only as good, merciful and true. They do not talk of him as beautiful, for fear of making him finite. They do not seem to be aware that God's beauty is as infinite as the rest of him. His beauty cannot be contained in any expression of it. His expression as beauty is only as incomplete as his expression as truth and good. Even if we try to imagine God as beyond beauty and beyond shape, his Beauty compels our mind to visualize him with some beauty and shape. This is something that even Shankaracharya, the philosopher of the abstract, and Nagarjuna, the philosopher of void, could not help.

While Beauty makes the abstract concrete, Truth, on the other hand, has a tendency to take us from the concrete to the abstract. The Vedic seers checked this tendency of Truth because they did not worship Truth alone, but all the three, Truth, Beauty and Good, together. When saints started worshipping Truth alone they got lost in abstraction. There was no alternative. The demands of Truth are very exacting. Truth becomes a despot if it is worshipped alone. Nothing relative lasts in its blazing flames. '*Neti, Neti*' (this is not truth) cried Shankaracharya to everything thinkable, because it was bound with something. Nagarjuna was a follower of the Buddha. However, driven by his exclusive pursuit of Truth (the principle that turns tyrannical on being pursued alone), he had to concede that judged from the standpoint of Truth, even the Buddha, was 'a magnificent illusion'. Nanak, therefore, made a simple and poignant observation that "more important than truth is true life". Truth, when pursued alone, gives us unavoidable wings to fly to abstraction. Or it lands us in void that sucks us and does not let us return to earth.

Similar is the case regarding Good. If pursued alone, without the balancing influence of the pursuit of Beauty, Good also becomes a tyrant. It, too, takes us beyond the context of life, into abstraction. In medieval India, when Beauty became a *taboo,* thinkers and saints who took only Good and Truth to be the symbols of God, developed a decadent faith in the ideal beyond good and evil. They started believing in something in which the Vedic rishis never believed, in which neither the *Tirthankaras* nor the Buddha believed. Mediocre interpreters started misinterpreting the ideas of the enlightened ones, by saying that even doing good deeds fettered the soul, and thus good was a hindrance to Nirvana. They said the ideal course for the true seeker was to do neither good nor evil but to give up all actions. Thousands of years back, when Arjun showed reluctance to fight in the battlefield, Krishna had told him the truth that nobody could renounce action, because even inaction was some kind of action. Therefore one should fight for the sake of truth and justice, offering all action and fruits of action to God. This lesson had been forgotten by the time of the Gurus. People had started yearning for a state of repose where one did neither good nor evil.

The Gurus gave a wild shock to the coiled serpent—the genius of India—that had discovered the philosophy of inaction. Inaction was a cosy corner where it could sulk and sleep. They said emphatically that good actions were the sole instrument that prevented evil from coming close to man. Besides, good karma cut the fetters of bad karma. Good actions were the carriers to Nirvana. They explained convincingly why it was an error to think that good actions were fetters like bad actions. Doing good action was imitating God, and imitating God created no fetter. 'When God does not bind, how could good actions that are born of his nature?' The tenth Guru prayed, "*Shubha karman te kabhoon na daru.*" ("O Lord! Give me the blessing that I may overcome the inhibition against good actions.") The Gurus dispelled this age-old philosophic error, and awakened the people to do good without fearing any unpleasant repercussion from the Law of Karma. They said that this Law did not count good actions as karmic fetters. It rather counted them among cutters of fetters. He assured his knights of Light and Love "When a knight dies in the battlefield divinity celebrates it with Divine joy." He produced this sentiment in a moving prayer: "*shastran te ativeer ran bhitar jujha mare to sanch pasije*" (Bless me O Lord with the boon that when a knight sacrifices his life you melt with compassion.)

I see a deeper meaning in repeated references to Brahma in Sikh scriptures. It was intended to remind the people of the third - nearly forgotten - God in the Hindu trinity. The objective was to restore Beauty in the intellectual temple, so that it may wield its sobering and earth-bound influence on seekers flying toward abstraction. Isolated pursuit of Truth or Good had made yogis and philosophers men of inaction. They had retired to caves, getting frustrated and heartbroken by the inhumanity of the rulers. They meditated and relaxed on luxurious tiger-skins, unsympathetic to the cries of the persecuted fellow countrymen and women. The yogis had hardened themselves against royal cruelty to innocent people, only because their wails only opened their own wounds. They only reminded them of their own impotence against the evil in which the children of mighty Bharat, "the playmate of lions", had been trapped. The Gurus thought that reviving veneration for Brahma might awaken their unconscious, and ancient memories buried in it. They thought that it might help people remember, "once upon a time we worshipped God as Beauty, and that was our golden age." They might realize that mere abstraction had made them "ineffectual angels beating their wings in void." They might see the truth that it was not impotence but petrifaction, only because they had given up the worship of Beauty that alone provided muscles to the skeleton of Truth and Good. The Gurus were quite hopeful that the day the people of India began worshipping the Trinity—Truth, Beauty and Good—not the lame Trinity—Truth and Good—India would awaken to a new Golden Age, brighter than all earlier ones. They looked more to the future than the past. They wanted India, their beloved nation, to awaken like the legendary city in which all citizens had fallen into a charmed sleep, and were revived back to life by a beautiful girl. Pursuit of only Truth and Good had led all the great ones from concrete to the deadly sleep in the abstract. Their minds had been lost in the void. Only the pursuit of Beauty could charm them back to earth, so that they might fight for the honour and freedom of the Motherland.

The balance of the human mind is maintained only by worshipping all the three faces of the Divine. The mind remains in its place only if it does not run after Truth and Good, ignoring Beauty. While Truth and Good pull the mind to abstraction, Beauty pulls it back to earth. Thus the gravitation of the three helps the mind to stay in its place, and act nobly under their joint influence. It was by maintaining thus the balance of their minds that the rishis of *Ishopanishad* had realized their goal—Brahm the Absolute—that is neither totally beyond nor totally within this world.

He walks and has walked away never
He is far away and the distance between us is nowhere
He is inside, but hark who is outside there!

The higher intellect of God integrates all the three aspects of Reality, e.g. Truth, Beauty and Good. But the intellect of intellectuals and the common people excludes Beauty, fearing its sensuousness to be sensuality.

R. E. Friedman summarizes the phenomena of the rise of the dry intellect of the jurists in the Western religious consciousness. The council of the Rabbis, separated from Moses by a millennium and a half, declared "that their tradition, decisions, and expositions of text are Torah." He further says, "The Torah is now in the hands of humans, and not even God can change It." He goes on explaining this amazing development, "A thousand prophets would not, therefore, overweigh a thousand and one jurists, for the judicial principle of majority rule, absolutely indifferent to claims of special inspiration or heavenly instructions, would prevail." Islam is opposite of Judaism, yet it also grants absolute authority to the jurists. This was never the case in India. But this spirit having dominated the Hindu intellect, during slavery, for a millennium seems to have partly seeped into it. It was this juristic importance in religion that the Gurus flouted with their beautiful songs of love and devotion. They boldly declared religion to be more a matter of love than of logic. It was nothing short of a miracle that this view of religion as a subject of lovers and not of jurists had successfully re-asserted through the Sikh Gurus, at a time when India had been conquered and placed under the theocratic rule of those who gave prominence to the juristic view and had imposed their laws on the Indians too. It helped the Indians immensely in keeping their intellect free. It saved them of the rebellious intellectual path of the West that culminated in the declaration that God was dead. The Ananda Marriage Act was a brilliant piece of the combined manoeuvring of the missionaries and British rulers to introduce their rebellious intellect in Sikhism, and deviate it from the path of love.

Beauty as an intellectual view of God got ousted from the Western religious consciousness. This ouster of beauty was marked by a phenomenal rise in religious violence. It began with the Crusades that were gory stories of religious carnage lasting several centuries. Religious arguments were rampant, but religious violence was absent in India until the arrival of the Muslim invaders, only because the Indians had kept devotion and love at the centre of their religious activity. Lovers, not jurists, had been the leaders of all Indian religions. Their intellectual view of God too had been different than the West. They never made the jurists their leaders, so much so that the Hindus, Buddhists, Jains and the Sikh religious leaders never created any law books. They practised love and human values, like non-violence, selflessness and equality of all living beings, and compassion for animals too. They thought that justice did not grow from law books. It grew from love, selflessness and the bestowing spirit. They trained their intellect to think of God or the Ultimate Truth as the centre of creation that was at the same time truth, beauty and good. They went to the two sources of action in man, man's nature and man's intellect, and gave them two separate disciplines that made both self-bestowing rather than self-acquisitive. From this disciplined self, they said, dharma i.e. justice took birth every moment afresh.

The Gurus fortified this noble tradition. It stands testimony to the great vision of the Indian intellectuals that in spite of the most outspoken criticism of each other's creed they never let the people forget that religion was love and its test lay only in its ability to generate spontaneous love and human values in every individual, not in rational arguments. The test of a religion was its ability to help the individual attain the four-fold freedom of the body, mind, heart and the soul.

In India the religious man had to discipline his intellect by pursuing the truth that was beautiful and good too. Truth that was not beautiful and good too was not considered truth, howsoever logical it be. Beauty was the principle of creation that the religious man's intellect pursued as a part of the religious discipline. On the other hand, it was only the intellect of artists, musicians, poets and writers in the West that comprehended Reality as Beauty. The intellect of the religious man, except the prophets and the Son of

God, was busy in two activities – judging others and proselytising. The clergy never took the observation of geniuses seriously. As a result the intellectual concept of Reality that was not essentially Beauty too got established in Western religions. This view of Reality generated extreme hatred between the followers of Judaism, Christianity and Islam. This view of Reality was brought to India by the mullahs, and with the backing of the kings they forced it on the Indian intellectuals too. Many medieval foreign kings of India rejected the idea that beauty was a part of God. Many of them banned music, painting, sculpture and all beautiful ways of worshipping Reality. Aurangzeb was foremost among them. Breaking of beautiful idols and temples became a religious passion. It created disintegration in the intellect of the Hindus too. They gave up the worship of Brahma, the God of intellectual beauty. When the politicians of 21st century India talk so much of secularism one wonders whether they are afflicting the illiterate masses with some Western disease or curing some ailment. One wonders whether they know that secularism was an intellectual challenge to the juristical view of religion, and nothing more. Could secularism be a substitute of what the Sikh Gurus and all great founders of religions in India had been saying time and again – religion is all about love and the cultivation of the self-bestowing virtue?

Only during the last decade of the 20th century the Western intellect woke up to include beauty as a constituent of Reality. Ironically, it were the physicists whose mathematical intellect was seeing beauty as an inevitable part of reality. Paul Dirac said it bluntly, "It is more important to have beauty in one's equations than to have them fit experiments." Physicists like Steven Weinberg, David Gross and Murray Gell-Mann have raised the questions: "Is beauty, by itself, a physical principle that can be substituted for the lack of experimental verification?" Whether "the solutions to the most difficult problems in nature had been the ones with the most beauty?" Whether the Final Theory is proving elusive because of the lacking in earlier physics of 'beauty', which is the principle of unification?

The Gurus fought against the idea that God could be imagined without the principle of Beauty. They made their holy book entirely out of beautiful songs of love and beautiful behaviour. They told the people that God could not be comprehended as an abstract Being. He was the wonderful *Waheguru*, the epitome of beauty as much as of truth and good. The Lord was subtler than all his Divine manifestations, even the Trinity. For them God was what He was to the ancient sages, Vamadev and Yagyavalka, Vashistha and Atri, Agasta and Jaimini. It would minimise their importance if we insist only on the doctrine they finally preached the Sikhs. They were leaders of the people of India. They were born at a particular crisis in Mother India's life. Fears and worries, humiliations and deprivations were rushing toward India's lay humanity. The Gurus challenged them to come to them, and leave the lay people in peace. They knew that though humanity was cast in the mould of divinity it was too delicate to face this unnerving attack. It was for the soul to divert this attack to itself, and the souls of the Gurus were fully awake to do this. They knew humanity to be a strange mixture of fragility and strength. It was strong in the sense that every moment Divine qualities like love, non-violence, compassion and kindness to animals kept growing in it incessantly. They grew spontaneously, not as a result of education. A wonderful thing about them was that they were fresh every moment. At the same time, humanity was very fragile, since it withered like a flower at the slightest attack. If the soul diverted the attacks on humanity to itself, humanity would keep providing these virtues, without disturbance. Since the soul was the strongest thing on earth, taking these attacks to itself would not harm the soul in any manner. This idea of collaboration of the soul and humanity within each individual was one of the greatest gifts of the *Prashnopanishad*. The Gurus were personifications of this unity of the soul and humanity.

Humanity is a God-created emotion as well as a species. As a species it may be perishable, not as an emotion. In these lectures all discussion of humanity relates to humanity that is an emotion. Humanity is God as a child. Its value lies not in its power but in being the endless source of an ever-fresh supply of Divine virtues.

It has to be saved at all costs. Humanity's enemies could shatter it because God had given it all the values but no strength. Its enemies could cause no harm to the soul since the soul was stronger than the Himalayas, vaster than space and quite beyond the reach of time. Knowledge of this secret truth of humanity and constant practice of it in daily life had made the Gurus fearless. They extended their helping hand even to those who did not become their disciples. Their wisdom showered its rays on all the people for they intended to lift the cloud of torpor from the heart of India. They had realized that though the masses had deep-seated faith in the Trinity yet by throwing Brahma down the pedestal the priests had developed an imbalance in their minds. This folly was proving to be the worst soporific of its kind. They reminded the people to reallocate a place to Brahma—the principle of Beauty—in their worship.

Their aim was not to give any new religion to the people. They were champions of humanity that is an emotion. The Sikh religion had grown as an automatic growth around the ten Gurus. Only the tenth Guru turned it into a military organization, since his clarion call as the champion of humanity had filled the unjust king with the passion of butchery. The canvas of the Gurus was nothing short of the whole of life. They were vitally concerned with the superstitions and the inertia of the souls of the Indians of their time. Their aim was to pull their humanity out of self-forgetfulness. They were keen that people did not take them for propagators of some new religion. For this they freely used the names of Shiva, Indra, Gobind, Hari, Brahma and others in their sermons and songs. The narrow religious enthusiasts, often in their separatist fury, have tried to portray them as non-Hindu thinkers. They have ignored this greater and nobler aspect of the Gurus' personalities.

Nama-Yoga

Yoga is the practical system of turning intellectual ideas into emotions and sensations. It has turned the high philosophy of the rishis into the emotions of the Indian people. It is a tribute to the success of yoga that the philosophy of life of the lay people and the learned is the same in India. The values that the learned practice intellectually the ordinary folks practice as emotions. The values are the same that the rishis had discovered in their disinterested quest running over several millennia. This philosophy has stood the test of time, and also the test that modern science has applied to it. All Indian philosophic schools have their corresponding yogic disciplines. They do not differ much from one another except in the case of *kapaliks*, and *tantriks*. These two leftist schools mystified yoga in medieval days and aroused suspicion due to their uncommon practices. They made wine, meat and woman parts of their discipline. They practised sexual union as a means of deliverance from all bondages, including the bondage of the forbidden. Many *tantriks* and *kapaliks* called their yoga by the name *Sahaj*, which literally meant 'simple', to emphasize that the best way to overcome a temptation was to yield to it and to let the soul get reborn of it. They believed that to experience all chthonic revelries and horrors was only a way to learn from first hand experience that there was no dungeon or hell where God was not to be found. They did so to prove their faith that there was no devil that could challenge God; that there was no other than God; that even the devil was a servant of God. They said that man should know that what he calls devil is his own mind working under the excited and ignorant pursuit of pleasure. They faced all sorts of darkness with the avowed purpose to prove that every evil was subservient to God and could be used, with a change of attitude, to attain Nirvana.

Guru Nanak condemned their approach and redefined *Sahaj*. To him *Sahaj* did not mean any relaxation of morals or an attempt to realize God through sexual union. *Sahaj*, according to him, was nothing but *nama-yoga*. The seeker was asked to concentrate on His name in his heart. He said that sincere effort in this direction made His name the pivot and the core of human life, thoughts, emotions and actions. This was the same as total self-purification. It was senseless to destroy the components of human nature. Its feelings, desires and thoughts were marvels of culture that had been attained after great research and sacrifices on part of Brahma during the time he evolved life from rudimentary forms to the human. If the seeker only made God's name the core of his existence, by constantly remembering him, all the components of human nature would take man to happiness on earth and hereafter. The Gurus would say that the black colour, when properly used by a painter, instead of creating darkness, would help in showing light. Similarly, all the components of human nature served in spreading God's light, if people took to the path of simply remembering God in their hearts.

This new definition of yoga was no defiance of the Hindu tradition. In fact, Nanak was emphasising the same perennial concept of the yoga of devotion that prior to him had been condensed by Narada in his *Bhakti Sutram*. Nanak had many discussions with the *siddhas* and he was grieved that they had hidden themselves in caves at a time when the people needed them most. It would be more appropriate to say that he revolted against the medieval *Siddha* concept of yoga. However in all that he has said about yoga he has only helped to flower the best traditions of the *bhakti-heritage*. *Bhakti-heritage* was a school of seekers of God who believed that God could be realized only through love and devotion.

I would like to tell you, in brief, the special features of *Nama-Yoga* as conceived by the Sikh Gurus. You can see for yourself that none of its aspects is in any way a defiance of the Hindu heritage. It is only a simplification, done with the sole motive of making it a thing of utility for the common masses. The *tantrik* web had struck a note of terror in the hearts of the ordinary people. Guru Nanak lifted that magical cloud and prevented the *tantrik* wave from severing the links between the masses and the enlightened men and women of India.

Nama-Yoga is an important feature of Sikhism. Some great yogis, too, had mystified yoga in the medieval days. It had become a science to which only a few had access. The Gurus broke this magic ring. Their aim was to make it as simple and common an affair as breathing. It would be wrong to say that in this they were discarding the Hindu heritage. In fact, yoga to the Vedic rishis and Narada was what it was to the Gurus. It was no artificial and external link between the individual and the Divine. It was the awakening of the Divine in the individual soul even as the flower awakened in the bud. In this process the bud was at once both destroyed and preserved. The green leaves of ego that enfolded the bud, i.e. the soul, got torn, but, at the same time, the soul got revealed in all its lustre and purity. Whatever best was hidden in the bud is preserved in the flower. The individuality was not to be destroyed yet it had to be realized that individuality was nothing but a coloured dome that covered the Divine. The simple awakening of this knowledge was the purpose of yoga, according to the Gurus, and for this they preached *Nama-Yoga*. They brought yoga back from the mystical isolation in which the medieval *tantriks* had imprisoned it.

No ardent yogic exercises are preached. No control over breath is considered necessary. Only the heart should constantly remember the *Waheguru*, i.e., God. This simplification made Sikhism most attractive to the masses. But one should not understand from this that the profundities of yoga were sacrificed for the sake of popularity. This simplification has philosophic depths. The Gurus eased the problem of the common man by not asking him to search in the depths. They did the searching themselves and offered to the common man the shining pearls that they fished out of the depths. Much that the Gurus found after rigorous self-discipline and philosophising they asked the common man to get through Divine grace. The common people could not have made the arduous spiritual journey. To initiate them into it might have thrown them into a listless state of confusion and despair. It required some strength of soul to bear the many agonies and frustrations usually experienced by seekers on the spiritual road. The Gurus knew the easier way too and they asked the common man to walk over it. It was the way of remembering God, silently or loudly, while working or while lying vacant. Mere remembering invoked His kindness. The Gurus said, "He is all powerful. He can cut in a minute all our fetters of sins. He can lift us to eternal freedom, to *Sachkhand*. If our soul remembers Him sincerely it gradually starts living in Him.

We get a secret inflow of the character of the person we love in our soul. I become him. Each becomes both. Love of Lord imbues the soul with Divine qualities. Its sinful tendencies to rush downwards, and its wasteful tendencies to run around get checked. A spontaneous upward tendency, *urdhvagati*, transforms individuality ultimately into love, i.e., God, the *"Waheguru."*

Sikh thinking shows that the One changes into many. It is the same spiritual clay that moulds itself into *haumey* (pride) in an ignorant person. And the same spiritual clay transforms into the loving soul, the blithe spirit under the spell of *Waheguru*. The difference between a delivered soul and a soul in bondage is also very obvious, according to the Sikhs. The spiritual forces are the same in each individual, since the soul of man has all the powers of creation. A delivered soul knows the spiritual art of transforming these forces into love. This is achieved through a process of self-discipline on part of these forces. The sum total or aggregate of these forces in each individual is his *haumey*. These forces cannot be disciplined at *haumey's* command, for, though their aggregate, it is no better illuminated than those forces. They have a strong tendency to defy and revolt against its command. Hence the often-lamented experience of spiritual men that in spite of their strong determination and self-suppression, their passions and thoughts act contrarily and breed pestilence inside. It is because suppression of these forces is also a way of strengthening *haumey*.

A true Sikh has first to realize this: "I am myself each of these negative spiritual and psychological forces. I should not be, but the fact is such today. I cannot gain anything by getting blinded to facts. The sum total of my past karmas has resulted in this ignorant lower state —a state of diffusion in me. Instead of claiming outright that I am one with my Love, let me strive correctly to become one with my Love, i.e., *Waheguru*. After realising myself to be these many powers within me, I have to learn that I am *Asat* (non-being) only as long as I remain these powers. I have also to know that it is *Sat* (Being) that has transformed into these various *Asat* powers. I can reverse the process and transform *Asat* back into *Sat* if I continuously and sincerely remember the name of *Waheguru* every day for some time. During this exercise called *Nama-Yoga*, the negative spiritual and psychological forces that have become slaves of *haumey* will automatically learn the Divine art of extinguishing themselves. This will not be self-destruction. It will be philosophic dying out that visionaries everywhere have known since time immemorial. It is a unique dying process that results in the birth of love."

Thus all the negative spiritual forces disappear and only love is left as the *Sat,* the existent. Speaking in the ordinary sense, all the powers still remain in us but oblivious of their individuality, totally at the disposal of Love, with no personal motive or objective for themselves. They have burnt themselves in homage to the white radiance of love.

The Sikh faith does not teach the killing or suppressing of any instinct, desire or passion. It is thus a creed that teaches total non-violence with oneself. Anything grown inside the soul, other than love, is a symptom of imperfection. By destroying it we shall only be losing the symptom that helped us in detecting the disease. Killing imperfection is strengthening imperfection. Instead of killing it and thereby building up a formidable *haumey*, ridden by inner conflicts, we should rather try to cure the spiritual disease— why we cannot love? The lamp of love gets kindled in the soul when the very winds that blow it out kindle it. Love in the heart is easy to come. But love in the soul is what the wise honour. The soul in love makes even God pay attention to it. Nanak did not call sexual love between legitimate couples profane. He disarmed those who wanted from a seeker of truth total celibacy. A song in the *Granth Sahib* goes as follows:

> If celibacy was the key to meet my Love
> Ahead of me, eunuchs would have met my Love!
> A bird is singing, says Kabir, in my ear
> To God a heart singing of Love's names is dear
> Whether you call him lay, foolish, or wise superior

> Kabir, *Gauri Rag.*

The Gurus had to find out a way whereby the soldier, the farmer or the labour could turn his very job into worship. They were sure that there was a way that could make the soldier absorbed in fighting, without losing concentration on fighting, at the same time absorbed in God too. Even while wielding the sword in the battlefield, the soldier's soul could be in communion with God. Such a soldier could alone be called the soldier of Light and Love— *Waheguru*. This was achievable by as simple a practice as the constant repetition of His name in the heart and, finally, in the soul. 'The Word' (*shabda)* was the source of all creation. The world of the five elements and their finer material essences (*tanmatras)* had its root in the Word. Modern science calls this original word big bang. The Gurus had called it sometimes *Om,* sometimes *Waheguru* and sometimes *Ram.* The Gurus had known the secret— one who learns to enter this source of all creation (God as the Word) has known the art of controlling the lives of people and their activities in this world. A soldier who constantly repeats the name of God gradually enters inside his name. It does not mean that he can make people bend to his will. He can only make them bend to the will of the God of all beings, not the God of some religion, that is some strange God who favours that religion. Such a God who is impartial and equally just to all the people irrespective of their religion has not been popular with those who call themselves 'believers' and others 'infidels'. Most of the clergy of the religions born in the Middle East, engaged in India in proselytising, have a problem. They believe in a God who harms the followers of Indian religions. They believe that the followers of the religions of India are marked by God to be put in hell for eternity, no matter whatever good karma they do. This was the view that the Muslim priests propagated in India, believing their personal ill will as the will of God. Most of the European and Australian priests that proselytised in India during the preceding three centuries had propagated almost similar convictions, believing their prejudice as the religious authority. On the contrary, every religion of India believes that whoever does evil will go to hell, whether he believes in Indian religions or Western, because God is absolutely impartial and does not favour any religion.

The *Japji* gives a very high precedence to the Word. It is prior to the Trinity. 'From the self-existent proceeded *Maya*, whence issued a Word that produced Brahma and the rest.' The Sikhs believe that if all the people of the world pray to the God of all beings that He may help in bringing peace and happiness to all the people, irrespective of their religion, there is no reason God will not listen.

Nama-yoga begins as a physical discipline that grows with exercise from physical to psychological to spiritual. It thus unites the entire visible and invisible existence of the true seeker with God.

Nama-yoga was no revolt against the heritage of yoga. It was rather a fuller way of accepting it. The Vaishnav saints had been singing of the pious and uplifting effects of repeating Ram's name with devotion. One who utters the name of Ram with sincerity paves the way to union with Him. He enters the world of name, which is a subtler model than the mathematical model of this visible universe. Another important difference between the two is that while no mathematical model has agreed so far with reality, i.e. the universe-in-itself, the name-model fully agrees with it. When the Vaishnav saints pray to Ram they do not pray to Him to be favourable to Vaishnav people. They pray that if they have followed the religion of humanity and have known Ram to be equally the God of all, and if they are true to the principle that all living beings are equal, then justice may be done to them. They never pray to be favoured against followers of other religions. They pray Ram to promote human values by helping those who are working for humanity selflessly. This universal approach can be seen anywhere among the followers of Indian religions. The Sikhs follow this tradition of the Gurus.

Nam-Yoga was the simplest form of yoga that certain very simple and humble men had developed. Nanak, Kabir and Namdev, were some of them. Certain Muslim saints had also adopted *Nama-yoga*. In accepting and popularising it, the Sikh Gurus did not revolt against the Indian heritage, for it called for no revolt. The Indian heritage alone has the courage to say that a good and virtuous man who follows some Middle Eastern religion is as good as a sincere follower of Ram, not one who believes in Ram but does evil. The same has not been found true of many other religions proselytising in India. One of the false hopes they gave to the illiterate Indians, and one of the most disturbing ideas that they have taught to the followers of the religions of India who they had targeted to be converted from Indian religions, is that if they simply get converted no matter how evil their karma are they will go to heaven.

Not Beyond Good and Evil

The goal of the Sikh Gurus was not beyond Good and Evil, if it meant ignoring the distinction between the two. This philosophic concept had been highly misunderstood in the Gurus' times, as it is generally misunderstood even now globally. Misunderstanding of it had already taken some misled followers of Shankaracharya to a flight from which they could not return. They had failed to abide by the distinction between the two states of the soul that their master, like the Sikh Gurus, had known.

Shankaracharya had asked only his highly evolved disciples to realize the oneness of good and evil that existed in the highest state of the soul. It was possible since evil had no independent existence. Evil did not exist at the highest level of the evolved soul. The highest level for the soul was to identify itself with God (*Ishwara*). Only after realizing this identity, Shankaracharya had known evil to be non-existent. The duality of good and evil existed only at the lower levels of the evolution of the soul.

Shankaracharya had prescribed an entirely different discipline for the beginner soul. It could realize its identity with God only by purging itself of all evil. There was no other way. Penance, selfless good deeds and knowledge were the ways to achieve the hidden identity of the soul with God. It was not possible to attain it without first attaining the rational knowledge that has the ability to separate good and evil clearly and thoroughly. He had asked his beginner disciples to first realize and establish this duality between good and evil in their souls.

Then they were supposed to live only by good. They were supposed to make no use of evil under any circumstance. This discipline alone qualified them to transcend the duality of good and evil. One who underwent it developed the extreme thirst to go to the higher state of the soul in which, even if evil surrounded it, the soul did not experience evil as an existent. It was essential for a soul thirsty to unite with God to attain this state in which it experienced nothing except God. Here the role of rational knowledge (or discursive knowledge) ended. From this state onwards identification with God was left only to love.

Some of the misled followers of Shankaracharya had shunned the practical course of rational knowledge and total abstinence from doing evil, even in the most trying situations. They had to win the battle of life by doing only good. They were not supposed to answer evil with evil. This extreme discipline of practicing only good had been made extremely difficult by the invaders who also occupied all the powerful seats in the administration.

The Gurus did not change the principle in a situation where the enemy lied and practiced cruelty shamelessly, and had no use for human principles. The Sikhs were supposed to do only good in such a situation too. But the Gurus gave the ideal of doing only good a more effective form. It proved a deterrent to the enemy's devotion to evil. They contemplated only 'the all comprehensive good,' in which evil merges and disappears for the seeker. Henceforth such a soul did not see evil even in the evildoer. It saw only the little glimmer of good that never disappears from a soul, however deep it might be drowned in evil. This ability to perceive only the little glimmer of good in the soul of the evildoer, and not the vast evil in it, is not blindness to reality. It is a sublime quality of the realized soul. It was this sublime attainment of the soul of Mahavir that had charmed the personification of evil (Kamath) so thoroughly that it gave up doing evil. It was this same sublime quality of the Buddha that had broken down completely the personification of evil (Mara).

In a sense the misled followers of Shankaracharya were no different than the *kapaliks* and *aghoris*, since they too began their spiritual journey by blurring the distinction between good and evil. They too did not have any use for discursive knowledge. In fact the ideal of going beyond good and evil has often been identified with depravity. It has been identified with the losing of the wit that distinguishes between good and evil. The Gurus had warned the people not to give up the choice of doing only good. They said that it was the path to unconditional good that took to the ideal state of being beyond good and evil.

Actions belong to the world of *Asat*. Therefore the good and evil actions both are *Asat*, illusory. Why then be so particular about their distinction? This seems to have been the argument of the misled followers of Shankaracharya. This resulted in indifference to political miseries, and also, to sincere and true human relations of love and friendship, and the joys and sorrows of life. It also helped in the growth of callousness, cruelty and insensitivity to human misery.

Guru Nanak recorded in the most dark and pathetic words the miseries and agonies of the people of his time. He suffered for the commoner's life—a true sign of greatness. Sikhism holds only God or Love to be the Truth. The world is a multi-coloured myriad show with no substance. Actions in such a world are also of the nature and stuff of which the world is made, i.e. *Asat*. But, the Gurus would say, this was no logic for not doing strictly good actions. The task before man was not to live in the world of *Kudarat*, with indifference toward the evil that rules over it, only too often. Those saints who ignored evil had allowed illusions to persist. They had shirked their responsibility. Man is expected to conquer evil in this world with the power of his spiritual knowledge and devotion. The evil in this illusory world has to disappear, has to become a nonentity first in the soul of man. Evil can be wiped out completely from this world if all the souls attain first the discursive knowledge of the distinction between good and evil, and then transcend it and attain the higher state of the soul at which it sees no evil, and sees only the hidden glimmer of good even in the evildoer. Such a purified soul alone can realize unity with the *Waheguru,* since the Waheguru is absolutely good. Evil loses its identity before him, and melts into *nothing.* That is why the Gurus never allowed their followers to worship them for the good work they had done. Throughout the Holy *Granth Sahib,* the voice of the Gurus resounds in many echoes— "He who is Love, He alone is True. He cannot have any evil. He is absolute Good. Worship that *Nirankar.* Surrender your Ego, your *haumey,* to him, so that the Lord, the Lover, may purge all traces of evil from your soul." Guru Gobind Singh, after having brought so much glory to the Sikhs, at a time when they were prepared to accept the Guru as their God, smashed the very tradition of Gurus, and gave his disciples only the name of God, the *Waheguru.* He gave them the Holy Book and the sword to walk on the path of God.

The Sikh Gurus believed that all actions are outer manifestations of certain inner spiritual activities. In fact, real actions are committed within the soul; and all outer actions are only their projections in the outer world. Speaking from the purely spiritual point of view, their projection outside, i.e., doing them materially, is insignificant. If they have occurred in our soul as passions, desires, beliefs, or feelings we have already done them. The bondage has already resulted. No man can help hundreds of such feelings, desires and passions. They have got to be weeded out. The surest way to do this is to confess them before God, the *Waheguru.* It will, on the one hand, expose the soul before Him, and, on the other hand, before the individual himself. We shall have then to pass through the fire of self-criticism. It will help us gradually in having only such passions and feelings as do not make us feel ashamed. Thus inner purgation is achieved. The deepest and spontaneous fountains of action in man are not born of the haze that blurs the distinction between good and evil. The Divine appears in us as the impetus of only good actions. Evil is no opposite of Good, as an impostor is no opposite of a true heir, as a false Guru is no opposite of a true Guru. In fact, the impostor has no existence as the heir. Mere opposing good does not turn non-being into being. It remains non-being, however wild it might turn. The

Gurus dispelled vehemently the delusion that sheer opposition to good grants any status to evil. If the worldly people do so the wise should not. The Gurus said that out of the many tricks of evil it is one, and a very confounding one: to appear as the opposite of God, from non-being turning up as the rival of God. The Gurus remind again and again that there is no rival to Him. Only He is. He is good. Evil is essentially non-existent, which becomes existent and powerful when the soul grants it recognition due to its fear. Evil is not the opposite of good but a veil drawn by ignorance, a play enacted for the blinded by the blind; "a tale told by an idiot full of sound and fury signifying nothing."

Archetype

Each people develop a collective consciousness that is always far lesser developed than the consciousness of their best individuals. The flowered ones are only a few. The confused and the ignorant, as well as those that get awed by evil and call it heroic, are many. Their confounded will and corrupt ways arrest the awakening of the collective consciousness. It remains in a state of inner strife. It adorns its surface with the flowers of the wisdom of its best individuals, but inside it remains raging with the sinful, wicked passions of its numbers and leaders. This situation cannot change until the people strengthen the will to defeat evil by uniting their dull and frightened support to good. Evil remains free and unconquered in the souls of most of the people, even if they abhor its triumph. Like a huge serpent, the collective consciousness coils round the individual soul and obstructs, inhibits and cynically thwarts its will for good.

The constituents of the collective consciousness are archetypal in form, by which I mean that they are the same for each individual. The evil, stupid deeds of a people, and their sloth at doing selfless good deeds, turn during the course of centuries into compulsive forces that we call social and historical habits. The average individual soul loses its individual will for good, caught in the stranglehold of this sick collective consciousness. This is the price an enlightened individual has to pay for belonging to a people. Their social and historical habits turn them deaf and blind to his genius, while they promote those that are like this collective consciousness, stupid, dull and regressive, only because they look to be its children. This collective consciousness turns into the sad fate of the genius and the good luck of those who are devoid of humanity and of the will to sacrifice their selfishness. The fate is not written in the stars. It is the creation of the cynical, slothful, fearsome and frightened collective consciousness. Yet even a single man can change the collective consciousness from being the enemy of a good individual to being his/her best friend. Guru Gobind Singh did this to an ordinary baker within the twinkling of an eye. He told him, "the people gave thee the skin of a donkey, and I baptize thee with my sword, and see thy skin shines like the skin of the lion." This baker dashed straight into the enemy ranks and killed those who had kept him in terror earlier.

The collective consciousness is the leviathan. It is monstrous. It has no mind and no soul. Though born of the spiritual and mental state of the people in some past, it lacks soul. Therefore, it cannot see the changes wrought by time and cannot have any initiative. Yet it is held sacred by the people only because it had lasted with them ever since their ancestors had recognized their group's separate identity. They wrongly identify it as their culture. Culture gets born every moment afresh from an awakened soul and fills its mental and physical instruments. There cannot be culture without the soul, and the collective consciousness has no soul. To call it consciousness is a misnomer since it is always in stupor. Like Frankenstein, it has come to life though it should have belonged to the dead.

The collective archetypes sit as parasites on each individual soul. God has sent the souls to live. Instead the archetypes live and the souls are compelled to supply all their power to these parasites. The task before every soul is to dissolve its collective archetypes and express the freedom, sweetness and light hidden inside it. There is nothing to be proud of in the collective archetypes. The Gurus talked not of the peculiarities of different people. They talked of the only light of the *Waheguru* that illumines each individual and gives him soul, name and form.

With the advent of the Gurus, a struggle began between the powers of *tantriks* and the power of Love. Medieval India had largely surrendered to *tantra*. All institutions and systems that emphasise the form and not the substance can be classified as *tantra*. *Raajtantra*, i.e., politics, as it is mostly practiced, is as much a *tantra* as the *tantra* practised by wizards, jugglers and roadside magicians, because all of them earn their bread by showing tricks. The *tantriks* had become formidable and looked invincible. The public mind feared and revered them. The people had accepted that their fate was in their hands. They did not as much as dare to dream of altering their fate, and of changing the foreign masters with indigenous people. The people had forgotten that the ultimate substance of all creation is love, whatever the immediate substance. They had forgotten that the force of true love could compel the strongest *tantra* to yield or perish. The Gurus reminded the people of the power of love. They called them to liquidate the insensitive and deceptive *tantra* from their religious, spiritual as well as social lives, and install love in its place.

Surrender to *tantra* in all walks of life had caused regression in the Indian soul. What was once full of love and light had become diseased and crippled. A number of unbreakable fetters had grown within and around it as a result of this surrender. They were the archetypes, i.e. strong psychological fetters that had grown out of surrender to evil. India had become a game sanctuary to fanatic and racially incensed invading hordes. They did not need any permit to hunt humans in India. The fanatic raiders were racists that prided in their racial chains. They did not know what constituted human liberty. To kill anybody, loot and rape innocent people, and to become kings by simply throwing their turbans in the air was their definition of liberty. They did not know that a liberated man is he who values others' liberty. They were unaware that to have double standards, liberty for oneself and slavery for others, is the sign of the infidel, in the right sense of the word. They had no use for the liberating Indian philosophy that spoke of the world as a family.

Such was the galore of ignorant beliefs with them that they did not see in this sublime declaration the future 'Charter of Human Rights'. They saw in it stupidity, since the Indians had welcomed guests like them. Repeated defeats at the hands of such barbarians was not seen by the Indians as the inevitable start of the inevitable later success of great ideals. It had rather shaken their self-confidence to the extent that they had started believing that slavery was the price that those who wanted to live by human values must pay.

The substance of a soul is love. As long as it is emphasised, every soul expresses itself in an original way. When emphasis shifts to archetypes, love disappears. In its place, archetypal images occupy the soul. The soul then expresses only the archetypal images, created by the soulless collective conscious. The joyous variety of human characters and their originality withers with the disappearance of love.

The Gurus entered deep into the soul of the Indian people. There they exploded certain myths that were feeding and strengthening these life-negating archetypes. The archetypes throw a veil of ignorance over the consciousness of the individuals. This veil paralyses the ability of the soul to produce positive consciousness. It makes the life of the people false and stale. It stops expressing the light of their souls. This inability robs the self-confidence of the soul. Instead of believing in its ever-new inner light, the soul starts believing in the archetypes. This belief turns those soulless archetypes into spiritual archetypes that look like eternal truths. Such people live with superstitions, ignorance and delusions.

The Gurus told the people that archetypes are collective negative characteristics that terrorize and occupy the psyche of a people. They do not represent their true characters. They are parasites on the spiritual foundation of every human personality, which deprive it of spiritual light and freshness. Archetypes turn into strong and blind habits that people start calling fate. They mould their lives according to fixed and frustrating patterns. The moment the soul begins its earthly journey they capture it, intercept its course, and lead it astray. The Gurus told the people that they were captains of their souls and masters of their destiny. They had only to liquidate the veil thrown by slavery on their consciousness to see that in reality each of them was worth one hundred twenty five thousand slave owners.

When the Gurus appeared on the stage pessimism, regression and escape from society to forests had already become the habits of the sensitive and learned people of India. They had become victims of the loser mentality. The Hindus were wasting their spiritual powers and wisdom in the search of some inner heaven where there were no foreign rulers heaping misery and dishonour on them. The Gurus told them that their sufferings were not the dictates of fate or stars. 'The moving finger' is nothing but your racial archetypes that you can change by making spiritual efforts, like the ancient practice of *Atmayagya*, in which the soul sacrificed itself to what it did not like. This self-sacrifice was not self-extinction, since the soul could not die. Instead its adversary died as a result of its self-sacrifice. Self-sacrifice of the soul was the way of the soul to enter and destroy the adversary. Whatever opposed the immortal soul could not contain it once the soul had entered it. It was a categorical imperative that the adversary of the soul would have to give such a soul rebirth, and perish itself in the process. The soul had not to fight the fooleries of its adversary, since whatever the soul fought acquired its immortality. The best way of attack in such a situation was the self-sacrifice of the soul to the adversary. It had not to stop at self-sacrifice. It had to ask the adversary to reproduce it. It was the right of the soul acquired through self-sacrifice. It must exercise it. Exercising this right resulted in the good of humanity. The Gurus said it was the only way to overcome evil.

The Gurus told the people that what they considered to be the iron hand of fate was only a hand of clay for one who had realized God as Love. They said that what they in a despondent mood had characterized their fate of slavery and frustration was no fate at all. Our own follies, superstitions and over-rating of the chance success of the heartless invaders had blinded us to the infinite power hidden inside our souls. Only the domain of *Maya* had stretches for the time being up to their spiritual world, because of their reliance on ignorance. They had only to shake off the torpor from their soul. The morning of a golden age was waiting for them. With a gang of negative spiritual powers, ignorance was determining and misguiding the steps of their souls. A deeper faith in the truth that God was only good, and the evil created by the enemies of human values could be knocked down with a feather, was the cure against it. The feather was trust that the soul was the image of God. Since God was only good the soul too was only good. The Gurus asked the people to trust the will of the *Waheguru* that is always in favour of the oppressed never in favour of the oppressor.

The Gurus asked the sleeping collective consciousness to shake off its slumber. They showed the way to neutralise the poisonous and suicidal archetypes. The spiritual powers, coiled and fossilised by this magical spell of archetypes, could be recovered, they said. The archetypes have no power, if they are left alone. It is ignorance that throws a soul in their snare. They said do not be ashamed of your weakness, because it is the raw material that can be converted into strength. They did not feel despondent on seeing that the Indians had lost vitality and spirit and had turned into sparrows before the enemy who had been falsely emboldened by his tricky nature, since God did not like tricks, and was always with the innocent and the truthful. Deluded by his easy success over a people who did not rob others of their freedom, the enemy was behaving like a hawk. Guru Gobind Singh proved that before the hawk of truth the hawk of lies and injustice had turned into a sparrow. Finding no truth in him to face it, the cruel ruler had stooped to torture the brave heart of a father by entombing alive his two little boys in a wall. The enemy lost the little support of his soul when he saw no trace of fear on the faces of the little boys, whom Mother Nature was asking, "who was the immortal mother that produced such fearless boys?" Later on, the enemy was baffled to see their brave father who did not express any sorrow at the loss, and instead composed a hymn to commemorate their martyrdom. Fanatical and senseless cruelty cannot deter the determination of those who take to no refuge except God. Guru Gobind Singh declared, henceforth sparrows shall kill

the hawks. Who knows whether he was thinking of the tender faces
of his boys and the ferocious hawk like eyes of the Emperor when
he said:

> "Sure shall I make the sparrow fight the hawk
> One sparrow shall fight hundred thousand hawks
> Shall sing my name Gobind Singh on their rock
> All and one and one and all the rocking hawks."

Thus, gathering whatever was left of the vanquished race of
the once mighty sons of Bharat, and without blinding himself to
their sore weaknesses, he guided them like the wind guiding a storm.
They moved like rushing waves, Guru Gobind Singh ahead on a
steed, charging as if it was a wind. Much before the enemy could
know, the sway swept him aside. Few parallels can indeed be drawn
from world history to such a determined and successful uprising.
The Indians had succumbed to the way of cold grief. Not only this,
they had employed their philosophy to give false tilts to passive
suffering. The deepest destructions in the soul had been borne
silently by the Indians during the dark medieval times. A proverb
had taken birth from this new archetypal habit — "it is vain to cry
out your sorrow. Laugh with the world; and bear your sorrow alone."
The Gurus refused to accept this counsel of lull. They said — Sing
your sorrows together. It will make a hymn of your sorrow, and the
Lord will listen. Report your sorrows to the *Waheguru* in all truth,
without exaggeration and without under-statement. Do not vomit
impotent wrath and poison against the enemy. Stick to truth while
reporting his injustice to the Lord. Ask the Lord, with a sense of
justice and in exact words, what action you expect of him. Clarity,
brevity and truthfulness of your expression will surely invoke God's
justice. No tyrant can stand on two legs after what he has done.

The Indians had been bearing all destructions of culture and
social values by certain unjust foreign kings coldly. A fallacy had
developed among them that to grow indifferent to pain and inhuman
tortures was to conquer them spiritually. The Gurus exploded this
myth. They said, better a hot-blooded expression of your grief than
a cold one. They realized that what their people had styled a spiritual
reply to atrocities was in fact hatred of the worst order. It was cold

hatred—the type we find in the eyes of crushed snakes and wounded tigers.

The racial habit of cold grief was an inhuman adjustment with the monstrous situation. The most valuable thing given to men, love, had been butchered. To this day this inhuman adjustment springs from our unconscious. Whenever love is killed, we willingly accept cold grief as an alternative to active love. It is considered heroic not to weep, not to protest, not to question. Such perverted virtues are the outcome of the collective sin of coldly accepting the murder of this most precious Divine element in us.

The Gurus exploded this myth. They showed that it was no virtue to hide your face from the butcher, lest your wrath burns him. It was rather like carrying his shame in your eyes. Thus you only help him to be more wicked. The shame would have been fruitful had it been confined to the eyes of the evildoer.

The Sikh Gurus have also upheld the same age-old perennial virtues but with a difference. They did not agree that the vices and sins in man deserve to be crushed. What prevented them was a better understanding of human psychology. They seem to have drawn a distinction between the sins that a man commits out of anger, lust or pride and the sins that appear in him as reflex, or involuntary response to others' inhuman deeds or sins from a nerve-centre, after initially turning back upon it. Not to react to others' sins, but to act against the adversary's evil action is the ideal situation, since in initiating action all our mental faculties can consult each other. In reaction the enemy guides us. A soul that is convinced of the wisdom of action, not of reaction, will soon find his faculty of reaction gradually turning inactive, and his faculty of taking action against an unjust action taking over from the faculty of reaction. It is in advising to act rather than react that the Gurus' unique contribution to the quest of liberation from psychological complexes and diseases lies.

The Gurus knew that the collective sins of the people couldn't be cured so easily, for the individual was not their cause and yet he suffered for them more than he suffered for his personal sins. The whole race was the cause. The collective sins had inhibitive influence on the individuals. Personal sins did not have any inhibitive influence on the individual. One could neither isolate him from his people, nor prevent the effect of collective sins on him. This predicament of man is unique and has not been addressed by the learned. Most of the Indian systems had advocated relief from both collective and personal sins in renunciation. This was not just. It had blinded the masters to the need of liquidating collective sins collectively, so that they did not plague every individual separately with their tremendous force that no individual could bear. The result was that the individual consciousness had simply petrified in face of racial sins, like caste distinctions and degradation of women. The Gurus invoked the people to liquidate the collective sins. They found it rather too easy to liquidate the collective sins that looked earlier impossible to liquidate. They said that if every individual disowned the collective sins sincerely they would liquidate. The soul had only to sacrifice itself to every collective sin and get reborn of it. The process of their liquidation was as simple as this. This great contribution of the Gurus to the science of applying philosophic wisdom to collective sins has not been appreciated so far. The efficacy of this simple method of liquidating the tremendous, negative and paralysing spiritual energy of collective sins can be seen in its historical outcome. The disciples of the Gurus showed great independence and will for amelioration, while their Hindu kith and kin, who had no knowledge of this practice, remained inhibited and passive. As a result of this simple exercise the Sikhs got filled miraculously with tremendous energy that nailed superstitions and redundant customs along with the enemies of the nation. The Gurus were not concerned with individual Nirvana alone. More important than it was collective Nirvana of the people from collective sins that had been draining three fourth of the energy of every Hindu.

Most of their contemporary learned men and yogis were advocating that crushing of negative emotions, like anger, pride, greed, lust, attachment and jealousy, was the only way to overcome them. The Gurus said that crushing was not the same as conquering them. Moreover, crushing rather strengthened them. Often crushing, instead of killing negative emotions, killed the spirit. The Gurus taught a new way to practice the rishis' call to conquer negative emotions. They said conquest was possible only by changing the spirit inside the emotions. Instead of suppressing or expressing them, if the lamp of love is kindled inside the negative emotions they would become willing slaves to love, since love was the most charming activity of the human heart. It had been given a central place by nature among all emotions, thoughts and sensations. Every power inside man willingly bowed down to love and to no other power. The Gurus, therefore, asked their disciples to cultivate love as the lamp that illuminated every faculty and power of the individual. They had found that by its very nature love neither suppressed any faculty nor encouraged its unrestrained activity to the chagrin of other faculties. It did so because of its intrinsic intimacy with the principle of beauty and proportion. Love's beauty-consciousness got transferred to the mental faculties through touch and direct contact. More than any sermon, love imbued every faculty with a sense of rhythm and beauty that acted as a deterrent to hyper activity. Since it was no external suppression of the hyper activity but an internal self-restraint by the faculty itself there could be no psychological repercussions. This has turned out to be the only practical way, within the call of decency, of controlling the plethora of faculties and energies inside man against their tendency to go wild.

One of the collective sins or archetypes was the suppressed feeling of revenge. Much wrong had been done to the Indians by various invaders. So shamelessly had their noble dreams for all mankind been shattered with brutal force that every heart spouted the venom of revenge. It was largely a passive feeling of revenge. Long misunderstanding of the virtues of forgiveness and non-violence had taught them only to curb this feeling. Such curbing could prevent its direct outburst, but surely it did not cure them of the negative emotion of revenge. It was finding expression in wrong directions. If you do not direct your anger to its cause, the anger will spend itself on some good person close to you. This would be inhuman as well as an act of cowardice. Unless this passive feeling of revenge was transformed into some positive feeling it would not leave the heart. In that case the Indians could not experience again the open sunshine that they had experienced at the dawn of their civilization. The passive feeling of revenge would remain overcast on their souls like still clouds that neither moved nor rained.

The most difficult task before the Gurus was, therefore, to find a human expression for this feeling of revenge. It was not that they treated it as any part of bravery. It was the necessary narrow passage through which every pilgrim of immortality had to pass. They neither eulogized revenge like the fanatics, nor resorted to crushing it, thereby making it all the more real and permanent.

The Gurus had realized that instead of being a natural reaction, revenge had become a subtle archetype in the Indian soul. The people in their thoughtless hurry to remove the bad feeling of revenge had suppressed it with their spiritual power. It was an abuse of the spiritual power that would not go without causing some greater injury. The injury was obvious. The spiritual power while suppressing contaminated the negative emotion with its spiritual radiation. As a negative emotion it was limited to the world of emotions. Contaminated by spiritual radiation it became infinite, in a perverted sense. Spiritual radiation was a sickness even though it transmitted infinity. An emotional malady has to be cured by some emotion, for like deals with like in nature, so said the rishis. A positive emotion grows out of a negative emotion the moment the soul sacrifices itself to the negative emotion and asks it to give it (the soul) rebirth. Contaminated by spiritual radiation, it turned into an archetype of the souls of the Hindus, and arrested it in its coils. In *Ramayana* Valmiki wrote of the *Naagpash* (the serpent fetter) with which Ahiravan made both Ram and Laxman ineffective before hiding them in the underworld. This *Naagpash* was an example of the archetype. Ahiravan was an expert in contaminating negative emotions with spiritual radiation and thereby turning them into archetypes. The souls of the Hindus were fettered by a number of such archetypes. The Gurus had realized why they were feeling powerless to use the wisdom of the rishis to remove the superstitions and supernatural fears that had been planted in their psyche by several unscrupulous invader-rulers.

Wicked emotions of the heart have got to be rooted out. There the Gurus agreed with Patanjali and the whole of Indian tradition. They, however, differed in their method. They were against the use of spiritual power to crush negative emotions. To make such use of the spiritual power was to create serpent-fetters (archetypes) for one's own soul. The archetypes did not arrest the power to act by free will of the individual alone, but also of his forthcoming generations. The Gurus practiced *Viniyoga* to liquidate the archetypes. *Viniyoga* is the science that can unite as well as disunite two dissimilar powers. Only *Viniyoga* could break the sinister compound of spiritual power and negative emotion.

This explains the Sikh Gurus' willing self-sacrifice. They found the coils of the racial archetypes of fear and the will to escape from social realities too strong to be loosened by reasoning. They knew that on such occasions a cheerful self-sacrifice, if one could not live with honour, making the hands of the wicked subservient to one's own will to self-sacrifice, gives rebirth to a brave man in the very heart of the archetypes. He gets the powers to melt this inhuman archetypal fetter without becoming inhuman. When one dies for truth without malice or ill will, without fear or hatred, rather with abundance of compassion and forgiveness for the killer, one gets rebirth in the very soul of the killer. A true hero thus reappears as the conscience of the killer. This conscience fills him with repentance and fear of the Divine. All his wicked designs become weaker. It is on historical record that Aurangzeb had reached very near lunacy after the sacrifice of Guru Teg Bahadur. He suffered terrible visions as his bigotry had shattered him. Not only he, the entire grand edifice of the Mogul empire was shattered after those irrational and brutal acts of Aurangzeb.

The hero gets a two-fold rebirth after self-sacrifice in this manner. He reappears as the conscience of the murderer. He also takes rebirth, as I have said earlier, in the very heart of the archetype. He scatters that archetype as a cloud of smoke by *Viniyoga*. His words become scriptures for the life force of his people. Those words flow gently in the blood stream and in the veins of his people.

The Gurus had all their lives battled against archetypes. Their activity had basically one aim and that was—not to let the will to live regressed, due to unbearable humiliation and frustration created by the rulers. Their beautiful songs, on the one hand, cut like sword through the lulling superstitions. On the other hand, their arguments, battles and willing acceptance of death destroyed the archetypes arresting the souls of the people. They strove tirelessly to keep the people awake. Nirgrantha Nathputra Mahavir, nearly two thousand five hundred years before, had told his principal disciple Gautam Ganadhar, "Do not let the soul sleep, O Gautam, nay not for a moment even. Do not forget that it is your best friend, but, if it turns lethargic and sleepy, it turns into your worst enemy." The *Gurbani* for nearly five centuries has been doing the same work — awakening the souls from indolence. The embrace of the archetypes is too comfortable, though paralysing. Those who come to walk on the razor's edge have no comfort in it.

2

The Real

$\mathcal{U}$ltimately only God, the *Waheguru*, is real. There is no dualism in Sikhism. But from the practical point of view, Sikhism calls five things Real — God, the individual soul, and God's three powers, wisdom, nature and love. The three *Divine powers* are also known as *Gurbani*, *Kudarat* and *Bhakti* in Sikh scriptures. Apart from these five realities, all else is unreal, a play of shadows staged by ignorance.

These five realities deserve to be dealt with separately. That will help in understanding the philosophy of the Gurus.

God

Strictly speaking only God exists. *Waheguru* or *Akaal Purakh* is the only reality. The position of the individual soul at first sight is not very clear in Sikh texts. Sometimes the tendency is to retain its individuality even after Nirvana. The *Japji* records that it dwells in the *Sachkhand* along with the Lord and partakes His bliss. The belief that God selects some of his servants and inspires them with a new vision to bring the lost world to order again, confirms belief in the individuality of the soul, besides the Lord. It would appear that the *Sachkhand* is peopled with several blossomed souls. It is a community of blissful and blithe souls.

There is, however, another refrain in Sikh scriptures. It is nearer the Upanishads. According to it, the individual soul loses its separate identity on attaining Nirvana. All individuality other than God is ignorance. Guru Nanak says:

'Where self exists
God is not,
Where God exists
There self is not.'

Rag Maru

This ambiguity about the individual soul disappears if we remember that the Sikh Gurus have spoken of two Gods. One is *saguna*, i.e., full of Divine attributes. He is the personal God. "His eyes are radiant and teeth exquisite, nose stately and hair long. His skin is golden" He is the same God full of noble attributes who the Hindus worship and love—Gobind, Murari, Hari, Kanha. All these names are among the 1000 names of Vishnu recorded in the scriptures.

The other God described in the Sikh texts is *nirguna* or the Absolute beyond attributes. He is beyond space and time, beyond intellect or imagination, beyond all categories of the intellect. "He is inaccessible, unfathomable, altogether distinct from His creation", as Macauliffe concludes. He is described as *Niranjan, Adi Purakh, Akaal Purakh, Sat Purakh, Karta Purakh*. He is nearer the Brahm of the Upanishads. Nothing exists other than Him. The individual selves form the 'multicoloured dome' in which the same white radiance of God shines.

Both of these Gods are in fact one and the same Reality, realized from two different roads, one, the road of love, i.e., *bhakti* and the other, the road of knowledge, i.e., *gyan*. The Gurus were enlightened souls. They had realized Him from both these roads. It would be wrong to say that the *Saguna Ishwara* is inferior to the *Nirguna Brahma*. No such gradation issues from Sikh texts. There is no authority to maintain it. If some scholars have maintained it, it is because of the habit of the intellect to categorise and put things in a hierarchical order. The truth is away from such attempts. In fact if hierarchy must be there then it would be nearer the spirit of the Gurus to place the *Saguna Ishwara* above the *nirguna Brahma*. It is because *Saguna Ishwara* responds to love, and love is higher than intellect. The devotee need not bother that all the attributes that he ascribes to God are finite, and finite cannot be ascribed to

God who is by nature infinite. His love for the Lord will tell him that attributes are only an imperfect way of describing the Perfect Beloved. Attributes are only an expression of the exuberance in the heart of the lover. Attributes born of the intellect put limitations on God, but attributes born of love have no fetters, just as true love has no fetters.

When the Gurus spoke for the heart they retained the individuality of the soul, but when they spoke for the mind they said that the realized soul became one with the Absolute, the Wonderful God, the *Waheguru*. The dispute, whether in Nirvana the soul is retained or not, is equally born of ignorance.

Intellect is rigorous and very exacting and for this reason it has been considered a lesser faculty. It moves by dry logic and it cannot be satisfied by any Reality except the Absolute. But the lover knows a higher face of Reality where the dispute of one and many becomes meaningless. There each becomes all and also all become one. There the individuality is retained without any dualism, even as the beloved lives as a distinct individual in the mind and heart of the lover and still there is no duality. The experience of the lover is more monistic than monism as a theory.

Self-realization is poetry in action. None but a poet understands the philosophic truth. One should not forget that the Gurus have spoken in poetry, and that too musical. To ask them to satisfy the dry intellect alone would be a basic error. The whole in us can alone understand the whole. For one who knows this basic difference between realization and intellectualisation there is no ambiguity about the relationship of the soul and the Absolute in Sikh scriptures.

The Sikh scriptures repeatedly assert that God is beyond time. He is *Akaal Purakh*, i.e., the Lord who transcends time. It had a special purpose. It would, therefore, be necessary to deal with this special attribute at some length in order to understand the Sikh concept of divinity correctly.

One important point of beauty about the language of the Gurus is that it is mostly clear and unambiguous. It reveals in its brevity and limitations. The Gurus have not used the language of the mystics even to describe their mystical experiences. It is rare that one finds such mystical language in Sikh scriptures as the one used by Guru Nanak in his poem 'Aarati': "Thou hast a thousand eyes but without eyes thou art." The refrain, however, is so full of joy that it would be unfair to read meanings in it. Only the joy coming out of it is its truth. Those who go for the meaning might get misled.

It appears that the Gurus knowingly avoided the mystical language. They knew its disastrous effects on the ordinary intellect. I shall also deal with the mystical aspect in some detail for it is essential in order to understand their concept of the Divine. I would also like to discuss a typical Sikh name of the Divine, i.e., the *Akaal Purakh*. I shall endeavour to create an image of God as conceived by the Gurus, through these discussions. It is not possible in these brief lectures to discuss all the attributes of God. I shall, however, speak of the *Akaal Purakh* and the mystical experience of the Gurus in this context.

Beyond Time—*The Akaal Purakh*

They called Him 'beyond time'—*Akaal*. No doubt several religions have called God 'beyond time'. It is one of the many names attributed to Him. But it is the Gurus who enshrined this name. To remember Him as the one whom time cannot touch, being itself only one of His manifestations, was highly exciting. It was also hopeful to a people in despair. Time seemed endless, for they were hard times indeed. The foreign rulers had established themselves on the soil, and were busy teaching the Indians religion through atrocities. Life hung on a thread. There was darkness all around. The hard times had assumed a gigantic shape and it seemed they would never end. To worship Him as the abstract Brahm was not enough to wipe out the gloom from the eyes of the common man. It did not enter the dark recesses of time where his soul was imprisoned. It was, really heartening to learn that the Divine could not be touched by time, and was greater; and, in fact, was the creator of time; and that, in this insignificant, enslaved, dishonoured body of ours lived none else but He Himself, as our individual soul. Thus even we could not be touched by time, if we willed so.

Through this concept Nanak sowed the seed in the minds and hearts of his people that was surely capable of removing the complex of being a subject people. Intellect cannot think of anything beyond time. To the intellect, the bird of true love can take a flight only up to the skies of space, but within the bounds of time. The space seemed to belong to foreigners for nothing belonged to a subject people. Even the freedom to worship and sing His praise up toward the sky was denied. A people who had been taught religion for several millenniums as the instrument of absolute freedom were being taught religion as the instrument of absolute slavery. Time seemed to have accepted the dictates of the trampler and the invader. Thus within the realm of space and time there was only darkness. God who dwelt in the world as the immanent Reality in His creation was obviously powerless to save His children from cruel rulers. This revelation was indeed horrifying and this seemed to have become a common revelation. Except in the case of the gifted ones, this seemed to have become the common knowledge. It was the view of deep despair. Natural logic in untrained minds of millions was leading thought to this impasse. Unless something was done to prevent this deduction, unless the natural logic in untrained minds of millions was helped to find the road to hope with ease and effortlessness, there was no future for the people.

Nanak found the solution in the concept of the *Akaal Purakh* — the Man whom time cannot wither, whom space cannot bind. He walks into the house of space and time and goes out of it at His will. Once inside it, He cannot be imprisoned like the ordinary mortals. He does not age at the touch of time. He does not fall at its final knock. Rather the clock of time has to run in the reverse order if He so wills. Time is nothing more than a clock hanging on His wall, and space is no more than the window through which He sees the constellations and the universes that He has created and which are a source of delight to Him.

It is not without significance that Nanak used the word *Purakh,* which means a man. He has knowingly used it in the anthropomorphic sense. No doubt the influence of Samkhya philosophy can be traced on his thought. Both Kapil and Vigyanabhikshu have talked of the *Purusha* whose mere presence activates *Prakriti* to unveil her beauty in several forms, from *mahat,* i.e., the feeling of self-importance, down to the five elements. Nanak used the word *Purakh* also because it aroused the memory of the *Virat Purusha,* the first man of the Rig Veda who was greater than the greatest; who was not subject to space and time.

Thus though Nanak's *Akaal Purakh* was a different being, more concrete than abstract, who suited the devotional needs of the masses, yet whatever links could be traced between Him and the *Virat Purusha* of Rig Veda, and the *Purusha* of Gita and Samkhya philosophy were to the advantage of Guru Nanak. He has therefore nowhere made any attempt to distinguish the *Akaal Purakh* from the *Virat Purusha* or *Purusha.* His aim was to build an idea in the popular mind of a Being, who though concrete was yet beyond the withering or all-ruling hand of time. In this, Nanak fulfilled a long nurtured desire of the popular mind without sacrificing the philosophic truths. In all folk tales and legends, the popular mind has been in search of a hero — be it Hanuman or Hercules, Hiawatha or Khidr or Gilgamesh — who is beyond the clutches of time. He is immortal, for His flesh is not meant to decay, or his bones to tire. Even to those heroes who the scriptures show to have died a natural death — Krishna for example — the hearts of the people have provided a mysterious, warm and cosy niche that turns their death unreal. The people have retained their memory with such fondness that it appears that they had never died. To this day, the cowherd boys and milkmaids of Vrindaban believe ardently that Krishna will appear some day, as if he had only gone to other lands or hidden somewhere. As if He is not dead. He has only transformed Himself into a flesh that never changes and never withers, and his skin is forever, of the same blue hue of a fresh lotus.

It appears that Nanak used the term *Purakh* knowing well that it arouses the figure of a man in the popular mind. He did so for a psychological reason. He wanted to awaken hope. When reason had closed all the doors and showed nothing but doom, he used the door of wishes and their fulfilment, which is always neglected by the philosophers and the seers. Where intellect fails, a deeper faculty, i.e., *pragya* works, so said the ancient seers. But it worked for the few who had already made full use of the intellect. What about the commoner who was neither willing nor had the capacity to walk to the frontiers of the intellect? Nanak was concerned about the millions. They needed hope more than the seer. He, therefore, gave them the idea of the *Akaal Purakh*, in a bid to save the crumbling roof of their ancient faith. He knew *Akaal Purakh* would be the bridge between their dark night of despair and God. His image, established firmly in their minds, will enable them to feel the *Nirankar* in their veins and blood. It was no use making Him a distant and perfect God. He should first be a palpable reality for the masses. When gloom encircles and all doors get closed, the human mind indulges in fancies and yearns for heroes who come to man's rescue. Such a one was the Matsyaavatar, the Divine fish. Another was Narsingh, the Divine, lion-faced, who saved Prahalad. Instead of taxing the tired intellect and asking man to think about facts, Nanak used the faculties of hope and wish-fulfilment to awaken the souls of his fellow beings. He knew once the soul got awakened the intellect would get rejuvenated. Then alone could it see hope and reason that seemed to it an impossibility in those days.

It is not without significance that above all other names of God besides *Akaal Purakh*, Nanak preferred the name *Waheguru*, i.e., God the Wonderful. He has emphasised the wonderful aspect of God more than any other. He did so as a supplement to his attempt at wish-fulfilment. It is only the wonderful God who can appear as a man and still remain untouched by time, and who can grant wish-fulfilment.

Wonder precedes all fruitful thinking. Man wondered: What are these stars? Why the birds fly while man cannot? How does lightning appear in the sky? The result of this wondering attitude is the progress of science and philosophy. Nanak traced the way back. When the intellect gets blinded, let us return to our original wonders. Instead of thinking, let us first wonder at the glories of God. A wondering mind sets a faltering intellect on the right road.

Scholars have often translated *Akaal Purakh* as 'God who is beyond time'. To call him beyond time is to limit Him in some space that is beyond the bounds of time, for the term 'beyond' is basically spatial. He is not only beyond time but beyond space too. For a Being to be such in a real and *graphic* sense, instead of being beyond, another quality is needed, that of entering inside and going outside freely of both space and time, and getting affected neither by entry nor by exit. Such a Being has to be wonderful. *Akaal Purakh* was therefore conceived by Nanak, not only as the one beyond space and time, but as the wonderful *Waheguru* who appears at His will inside the folds of space and time as well as outside, without getting changed in any manner.

Mysticism

The Divine experience is indeed too full to be expressed in words or actions. Those who use the mystical language either confound the commoner or create a distance between the commoner and themselves. One of the main aims of the Gurus was not to create this distance. They paved the way for the mingling of the elite with the commoner. The scholar and the seer were to share their lives with the common people. By mingling with them they were to illuminate and elevate the life of the common people. This can be done only by one whose character and insight is beyond questioning; one who has nothing to hide from the commoner's eye. The Gurus had entered into the final halo of the Divine, which has the infectious purity of a child. The Gurus have called God Love in positive terms. Their concept of God views love as his main virtue. They used language only as far as it could convey coherently, consistently and with clarity. Language was not allowed to indulge in mysticism. They left mysticism to silence and personal experience.

I shall try to explain this point further. It can be appreciated if it is borne in mind that my contention is only that the Gurus did not use a mystical language; not that they had no mystical experience.

All deeper experiences have something that language cannot express. Still there has been a strong fascination of language for the saints, and they have been using it to express their unique experiences of the Divine, without expressing anything comprehensible. Their futile use of language has given rise to several warring creeds within their systems. One of their disciples gives one interpretation to their utterances while the other, with equal authenticity, puts forth a completely different interpretation. This has led to much confusion.

Buddha was silent when questions regarding the existence of the soul and God were put to him. The reason that he gave to Ananda for this silence was that his reply would have confused the questioner further. Yagyavalka stopped replying to the too eager and inquisitive Gargi when she asked him question after question to explain the Light behind all phenomena. He said, *'you have asked too many questions about a thing about which so many questions are not to be asked. Take care Gargi lest your head falls.'*

Mysticism is often born of a certain misuse of language. All mystics have, at best, used equivocal terms. It explains nothing. A better way with the greatest masters has been silence, when the burden of language becomes too heavy. Language is a tool and it is for clarity. The logical positivists like Mr A.J. Ayer and Mr Gilbert Ryle are indeed, to some extent, correct when they insist upon a mathematical language. Wittgenstein was a modern mystic who had also discarded the use of language to convey inexplicable experiences, for it involves one into another snare—the linguistic lust. His philosophy was a 'linguistic therapy' that addressed itself to the peculiar *'sickness'* of his time.

Ram, Krishna, Buddha, the Sikh Gurus and the twenty-four *Tirthankaras* have not used language to express anything that could not be clearly and precisely described. The Indian tradition is against expressing the deeper experiences mystically. At a higher stage, therefore, they do not recommend scriptures. The ultimate truth grows in the heart, and language fails there. Many Indian rishis had called themselves 'the sky-clad', and the sky stands for space in Indian thought. They enter space intuitively after a thorough discipline of the senses and the mind. There is no language in space. The 'word' is lying there unuttered and each seeker has to awaken it to speak to Him. Ancient scriptures say, billions of years ago when there was no universe, *Siva* (Absolute) was dancing ecstatically. He made a sound '*Om*' and space and time were born. Sound made space its home. The modern astrophysicists also say the same thing—there was a big bang and space and time came into existence. Modern scientists have provided proofs for many findings of the rishis that were earlier ignored as figments of an imagination that had gone wild. There is need today to distinguish between the two kinds of imagination—the wild imagination and the vision of the rishis. It will unite all truth-loving people, and provide a new impetus to human values.

The Sikh Gurus have also made a limited use of language. They have not used it to explain the inexplicable aspect of the Divine. They have used it to explain only that glimpse of the Divine that can be clearly expressed in definite terms. Their aim was not complete self-expression. Their aim was to express only if the listener could be benefited. They have, therefore, described Him as pure love, untainted by worldliness. Another attribute of the Divine, according to them, is being beyond time—*Akaal*. He has also been described as the kind, just and forgiving creator of all. All these terms are positive. Language can be used here with clarity. Beyond this is the mystical experience that is not accessible to language. The Gurus have not described it. They have not permitted Sikhism to indulge in the luxury of equivocal mysticism.

I have already said that mystical experience and its equivocal expression are two different things. No deeper experience of truth is devoid of inexplicable shades. Even the scientists have such experiences when they enter into the mysteries of the universe. But they express only that much of it that can be reduced into equations and clear terms. Similarly the Gurus, in spite of their mystical experiences, have not resorted to mystical expression.

The Mystical Sway

In the days of the Gurus, due to a long history of sloth and inertia, of suppression and slumber, mysticism, which charlatans and spiritual leftists (*vamamargis*) also practised, had degenerated into occultism, superstition and escapism. The Upanishadic mysticism was an expression of overflowing joy. It was not an intellectual expression. After the intellectual adventure, when the seers had found it incapable of revealing the Lord, and saw Him in a blaze of love, they sometimes used a language that did not convey a definite idea. Later on, after the invasions had sacked the vitality of the people, certain confused and beleaguered thinkers used mysticism as an escape from all cruel realities. Soon it became a fashion. The Gurus refused to call it mysticism, since in their view only a lover could be an honest mystic, not a thinker. They banished it from their *Sangat* (assemblies, congregations). It was a mark of the limitation of the soul. They believed that it would be great to be rid of it even in spiritual discourse. To them the awakening of love was freedom from the bondage of intellectual mysticism. Love was direct experience of God. After the intellectual efforts come to their climax, the intellect discloses the last secret to all intellectual mystics. It had whispered in the ears of a famous intellectual mystic, Omar Khayyam, "I am sorry, after taking you on this long Odyssey of mysticism toward Truth I must confess now that I did not have the map to locate the island of Truth." This kind of subtle deception played by the intellect had alerted Nanak and the nine Gurus against mystical expressions.

C.G. Jung says, "The possession of the mystery cuts one off from intercourse with the rest of mankind." The Gurus neither attained nor aimed at such isolation. They were in constant communion with the people. They broke all barriers of the mystique to communicate with the common people and to tell them the truth in a simple way that they could grasp. God to them was more of a reality than a mystery. They had known that no secret or mystical religious practices were required to be in communion with Him. One could be in direct communion with God if one sacrificed his soul to Him out of selfless love. They did not play the role of the carrier of God's word.

The mystical sway is the power often developed by misguided saints and spiritual men. It develops confusions and uncertainties into spiritual power. This helps in breeding superstitions, fears and ignorance. The Gurus had realized that the contemporary life needed impetus or inspiration for right action, and it could come only from love. Those who taught people to execute the command of a wrathful and revengeful God did not know God, because God was neither wrathful nor revengeful. Even the worst sinner did not surprise him and did not arouse wrath in him. In his supreme wisdom, God always remains forgiving and merciful. He never asks any human to punish any sinner on His behalf. Those who claim that they have received such communication from God are, to say the least, liars. The Gurus said, "God is Love and the way to come close to Him is love. Only such action that is born of self sacrifice to God is acceptable to Him."

According to Sikhism, *haumey* or ego and action born of ego are the reverse of *hukum,* i.e., God's will, and action to fulfil the will of God. What is the way to know the will of God? Only by sacrificing one's soul and will to God one could experience His will. A true Sikh has to change *haumey* into *hukum.* Though they have not talked in detail of their spiritual experiences, yet there are important hints. The true devotee sacrifices his soul and entire being to God i.e. Love, and thereby exchanges *haumey* for *hukum.* Such a devotee gets the Divine gift of mystical sway. This Divine gift creates enemies for him. His followers also become prone to folly, superstition and blind faith. The Gurus asked their disciples not to stop there, and to give no importance to the mystical sway. Even the mystical sway was a snare. Most of the saints prefer to utilize this gift. Their further progress stops here. Patanjali had also warned the yogis not to lay much price on the Divine gifts and powers. To value them is the same as to miss the goal. There is no magical power or miracle that the Sikh Gurus claim to be their special virtue. Like the finest of the rishis, and like Mahavir and the Buddha, they refused to attract people to religion through miracles. They invoked only the power of love. For one to be able to love truly great penance and purification of the soul is needed. To communicate with love (God) is difficult, since only love in the individual soul can communicate with love. Love in individual souls is often found shocked, abused and sleeping. It is in torpor, not at all prepared to wake up. It loves its cool slumber, its coiled repose. The soul loves the injury that puts its faculty of love to sleep. It is like the mother of a naughty boy who ignores a little injury to the boy that has rendered him incapable of doing mischief.

On the contrary, the Gurus awakened this spiritual and deeply hurt emotion of love in the hearts of the Indians. The emotion of love, due to the habit of self-negation, gets intoxicated with despair and lulled with spiritual morphine. Life in India had been dehumanised by repeated invasions of the barbarians. The invaders had varying tastes for human suffering, and they employed varying ways to cause suffering to innocent citizens. The Indian people had loved immensely all the people who had come to them. Repeated betrayal by the outsiders, whom they had loved whole-heartedly, had brought them to a stage of despair when love ceased to be active in their souls. Their sleeping souls had become the base on which every invader was planting his perverted psyche as a parasite. Like kaleidoscopic pictures, with unaccountable fastness, the common man's life was moving without consulting his love. An utter slave he had become. The Gurus realized the danger. For a country with such an enlightened past, it was all the more suicidal. In the remote past, the soul had touched the supreme heights of evolution in India. It had realized its essence, i.e., love. Now without love wisdom was becoming a subtle bondage. Wisdom insulted, humiliated and frightened by those who had benefited from it proves to be the worst enemy of its owner. Wisdom starts seeing as more important than wisdom the ignorance that audaciously and superciliously hurts it. In spite of its proximity to Truth, emotionally wisdom is a very fragile thing. After getting hurt, it becomes merciless to the soul in which it gets born, and makes it a prisoner. The Indian soul has suffered long this pathetic anomaly. The spirit of negation had poisoned wisdom. Wisdom was there, but it could not be used without the spark of love. Devoid of love, wisdom had turned into a slave of the invader's cunning. The sweet waters were there, but none could drink, for they had been poisoned. What should have led the Indians to higher conquests and fulfilments, both here and hereafter, had brought them disaster and pessimism. "Why?" This was the question that struck Nanak. "Why so much darkness in spite of wisdom?" asked Nanak, and his anguished soul cried, "How can I come out of it?" He faced the problem realistically. There was a fundamental difference between the approach of other contemporary saints and the Gurus. The saints feared aggressive stupidity most. Shankaracharya had paved the way for the resurrection of love with his brilliant conception of *Maya*. But his followers had misunderstood it. They mistook it for an escape-route from the humiliating and cruel realities of the life of a people who had been enslaved. This mistaken interpretation of Shankaracharya's approach affected Tulsi Das, Ramanuja, Vallabha and all other succeeding illuminated saints. They all agreed on one point at least; that it was possible to build a different world within this tormented world of ours, and instead of lamenting for what man had made of man, a wise man should build his private world of spiritual wisdom and live in it, establishing a close link with God. The Gurus said No. "Not for me," said Nanak, "any private world of self-exaltation. Where the common man suffers, there is my field." The Gurus were the first, in the medieval days, to make an attempt to win back the earth for lovers, the children of God. They were realistic enough not to be satisfied with any spiritually animated world. They were clear that they had to love and share the common life and its sufferings. They had not to use their spiritual powers to build an ivory tower of elevated thoughts for themselves. They did not go for safety. They were born of courage, and dangers were what aroused them to more activity. They exploded the myth of the private, elevated and capsuled life. This paved the way for the descent of the Lord of love in this matrix of space and time. They could not have done so without provoking the wicked and the ruthless. They did not bow to the forces of darkness. They did not compromise even with spirituality on the point of love. Spirituality was not a life of thought to them. It was rather a life of love. Whoever was an enemy of love was their first enemy. This approach naturally brought them face-to-face before a mighty empire, and as time passed, they had to fortify themselves militarily against royal plunder and ransack. This gave a new shape and concept to the Sikh faith. Originally, militaristic activity was not envisaged. Guru Nanak lived as an ordinary farmer with his wife and two sons. Never for once did the idea of taking up arms come to him.

The Sikh Gurus remained realistic in spite of a tendency toward the mystical. Their mysticism was confined to the emotion of love, and had nothing to do with the idea of love. They did not prefer the mystic's language or passion to transport oneself beyond space and time. This explains why out of all *bhakti* philosophies, Sikhism alone became militaristic. Their aim was to rebuild the changeable realities of this world. The mystic vision was a deep experience of love, not to be talked of but to draw inspiration from. Man's job was to create a change in the world so that the forces of life might imitate the Divine life of love.

The Sikh militarism is therefore not an essential part of the creed. It is the turning of philosophers into warriors of love as a matter of exigency, as a response to their time. Their history records one of the finest drama of the awakening of wisdom and love, both in the same wake. Their wars were only outer expressions of a deeper inner vow of total fearlessness in love. Lively and agile must have been the sense that led the Gurus to trace the maladies of the human soul. In the Mahabharata, Vyas discovered anger to be the root of sins. But in the time of the Gurus, fear had become the root of evil. Evil does not stick to a form. It rather prefers the latest form in which it is unrecognisable. Mephistopheles tells the bewildered witches—who fail to recognise him in new attires and without a cloven hoof and a tail—that there was nothing to wonder, for much water had flown down since they had met last and culture had gained time enough even to reach the devil.

The Indian belief is that evil is unreal, though it takes on shapes that appear more real than the real. All that appears as evil is only a play of ignorance and illusion compounded i.e. *Maya*. And *Maya* is most swift and fluid. She does not stick to any form. She keeps on changing. She can even appear in a very *Satvik* (noble) form. If she appears as anger, she does not confine herself to anger. By the time of the Gurus, she had had time enough to take on new forms. She had now taken on the form of fear. Instead of anger, fear had become the source of evil. It had become the root of all sins. It had grown and nurtured in a subtle way. The Indians did not begin with fear. They had only begun squaring off issues. They had left politics to the ruler, and society to self-acquisitive individuals. They had contrived this artifice in order to keep their peace undisturbed. But peace could not be retained in this way. The storm had entered the soul. It could not be quietened by leaving those torn by it to them. It was a hidden form of cowardice on the part of the philosophers to leave the layman alone to grapple with his problems, and to go for an isolated life, only because of a shallow desire to figure superior in the frightened eyes of lesser humans. It was the 'pathos of distance' that had enticed the souls of the higher ones. When their turn came to give a lead to the erring and confused masses, they stood aside. The bark had broken on a winter night, and against cold dark waves, millions were struggling. The captains at this time had preferred to retire with their puff of hashish in the name of God. This was betrayal. It grew gradually into a deep-seated fear. People started fearing everything. They feared the rulers. They feared the learned and the elevated almost as much as they feared the tantriks. They feared to love. They feared to worship openly. To speak the truth was out of question. In the medieval ages, even those known for their boldness, like Kabir, confined themselves to parables or such expressions that did not directly hit the wrong-door, i.e., the ruler. He darted couplets that hit both equally, the wronged and the wrongdoer. This kind of equanimity turned both complacent. Neither felt responsible for the wrong. As a result the rulers continued with their policy of favouring one religion and persecuting the other. There is not a single treatise composed in medieval days that speaks boldly and factually of the wretched condition of the people and the atrocities perpetrated on them. Fear had silenced wisdom. There is no history of those days, no other autobiography or any such record to give us a sensitive appraisal of the soul of India in that unprecedented crisis. Fear had crippled love. The Gurus, therefore, made courage the cardinal virtue. Fear has become the source of all evil, so shall courage become the source of all good—this seems to have been the thinking of the Gurus. Love for the oppressed and the humble was the spontaneous emotion that made them walk alone, leaving the path of other contemporary saints and savants.

Soul

According to the Gurus, the soul is eternal and real. It passes through a vortex of life and death before its deliverance. In essence it is Divine. It is a spark of the Divine Light shrouded, layer upon layer, by a complex web of the mind, the senses and the ego. They do not let the light remain Divine any longer. The shroud has an ever-active urge to dominate and lord over this inner light. The nucleus is the same Divine spark in all living beings. As a variety of atoms come into being due to a variety of patterns and pressure of the orbiting electrons, even so different patterns of union of the soul with the mind and the senses create a variety of individuals. Though born of the same Essence they can thoroughly betray it. The task given to the individual soul is to rule over the elements orbiting it and also to illumine them, as the sun illumines the solar system. Then alone the soul fulfils its mission, i.e., making the earth a little paradise, and illumining it with the Light Divine. To the Gurus, the Divine spark in the soul is love, not wisdom born of intellectual exercises.

Mankind has not fulfilled this simple task. Love inspires only a few. Violence and cunning against love inspire many. This duality inherent in the society leads mankind away from God. Birth after birth, man is busy building his ego into an unruly and godless fabrication. Its storms and clouds completely conceal the Light Divine. With the passage of time, such darkness becomes the rule, and, even though suffocating, the soul gets used to it, and generations pass sleepily. Then comes one like Nanak to tear this established darkness and to subject the elements of society to the inner light. Thus we find that there is a very thin difference between living by sin and living by the word of God. Those who live by the compelling force of the orbiting elements live by sin, but those who live by the spark, the nucleus, are the children of God. Their life is homage to Him, for He is the nucleus of each individual soul. He resides in the heart in miniature. The choice is given to every man: either to make the Lord slave of the elements or make the elements His slaves. The wise choose the Divine order while the ignorant go for the forces of darkness. This choice starts weaving the web of karma around each individual soul. Caught in the forces of darkness due to a wrong choice the soul gets subjected to the law of karma, and passes its days in sins and sufferings.

How can a lost and wandering soul rediscover its shrouded light? The Gurus one after the other in various ragas have answered the question—'by love, by *bhakti'*. It is only given to love, to disentangle the soul from the polluting alloy. *Bhakti* dispels the charm of the ancient magician *Maya.* The true pain of a lover's heart opens the stony citadel of *haumey* and breaks it like a house of sand. To love is given the power to lead us back through the invisible track of karma and to wind up their threads.

I have already said that the Gurus preferred silence to mystical and unclear utterances. They spoke only that much of the Divine that could be spoken clearly without creating confusion. A careful study of the scriptures shows that it is by love, more than any other attribute, that the Gurus have characterised God. If one knows that God is love, he need not know anything more, for nothing much about Him is accessible to words. From the first Guru down to the tenth, they have said the same thing that can be crystallised as, 'Love is God, and Love is Soul.' It is through love that the identity of the soul with the Lord is established. If we serve true love and if we live by love alone as the cardinal virtue, we are living by the Divine Light.

Thus, talking in a practical sense, to live by God or the soul is in fact to live by love. My objective in these lectures is to make Sikhism useful to the modern man, to illumine his agonies and interests with the light of the Gurus. I will now take up the problems of love to illustrate their teachings. I will do so because love is nearest to the Divine Light, according to the Gurus, and at the same time, it is the most common experience of all mankind.

One thing deserves clarification at the very outset. The Gurus have made no distinction between the love of God and the love of man. There is nothing like Spinoza's intellectual love of God in Sikhism. We are not required to love God as distinct and other than love of human beings. Contrary to it, service and love of human beings have been given the highest place in the Sikh discipline. In fact, the whole of *bhakti-movement*, of which Sikhism is a surviving part, makes no distinction between love of man and the love of God. It does not call the former profane and the latter pure. Rather, love of a human Guru is the first step we take toward coming closer to the Divine. The choice of the beloved is a sure measure of the stage up to which a soul has evolved. A beloved cannot be imposed. To ask a soul, lost in the colourful material play of clay and scents, to love the abstract *nirguna* Lord, is to send it to more darkness. It is only true love for some human being that can show it light through the confusion of the worldly strife. Love is a palpable feeling. It is a fine and decent alternative to our crude attachment to material things. Love is thus a spontaneous step toward spiritual life. It pulls from *haumey* (ego) and material greed, and gifts a person the exquisite sight that sees someone else as more important to him than his/her own being. Love is the bridge that helps to cross the gulf that compels one to live in selfish isolation. The heart that aches for someone else soon starts experiencing God as Reality. No argument can convince an atheist. Let him fall in love, theism will become his urgent need. What true love gifts cannot be borne by the heart alone. It can be borne only if the heart shares it with God. The heart needs nothing short of the infinite God to be able to bear the little drop of love. All desires and sins too lie hidden in the heart. How can one get rid of them unless they get charged with pure love, no matter for whom?

The *bhakti* tradition of India believes that it is love for human beings that flowers into Divine love. The love of Radha-Krishna

has been the ideal of the lovers for several centuries. The fifth
Guru had composed song after song seeing himself as Radha pining
for Kanha (Krishna). There is no Christian inhibition against
profane love and adoration of religious love for the Lord in this
tradition. Mira pined for Krishna like any ordinary woman for her
lover's touch, embrace and merry frolics. And yet her songs full of
sensuous spirituality were found holy by the Gurus. It was not
liberality but a closer view of human truth on part of the Gurus. It
gave confidence to ordinary men and women in their feelings. How
could they be intimate with God if they did not trust their own
feelings? It is asking for outright duality if a man is to develop a
separate love note in his soul for God. The Sikh question would
be, 'Is the Lord not present in the earthly beloved?' The seeker is
asked to love the earthly beloved so completely that his/her deeper
self gets revealed to him and, next, gets united with his soul. The
complete union of two souls transforms the two souls into the Soul
of souls. It is the same as discovering God in the beloved, for he
dwells in the deepest self of every individual. The flame of love
cannot be satisfied unless the souls of the two unite. Love is a
process too that compels the withdrawal of the veils of *Maya* from
the soul. It is repeated time and again by the Gurus that one's true
soul is the same as God. And the true soul gets uncovered only in
love. Thus, in truly loving an earthly being, we discover God in
our hearts. Rather we become Him.

I would discuss a few problems of love to illustrate further
how love for an ordinary human helps in the moral uplift and
illumination of a soul in bondage, like the soul of the modern man,
which is caught in the silken threads of archetypal and racial forces
as well as individual karma. It will explain the logic behind the
Indian unwillingness to distinguish between the human and the
Divine Love.

Two Guiding Realities

Besides God and the soul, there are two more realities which
men experience. One is the wisdom of the Gurus that is enshrined
in *Gurbani*. The tenth Guru finally gave the seat to the *Gurbani*

that was reserved for the Gurus. The *Gurbani* is not a mere assemblage of words and sounds. Beneath this flows the perennial nectar of wisdom. A true seeker has to dive deep to reach it. The Gurus have used simple and direct words, paying no attention to their beauty or rhythm. They did not try to endow the words with any arresting quality that might distract. Their aim had been to attract the seeker to the hidden rhythm and beauty of the true word. They want him to hear the faintly murmuring waters beneath the feet of Saraswati.

Gurbani is to be taken as the ever-guiding Guru by the individual soul. It tells us of the true Father and is the real mother. The Sikh belief is that everything is born of *shabda* (word). The Divine word *Gurbani* is the *shabda* of God as it was revealed to the Gurus. All individual souls are born of this *shabda* and this *shabda* is their true mother.

There is one more mother of the individual soul. It is *bhakti* or love. It is undying and perennial. God has left the individual soul to the care of these two mothers. *Haumey* (ego) a deluded and deluding synthesis of psychological forces blinds man and he discards both these mothers. Casting off the over-blown skin of *haumey*, he has to learn afresh, as a child, his alphabets from these immortal mothers. He has to learn from them how to walk, speak and work. Only then he becomes a true soldier of God and fulfils the mission of his life. Living and acting in this way he attains Nirvana.

Sikhism considers *Gurbani*, i.e., wisdom and *bhakti* i.e., love-devotion-reverence as the two guiding principles of the soul. They are *Satvik,* the immoveable and immortal principles, not *rajasik* i.e. transient and pragmatic. In no case should they be activated. Fanaticism and religious hysteria takes birth when instead of activating itself the soul excites these two Divine mothers to activity. *Maya* and *haumey* are known for misguiding the soul to commit this error. The soul in the trap of *haumey* starts enjoying lethargy and its own corruption and self-degradation. Such deluded souls start expecting these mothers to do for them what they alone can and must.

The soul has to take on the challenge that the world throws at one's life, for if life picks up the gauntlet it gets corrupted both ways, whether it wins or loses the battle. One of the first steps of the spiritual discipline is to restore *Gurbani* and *bhakti* to the original *Satvik* state of sublime passivity, in which they inspire action in the soul and also help a sincerely active soul in moments of crisis in several inscrutable ways, but never take up the gauntlet on behalf of the soul. An active soul that does not shirk its responsibility to the nation and humanity is blessed by these mothers. The proof of this blessing is that the soul starts hearing the *anahad* (soundless) music of wisdom that is ever flowing from the feet of these mothers. The power of ignorance and delusion starts leaving the individual. True love or *bhakti* can be discerned by such a soul from false plays of passions. To feel the fire of true love one has to restore the Word first to its original passivity. Then only the storm and heat of negative passions calm down and the soft whisper of love becomes audible.

The Sikh concept of reality is that God alone is real from the absolute or *parmarthik* point of view. However, from the practical or *vyavaharik* standpoint reality is five-fold: God, individual soul, Nature, *Gurbani* and *bhakti* or love.

Gurbani and *bhakti* are *Satvik*. The individual soul is *rajasik*. God is both, and more. The individual soul has to pave its way to the Lord. On reaching there it becomes like a transparent flame of love that aspires for nothing except merger in Him, even as rivulets pass into the river. *Gurbani* and *bhakti* are the two guiding mothers who guide only as long as activity is not shifted to them. They are best in their passivity, for as passive sublime presences they act as the voice and hands of God.

Kudarat

Nature or creation is a reality according to Sikhism. The universe has been called the body of *Waheguru*. *Kudarat* or Nature is the creative power of God. She is completely under His command. She is one with Him. When He wills to create, she gets separated and individualised to fulfil His desire. At no stage does she go astray. Whatever she does is entirely His wish. She does nothing by herself. She does not cast any spell, nor does she trap the individual soul. She does not aim at keeping the soul away from God.

Here Guru Nanak differs from the traditional view of the Western idealists, foremost among them Berkeley. The universe is not our dream or illusion. Like Dr Johnson, any of the Gurus might have kicked a stone and said, "Sir here I refute Berkeley!" To the Gurus Nature is neither a projection of ignorance nor a tempting trap. It is very much there. It is a material, substantial reality that has no intention to mislead the individual. It can turn into a trap or the very passage to God depending on the individual.

Kudarat is as much real as *Gurbani* and *bhakti* or love. These three are the powers of God. They are real from the practical point of view. From the absolute standpoint, however, there is nothing except the Wonderful God, *Waheguru*.

Soul and these three powers emanate from God. All these three powers appear in the soul too as miniatures. They are like mothers to a true man. They help him all his life to fulfil his mission. It is *haumey*, ego, born of individual greed and ignorance that weaves an invisible web around these powers, agitates and involves them and tries to break their motherly vow. Then they who were given to guide him all through life turn into their opposites. They become veils that no cunning can tear.

The soul partakes the powers of God. Therefore the soul can influence these three powers of Divine origin. A wise soul never tries to command them. A wise man surrenders his will to the will of God. He first teaches his will to learn to be completely a vessel of Divine Will. A will trained in this manner never tries to command these three powers. It looks at them as a child at his mother.

The beauty of nature, the majestic mountains and moonlit skies are palpable realities, according to Sikhism. The world of sounds and colours is no fantasy. Its joys are not to be despised. They are the many gifts of a mother to her child. A will surrendered to the

Lord knows how to enjoy these gifts without getting any bondage in return.

To awaken *Gurbani* in the soul right knowledge is not enough. It is also not enough to have *bhakti* or love full of devotion. Unless corresponding karma is there, one cannot be a free man. It is selfless karma and their fruits, both offered to the *Waheguru*, that unites a soul with Him. Unless action that actualises disinterested knowledge is there, one cannot be free of *Maya*. *Kudarat* or Nature is the Divine power that creates. Each one of us has it in some measure. It is the power that inspires us to work to make the life of others better. It gives us the fire to die so that others may live honourably. Nature is born both as the universe and the individual human nature. Unless human nature is disciplined under Divine Will, the human mind keeps tossing on the waves of stray thoughts without any progress. Even the proper flowering of the intellect and devotion do not satisfy the soul that has the Divine seed of activity right inside it. The soul wants to feel itself moving toward the goal. Hence the restlessness. Without finding the path, by getting rid of *haumey*, it remains ever restless.

In their concept of Nature (*Kudarat*), the Gurus had said something that was different than the views of Nature of many Indian and Western philosophers. The path of true knowledge had already taken the finer ones, the *Siddhas*, away from the bleeding life of the commoner. The path of love or devotion had also taken the same flight, high above the earth and its ignorant children. They were turning away in huge numbers from the thorny, unpleasant and vulgar life of the masses. Guru Nanak was worried by the instinctive escapism of both intellect and true love. He realized that something was missing from the popular view of religion. The Lord has sent the soul in the world. It cannot be His will that it should only trace the way back to Him. God's act of sending the soul to this world would be meaningless if the soul returned without creating an impact on this world. And no act of God can be without some purpose. Nanak realized that God wants the soul of man to fill the often-heard sad music of humanity with the joyous Divine rhythm. Man has not only to know the way back to God, he has also to use all his powers so that the earth may become a little paradise of God, in spite of all its thorns and barren rocks. "It is possible," Nanak said, "my brothers, to transform ordinary life into the Divine, while living on earth and amidst these mud-smeared faces. Were it not so, I would not say it is possible, my brothers." His life long argument with the *Siddhas* and *jogis* is pivoted on wonder. "Why, pray why, do thou run to the cave and the forest? The wonderful Lord dwells as much in broken homes, in the eyes of ignorant but honest people, and in the simple joys of children who partake His powers of creation unknowingly." All his life, Nanak wandered like one with an arrow stuck in his heart, bleeding for love for erring mankind, watching sadly the age-old drama of mortality enacted by people and nations in the slow aimless way.

Kudarat or Nature cannot be understood by the intellect. The intellect is as blinding as will. It has an innate tendency to run toward blind alleys and pessimism. The frustration of intellectuals is the gift of their enormous intellect that sucks all drops of love while unfolding itself. The intellect leads to correct results only when it is born of love and wonder. Wonder is the original impetus behind our faculties. Alas it withers too soon! It provides the necessary link with truth, but the intellect obstructs seeing. Wonder disappears only when intellect becomes arrogant. Intellect is born of the Wonderful Lord, the *Waheguru*, and only wonder can reconcile proud intellect with this truth. But the intellect seeks isolation, in which it sees nothing but itself. It turns everything that it sees into shreds and then wails that there is no charm in shreds. It finally gets horrified of itself and gets consumed by its own products. Intellect is invisible flesh that goes berserk pursuing abstraction, forgetting that all Nature is a compendium of the visible and invisible flesh of God.

Intellect, devoid of the refreshing push of wonder, builds *haumey*. It becomes *manmukh* or worldly. The five deadly sins take birth from it and create a veil between Nature and the mind's eye. The mind starts creating the web of *Maya* and projecting it on Nature.

Nanak is not inhibited against dualism even though he has realized the One to be true. God's creation is a play of the many and in this mundane world the many are Real. The way of knowing *kudarat* (Nature) is the art of using at least two faculties at a time. The world of the many cannot be known by one faculty. The ways of truth are strange. It is duality alone that knows duality. The pride of monism is also a pride and has no validity. All methods have their limit and a true seeker knows their limits as much as he knows their utility. Intellectual arrogance is the product of an over-stretched monism.

The lonely intellect when entrusted with the quest of Truth only leads to despair. It also becomes obstinate and unyielding. Finally it draws shutters and ruins the mind in closed isolation. It is this deadening quality of the intellect that the West has also been discovering sporadically. After the Renaissance, after the Romantic Revival and after the Victorian Age, the intellect of the Western critics has been busy exposing the follies behind each of these movements. This meaningless exercise has alienated the Western mind from the different forms of joy that had created those movements. The spirit behind each of them has been reduced to shreds mercilessly only to be swallowed by the intellect. The revolt against the intellect was the result of this error. Henry Bergson declared intellect to be totally unfit for knowledge. Even an intellectual like Kant found intellect unproductive after a few steps taken toward knowledge. He had to awaken the faculty of wonder to appreciate the starry heavens above and the moral law within, to remain close to knowledge. F.H. Bradley, another sharp intellectual, had to discover the higher faculty of immediacy, a faculty that was more comprehensive than the intellect, for intellect could give only discursive knowledge. His was an intellectual revolt against the intellect. Therefore, it was destined to die out very soon. As if annoyed by its brief resistance against the intellect, the Western mind has wedded itself now to the extreme and the naked intellect of mathematics that does not tolerate emotion at all, even in literature. It has alienated the Western mind from all kinds of natural joy. In order to get relieved of the resulting tension, one has no alternative left except going to the devil for entertainment.

Nanak said that the way to escape from the self-destructive steps of the intellect was to wed it to its lord and master—the faculty of wonder. When the intellect works subdued under the mellow influence of wonder, it leads to truth and light and shows the way to higher faculties when its operation ends.

Kudarat (Nature) is to be wondered at, if one truly seeks the key to its mystery. This is the method that modern scientists have at last started employing. Einstein has himself given out the secret of his knowledge—a constantly wondering mind.

The more the intellect sharpens the more fond of newness it becomes, so much so that it hates to be confronted with the same things, situations and even persons again and again. A thirst for newness that refuses to be satisfied makes everything created by God look stale and uninteresting. This attitude is entirely the opposite of the attitude of a child who simply wonders. He loses interest in nothing. Every day the same toys and faces reveal new facets to his wondering mind. But the moment the adult mind starts running after novelty, everything becomes immobile and jarring. The nature of intellect is suicidal to man. The visible creation of God has the same old mountains and stars, the same round and shining sun and moon and the same dirty-yellow or khaki soil and azure sky. He does not change them. If the intellect loses interest in them, there is surely something wrong with it. An intellect constantly in touch with the faculty of wonder does not run to its barren and stale excesses. The nature of the intellect causes the withering of the mysterious lotus of knowledge, the lotus of a thousand petals in the mind, the *sahasrar.* The petals instead of pointing upward turn downward at the touch of the abstracted intellect. An intellect that turns the petals of this mysterious lotus in the mind downward is a wicked thing. It leads even a wise man straight into the prison of *haumey.*

Sikh cosmology is not limited to the world of matter, visible or imaginable. There are other worlds that are revealed to a true seeker in the silence of his meditation. There are not only millions of universes like ours, and not only countless suns and moons. When the seeker ascends on the Divine road, he sees the light transforming continually into amazing shades. Apart from the visible and invisible external worlds revealed to cosmology there are inner worlds within the individual that start unfolding their splendour to the seeker of God. The ordinary man is given to live in *Dharmakhand* i.e., the world. Here he has to lead a life full of actions with the sole objective of spreading true light and love. If he does so he ascends to a higher inner world that has been called *gyankhand* in Sikh scriptures. It is here that the mind can meditate unwaveringly. The higher the ascent of the seeker, the more Nature stabilizes the mind, until it becomes like a lamp in a windless spot. Nature reveals to him finer arts of thinking and feeling. Here he learns how to stop the wasteful or frustrating activity of these faculties. One who has long meditated here finds one day the petals of still another lotus opening, a more luminescent lotus than the earlier. He sees a new inner world in his heart. His wondering eye notices celestial cataracts of joy gushing and flowing. It is here that he hears the Divine music and the *Nad Anahad*. This is the *Karamkhand*.

The true seeker of the Beloved does not dwell even in such a Divine and joyous surrounding. The mind has to put no fetters on the soul in the journey upwards, for though resounding with Divine joys, this beautiful inner world is still a reality of a lower order. Above it is the *Sachkhand* where the selected ones enter. They have been tested. No lust is strong enough to hold them back. No joy, even the Divine joy, is powerful enough to keep the determined bride, the soul, from uniting with the Eternal Bridegroom. He resides in a *saguna* form, with a body and all rapturous attributes, in the *Sachkhand*. There the wise reach to be constantly in His company to partake His unending joy and play. That too is not a place of halt for the true lover. It is only such ardour that finally lifts the soul above all forms of space and time where it gets merged totally into the *Alepa*, the *Nirankar Purusha*, the Lord beyond all forms.

One who ascends thus to be finally merged in the *Waheguru* does not lose his identity altogether. Strange are the ways of the Lord. On the highest peak of meditation He holds such ones totally merged and inseparable from Him. However, at the same time, they live with Him in the *gyankhand* that is a world of the many, where the liberated souls live in Divine Company.

Another point to be noted is that the liberated are free to travel upwards and downwards. Once liberation has been attained, there is no fear of the recurrence of bondage. The liberated ones do not keep confined to their blissful world. In the twinkling of an eye, they can appear in the *Dharmakhand* i.e., this world of ours to make life better for their fellow beings. They can walk with the struggling people to help them with their infinite compassion and knowledge. It was not a vain promise that Guru Gobind Singh had made to his followers. How can those, whose sole impetus had been compassion for and suffering with the common people, become indifferent to the fate of the common people after entering the blissful world of the liberated? What pleasure can hold a heart back, now when it has outgrown all the earthly imperfections? Now it cannot be enticed even if it incarnates as a mortal with mortal imperfection.

3

Love

$\mathcal{I}$ would like to speak of ordinary human love and its significance in God realization according to Sikhism. Prior to the Gurus, a belief had developed that human love was the same as *moha* or ignorant attachment. The Gurus spoke against this belief. They have asserted repeatedly that there is no need to leave the family life to attain Nirvana. Their view is that human love leads to Divine love. Only sincerity is required. Besides, the motive should be clear, i.e., union with *Waheguru*. Unlike the Sufis, to the Sikhs, the earthly beloved is not only a means of loving God. The path of the Sikh Gurus takes to the discovery of the deeper self of the beloved through love. The lover has to love the earthly beloved, not *Waheguru* through her. As his love deepens he gets the love and company of several deeper selves of his beloved, each succeeding self subtler and fuller than the former. Finally comes the state when nothing is left to be revealed in the individual self of the earthly beloved. It is at this point that the astonishing miracle happens. Both get transformed into the Waheguru.

Sikhism believes love to be a discipline involving several stages of consciousness. They correspond to the various layers of a man's personality. The deepest of them is God. A true seeker passes through and outgrows all those stages to reach the deepest layer, where he finds no distinction between the earthly beloved and God.

Instead of giving up human love, one is asked to pursue it to its end for the sake of Divine Love. This message has a direct relevance to the modern age and especially for modern youth. I would therefore like to discuss from the Sikh point of view a few problems that lovers face. I would try to show how Sikhism would solve them. No situation met by ordinary lovers is mean or unworthy of spiritual solutions. In fact, they are opportunities given by *Kudarat* to each one of us to transform the ordinary life into the Divine. There is no need to create a Divine life parallel and distinct to the day-to-day ordinary life. We have to discover the deeper language, the Divine symbols underneath ordinary events of life. Love is of utmost importance since even though an event of ordinary life it has all the ingredients of the Divine. If it is not wasted in the distinction of the flesh and the soul, and if in physical love the heartthrob of the Eternal or the voice that is Soundless, *Nad Anahad*, can be heard, love becomes the surest way to unite with both the earthly beloved and God at the same time. My objective, therefore, is to talk of this mortal love in this lecture and to show how it can lead to Nirvana. Love is a consciousness, devoid of self-consciousness, and the first rule to be observed is that it should never lead to self-consciousness. It should always lead to the consciousness of the glories of the Wonderful Lord. When love leads to self-consciousness, it develops ego and selfishness, and instead of opening, closes the heart and the mind.

Love and Grief

The ordinary lover has no reason to glorify it, if he finds some similarity between his love and the love of the Gurus. There is a major dissimilarity too. To him sorrow and tears are a precious part of his love. To the Gurus, sorrow belongs to the world of shadows. It is *Maya*. It is only unwise reaction to unhappy events. No sanctity should be attached to it. Rather by an act of will, the true lover should discipline himself so that no circumstance succeeds in producing sorrow from his love. Sorrow as a form of *Maya* has a tendency to attract violence. *Maya* clears her account rather too quickly. After appearing as sorrow, she appears as violence. It is aimed to wipe off sorrow. But human love gets trapped in its play. *Maya* creates a copy of the sorrow of love. This copy of sorrow is full of pure sorrow. It lacks the ray of joy that stabs and runs through the real sorrow of love, and turns love's sorrow into a Divine experience. Love's sorrow is neither pure sorrow nor pure mirth but a Divine mixture of both. It is this streak of joy inside sorrow that makes love something that cannot be artificially created. Love often remains blind to this trick of *Maya* and identifies its Divine sorrow with the copy created by *Maya*. *Maya* plays with opposites. It now brings violence in the play. Now violence and sorrow both creations of *Maya* grapple with each other. The ignorant soul cannot see the difference between the real sorrow of love that is stabbed with joy and the false sorrow that is pure sorrow. It identifies the two, and thus involves true love also in violence. The wise soul that sees the difference does not mix up the false sorrow with the real sorrow. Having already identified its sorrow with *Maya's* copy of sorrow, love of the ignorant soul commits another folly — it takes violence also as a part of it. Thus sorrow and violence become two essential parts of love. The history of human love has therefore often been written by violence and sorrow. Sikhism believes that true love in a true soul always succeeds. It does not get involved with violence. Those are ignorant souls that believe that the fate of love is tragedy.

A wise lover knows that the path of love is like the razor's edge. He does not accept the sorrow that has no ray of Divine joy running through it. He knows it to be *Maya*. He sacrifices his soul to both his sorrow and the false copy of his sorrow created by *Maya*. He also asks these two entirely different forms of sorrow to make similar sacrifices to each other and give rebirth to the soul. This simple act dissolves the false copy and the real alone remains. This is the ancient way of dismissing *Maya* from daily lives.

Guru Tegh Bahadur showed no grief when he saw his dearest disciples being murdered by the Moguls against all canons of justice. Sorrow is not the essence of things, the Gurus say. They do not seem to agree with the Buddhists on this. Sorrow is a form of *Maya*. It looks too genuine. It has the power to touch the heart. This should not mislead us into believing that it is a part of reality. The real is love, nothing but love. The wise choose joy as their expression, and peace and contentment as their robes rather, not sorrow. They do so in order to bring to halt the movement of the vortex of life and death. They want to make joy the true friend of love. They want love to succeed in this world of shadows. They are not satisfied with the ultimate conquest of love. They want the immediate conquest too. Sorrow should be a companion of the wicked and the tormentor, not of the human, and the lover. There has been some manipulation on part of the cunning to throw sorrow to the lot of lovers. The Gurus worked hard to turn the disc of fate.

Even though grief springs from the deepest core of love and gives touching expression to it, the wise should see in it a play of shadows with no substance. It is only a heart touching face of *Maya*. Mankind has not yet learnt to make joy as deep an expression of love as sorrow. As a result the finest and noblest experiences of a human soul are bedewed with tears. A new sparkling laughter has to come from the soul. Only he can make it a reality who has realized the Lord as Love. It is a pity that Nietzsche knew nothing about the Gurus. How tragic that this noble soul that knew itself to be "the greatest genius that Europe had produced after Aristotle" was driven to the lunatic asylum! What a colossal wastage of human virtues! What tender emotions must have been there in this man's heart that had wept so bitterly that he had lost sanity then and there for empathizing with the pain of a horse that he saw being tortured by human beings on a road of Turin!

Nietzsche believed that man became superman if he adopted the ideals of aggression, insensitivity and selfishness. The Gurus believed that unconditional love asserted against brutality was the way to be a superman. The Gurus succeeded in this very world, where Nietzsche failed. Their whispers of love proved stronger than hurricanes and shattered the greatest empire of the 17th century world.

The impasse and closure of all roads to love that bewilders and maddens sincere lovers after walking together a few steps is a test of love. It is an unreal phantasm, not the fate of love, though it often disheartens lovers. The Gurus say a true seeker trains his soul to sacrifice itself to the impasse to get through it, for there is neither some empire nor any fate that is stronger than the soul. The soul of a true lover sees in the hurdle a play of *Maya*. He has no doubt that there is no power other than the Lord's on earth, and since He Himself is Love, there is nothing that can cross His will. All forces blocking love's passage are illusory. Only a weak soul believes the hurdle to be real and gets caught in the four-fold play of *Maya*. Its belief in fate generates grief and disappointment. These in turn arouse general apathy and violence. Then comes false conduct that excites it, not action dedicated to God along with its fruits. These forms of *Maya* combine against a soul in despair and celebrate its fall. A true lover cannot become a prey to *Maya*, since *Maya* is the servant of the Lord that obeys His will. And the Lord never despairs a lover. It is written in words and inside words that the lover wins in this world, since it was created out of love, by love and for love. Even in utter failure the lover should never lose faith in the victory of Love. Only then the magical mirror of *Maya* shatters, and the lovers cross the turbulent sea of life and death and find fulfilment in this very world. More real than all scheming forces is the gentle breath of love in a true heart. One who knows this humbles all obstructing forces into slaves of love. "They go by the road," sang Guru Amar Das on his lyre, "which is sharper than sword and finer than hair."

The third Guru sang in ecstasy, in *Majh Raag:*
Salvation is the unsought prize,
Of the heart that loves and yet pines.

Spiritual love often falls prey to histrionics and postures. It has a tendency to look mystical. Love's attention on external behaviour robs it of inner content. It is the highest truth known to man, and one must be very careful on the summit, for winds are sharp there and steep is the decline. The slightest help of falsehood poisons true love, and turns the true lover into an ordinary juggler doomed to the fate of a juggler. This has been the cause of ruin of many a noble soul. When they are too close to their goal often frenzy overtakes them, and offers them some piece of mystical behaviour to convince others that they are in a special relationship with God. This little falsehood on the path of love proves for them the darkest cloud of deluge on their mental sky. Lies and false postures do not match even a single step with love. They turn into whirlwinds that sweep such souls away. Love turns into love of mystery to them. The love of mystery deviates slightly in the beginning from the path of God, but soon the deviation broadens suddenly, and the original path gets completely lost to sight. Mystery comes with its own package of charms, talisman and rituals. All rituals pretend to be symbols of deeper truths, but depth is no guarantee of truth. The higher road is full only of depth all around. Deep are labyrinths and dungeons too, and deep is the world of void too, where Trishanku, the ambitious, went in quest of happiness and has not returned ever since. No depth opens except the depth of abyss, if love for God is not artless.

The Gurus have not allowed their spiritual love to take the wings of mysticism. They have kept it very simple without elaborate mannerisms and rituals. It is the simple language of heart to them. It could be the babble of a child or the simple language of a highland lass, but never the sophisticated speech of a heroine or a queen accomplished in the art to rule over others' hearts.

All mystery, as the depth psychology of Jung says, tends to isolate its owner. The spiritual love of a saint has been often glorified as a strictly secret union of the saint with God. Love indeed is the most secret and mysterious spring in the heart but there is no secrecy when it flows out. Then it becomes the scent of a flower that cannot be hidden. To choose its recipient is not in the hands of man. Though it is a shaft that comes from the deepest and unknown core of one's soul it knows its target. Any manipulation here does not bring good to anyone. Any attempt to dramatize love leads to perversions and complexes. People fear, secretly doubt and also feel violently angry at such manipulations. The Gurus took special care that their spiritual love was not given any mystical air by their high position or by the reverence of the disciples. They knew that love and dramatics were opposites. It is all right for Shakespeare to write Romeo and Juliet. But for a real Romeo to act like Romeo in his personal life would be disastrous. Any histrionics for a true lover is not only unbecoming but it violates the aesthetic sense of the lover. The aesthetic sense is an integral part of love. It determines love's actions and expressions. The aesthetic sense is unique with every love. Not to abide by it and choose some other lover's expression would make him look ridiculous. At the same time it would falsify his tender emotion of love. Any dramatic expression of the real emotion of love is self-violence against love. Others' violence may not affect adversely but self-violence against love vitiates personality and may falsify its whole structure. In such a case the personality can alienate the soul and acquire a character that is entirely hostile and foreign to the soul, and that can never give expression to the soul. Such a man's personality may never let his soul express itself through it. His personality and soul become entirely opposites of each other. Emperor Aurangzeb is said to have acquired an artificial personality after the death of his only love, Hira Bai, in his early youth. The compulsion caused by his ambition to become the Emperor did not allow him the natural expression of the deeply shocked lover. He acquired an artificial character that never let his soul live again its life. His entire life turned into dramatics. He was mostly acting to look like a *dervish* (saint), and often felt his life worthless, for if life cannot express the soul it can do precious little. The Gurus expressed their love as naturally and simply as it chose to express itself.

The spiritual love, according to the Gurus, is only concentration of the total being of the lover in love. This concentration comes naturally to the first love of a man. Spiritual love is only an imitation of the first emotion of love that is marked by its tenderness. Therefore, the Gurus never give any high position to spiritual love. Many saints have made much of spiritual love. As a result it has acquired some mystery about it. The Gurus never talked much of mystical love either. They seem to have been driven to reticence about both spiritual love and mystical love for the sake of truth. Spiritual love was only an exercise to them that checked the spiritual power from turning to negative expressions. After taming all their spiritual powers by concentrating them and expressing them in spiritual love, the Gurus did not end their quest. They have talked of the tender emotion of love that Mira had felt for Krishna as the crown of all sorts of love including spiritual love. It reappears spontaneously only in that person who does not provide false tilts to spiritual love. One of the Sikh Gurus' greatest gifts is the truth that they had revealed about the path of love. While the Sufis were making much ado about spiritual love the Gurus said there was not much in it. Instead they valued the tender emotion of love that a virgin and a chaste woman felt. The love that Mira felt for Krishna was both the love of a virgin since it began when she was a little girl, and also of a chaste woman since it continued when she got married. She told her husband that she was already wedded to Krishna; therefore she could not be his wife. She remained the chaste woman of Krishna. The love of Mira has been the ideal of Sikhism, not the so-called spiritual love. All the Gurus followed Nanak in this choice of their ideal of love. It went to the extent that they called themselves women lovers of the only male Waheguru.

The first poet of mankind, Valmiki, had also sung of the love of a virgin and a chaste woman as the highest form of love. He had been a murderer and a dacoit before he took to the life of a rishi. He had to discipline his spiritual powers that had taken to the negative path due to a violent career. He had practiced spiritual love to change his spiritual powers from the negative to the positive channel. He too had crowned his spiritual love with the two loves of Sita for the same man Ram, first as a virgin when she saw him in a flower garden and next when she, as his married woman, had remained true to him as a prisoner in the house of Ravan. No man knew better about spiritual love than Valmiki. Being the tip of the volcano of negative spiritual powers he too had crowned his spiritual powers with the tender emotion of love that ultimately turned out to be the sealing of the volcano. It seems that the tender emotion of love has been given the highest place in the hierarchy of love by the Indian saints, including the Sikh Gurus.

Active Love

Love is God to the Gurus. 'A body untouched by the spark of love is already dead.' The Gurus have worshipped and loved God as His female consorts. Like Kabir, their souls had spontaneously grown the love of a virgin for their common bridegroom. This *priya-bhava* was essential to break the eggshell of *haumey*. It helped in developing the virtues that were dear to the Lord. It is the best-known way to get rid of dualism.

While discussing Dostoevsky's novel 'Poor Folks', Belinsky criticised the love depicted in it as 'passive Christian suffering.' No such passive suffering has any place in Sikh religion. You have not to turn your left cheek to the person who has slapped you on the right cheek. Slap him harder, for if he is unjust, he is Godless. If he punishes in the name of God, know him to be a liar for God does not need anybody to officiate for him.

The Gurus have given no importance to suffering for suffering's sake. Suffering does not elevate, neither physical nor spiritual. Only you should not be afraid of suffering if it comes to you on the path of love. You must be prepared to die for love. But if you can win the kingdom of earth for love by destroying the destroyer, so much the better. Nietzsche called Zarathustra the anti-Christ. Zarathustra said a 'Yea' to life, according to him, whereas Christ said 'Nay'. The Gurus would say that Nietzsche had taken too seriously the two opposites. There is no 'yea' and no 'nay' to life in Sikhism. Instead of deliberating about a thing that is not entirely in the hands of the individual, the individual would do better if he transcended both by sacrificing his soul to both and by his soul's rebirth from them. This is the ancient way to ensure that none else than God deliberates for you. Sikhism is all about involving God in your life. You cannot involve him forcibly, magically or by proclaiming to people that He favours you. You can involve him in your life only by loving him truly and artlessly, as Mira loved Krishna, as Sita loved Ram and as the tribal woman Shabari loved Ram.

To a lover, life and death are not opposites engaged in mutual opposition. His life passes several times through the agonies of death. But death proves in his case the best caretaker of life. A brave man has to take rebirth from death willingly. Death cannot shroud his life. It is only too obvious if we look at the fact that he lives in the memory of people. However, talking in a spiritual sense, death is no event. There is nothing like death to a true Sikh. To him the Hegelian or Marxian belief in the essentiality of opposites will sound as a myth born of philosophic leisure. Sikhism does not believe in the existence of pairs of opposites in the spiritual world. The soul is not obliged to recognise the existence of death along with life. At the merely physical level, this pair does exist. But it would be contrary to the idea of monism, as the Gurus knew it, to believe in the existence of warring opposites at the spiritual level. The negative and positive spiritual powers are preludes to spirituality. When the seeker overcomes the spiritual dualism he finds true spirituality that is no spiritual power. Instead it is the tender emotion of love.

The Gurus do not believe that in the spiritual world of a seeker that exists in his mind there is death, defeat, hatred or fear as the opposite of life, victory, love or courage. Only positive virtues exist in the soul as delicate emotions. Whatever is negative is not in existence. The negative is only the colour and appearance of the terrible mother, *Maya.* By appearing as the opposite of positive virtues, she blinds the soul into accepting it as their negative. *Maya* has indeed access to the soul. This high level spiritual intrigue takes place only because *Maya* has access to the soul. The Gurus had saved their disciples from it. They taught them to take every opposite of virtue appearing in the soul as an appearance that has no relation with the soul. The opposite lasts only as long as *Maya* can delude the power of ignorance that too belongs to the soul, like the power of knowledge. Whatever *Maya* creates in the soul appears to be more than the real but it is nought. Those who live by God know that to be lesser than truth alone is not falsehood. To be more than truth is also a form of falsehood. The artificial often shines more than the true diamond. 'We have no reason to accept the spiritual existence of evil'—this is a major contribution of Indian religions, which Sikhism did a lot to translate into common practice, during the dark middle ages of India. This gift of the great Indian thinkers—born of disinterested quest of truth—can never be over-estimated. The idea of devil as the opposite of God that certain religions propagate goes against spiritual monism that they uphold. It is time that they examine whether the idea of the devil was added later to suit the need of proselytising. People were so deep in evil that they needed to be assured that the devil was responsible for the evil that they had committed. The people needed a religion that assured them that mere conversion to it would earn them heaven. They needed to be assured that God would not judge them for their karma if they got converted. In the entire history of religion there is no idea that is more fantastic than the idea that the devil becomes instantly responsible for all the evil that they had done the very moment they get converted. Their seat in heaven also gets reserved instantly.

The Sikhs do not believe that there is any force that can challenge and stand before God after challenging his being as the only Wonderful Master of all good and evil beings. No demon or devil could have survived for so long after challenging Him. The Gurus thought that man's need to lighten his burden of evil has created the idea of the devil that willingly accepts to be the source of all evil in this world. This idea has done immense harm to humanity, since it has emboldened many wicked men in history to indulge in carnage, genocide, and evil against women and children. They were emboldened by certain priests who promised them that since they indulged in evil only to proselytise, God would rather award them with a seat in heaven. The Sikhs call him a brave man who has the guts to hold only himself responsible for all the evil he has done in his life. He who needs the devil to own his evil deeds must be a man who knows that he has done evil, fears his karma, but wants some religious authority to live in delusion that, not he, the devil is responsible for his evil karma. He has muted his reason, and has no idea that knowledge of truth and moulding of one's personality to pursue truth is the only way to burn evil karma. The Gurus say that only the seeker of true love acquires true knowledge that burns the seeds of evil in the soul. No Guru can wash out the scroll of one's evil karma. They also forget that true spirituality is not power. It is above power and weakness. True love, i.e. the tender emotion of love, is beyond the strife of all spiritual powers. The Indian heritage bypasses the spiritual power of love as the base camp before the final ascent to the Everest of true love. The Everest of true love is the tender emotion of love that had appeared in life in early youth and that the *premyogi* (the seeker of true love) recollects only when he has conquered the opposite pairs of spiritual powers. The entire spiritual heritage of India differs from the spiritual heritage of the Middle East regarding the nature of true love. While they call love the strongest spiritual power, India calls it a tender emotion. Indian saints call the helpless love of Christ for his killers and his reluctance to defend himself against the charges as the finest example of true love from the Middle East. But they would add that Christ's love is not spiritual power but the climax of spirituality, i.e. the tender emotion of love, the higher immediacy that has no opposite. The love of Guru Teg Bahadur for his slain knights is a tender emotion, not a wrathful spiritual power. Similarly the love of Guru Gobind Singh for his sons is a tender emotion beyond the spiritual powers of wrath and revenge.

According to the Gurus, evil cannot be immortal. Belief in the immortality of the devil seems to be the product of the coward's mind that fears to trace the source of evil within it. The Hindus have consistently maintained that no Reality other than God exists. All that is neither God nor godly is, again, a play of God. He has playfully created a power within man called ignorance (*agyan*, avidya) that jumps to act before thinking. Ignorance is the only source of evil in the world. It keeps weakening the soul. When knowledge starts flowering the soul, there comes a stage of illumination in the soul when ignorance totally disappears. That state of the soul has been called *Kevalgyan*, which means 'only knowledge'. It is the stage when only knowledge remains in the soul. Mahavir and Buddha both had attained it 2500 years ago. Prior to them countless souls had already attained it.

He who is perfect in the *Sachkhand* appears in imperfect form as man in the *Dharmakhand;* i.e., Earth. God wants to test this imperfect manifestation of His by placing him in the wizardly hands of the terrible mother *Maya* that can adopt any bright or dark form she likes. She can appear as perfect before this imperfect being. Only courage, love and truthfulness can help man to come out of her puzzling mazes. He cannot match her in cunning and cheating. These arts she possesses in full measures. If man and woman abide by the light within, if they do not lose faith in the sole existence of good, in spite of the fact that experience offers too much of evil, if their faith in the mercy of God does not dwindle even when they get no help in their difficult hour, they develop the power of Truth (*Sat*) within them. *Maya* does not share virtues and she has to give rebirth to such a determined soul. Only a soul that knows the secret of taking rebirth from the terrible mother, i.e. *Maya*, can be successful on earth (*Dharmakhand*) in spreading the light Divine.

> "How strange! *Maya* bewitches man
> And He who bewitches *Maya*
> Him seeks no man."

The Sikh faith shows a rigorous attempt to live by the little light that dwells in the human heart as a delicate emotion. The Gurus sacrificed everything to live by it. The lives of Guru Arjun and Guru Teg Bahadur are illustrations of total faith in God, and infinite courage born of it.

The Sikh ideal of love is aggressive, not passive. You have to win the earth back for humanity, which is the living image of God on earth. "Let us evolve a way whereby the blood of the wicked soaks the earth not the blood of the innocent."— Thus spake the Gurus, the children of *Akaal Purakh*, they that hath transcended time.

All the Gurus lived in a period of terror when one could not express his love of God in the way he chose. The Mogul Emperors offered the alternatives to at least two Gurus to give up their faith in God or accept death. Perhaps denial of freedom cannot hit deeper than when it tries to rule over love. Love is the very nature of originality. No two loves are alike. Every saint loves God in his original way, even as every lover loves his mortal beloved in an original way. The more intense the love, the more original it is. Shabari showed her love for Ram by offering him half-eaten berries. The love of the Gurus cannot be measured for it was all of them. They existed only in love, for the sake of love and by love. Outside love, they considered their existence illusion.

To ask a lover, under terror, to change the style of his love is the same as to ask him to give up love. It is again a trick of *Maya* not to ask directly for what it is asking—i.e., give up the path of love. Instead it asks for the surrender of the originality of one's love. Without its unique originality love ceases to be. Religion is only a style of love. If it preaches hatred, it ceases to be what it professes to be.

The Gurus would not have given their lives for their style of loving God had there been nothing unusual and so precious about it. Their style belonged to the time when they were born and the space or place where they were born. Love is so subtle a wonder that it cannot be expressed in any other style except the style that was born with it. The love of Mira, Tukaram, Chaitanya, Nanak, St. Augustine or Mansoor has its own style, in each case. Divorced from its style love becomes mute magic inside the soul that can be only vaguely experienced, but cannot be expressed.

Love is the closest image of God known to man. Love is pure essence. Hence its language, style and gesture are all original within each individual. The teachers of mankind know that their styles cannot be exchanged. The style of each blossomed soul has a special value for the world. To give up the original style means not to give expression to the originality of love – the only form in which every soul experiences true love. To give it up would be the same as spiritual suicide. They cannot communicate their experience in any other style. Their followers adopt their style and call it religion.

He who bows to terror makes it a parasite on his soul. Terror produces the feeling of absence of love in the terrorist. Absence of love is the same as turning infidel. A soul that frightens another soul gets frozen by its own spiritual power of terror. It is as good as absent. The playful terrible mother exploits it. She appears in the heart of such a soul as the lust for love. Lust for love is the name of the substitute of love.

The feeling of the absence of soul is an illusion caused by terror. The Gurus realized the enormous wrong terror was causing. Therefore they stood and said — those who terrorize are children of the terrible, not of God. They fear as much as they frighten.

'Fear I none
For frighten I none.'

Guru Tegh Bahadur

It was, therefore, as vital to stand against terror and flout it as to express one's experience of God. They were parts of the same scheme. What they taught at the spiritual plain, they exercised on the mundane for the understanding of the common men.

So much importance is attached in Sikhism to direct communion with God, and on the capacity of each individual soul to do this, that the last Guru dissolved the very institution of Gurus. Only the holy book was left with the Sikh as the guide. It contains no rules and no instructions as is generally expected of a religious book. It contains expressions of the experiences of love of great men and women. They are in music. If properly chanted within their musical discipline, they are likely to awaken glimpses of the subtle experiences of the love of the Gurus. That would serve as a beacon to a true seeker.

Music is an essential part of all the hymns contained in the *Guru Granth Sahib*. This fact should never be ignored. The Gurus have not left everything to the written words. They never strove for poetic excellence or original similes and metaphors. But they have all been meticulous about the musical discipline. It is the symphony, the melody and the lyrical power inlaid that is of greater significance to them. They have preferred intimate communication to brilliant communication. In simple forms they sang with their band of Sikhs from village to village, awakening in the soul of the common people the sublime experiences the Gurus had in their love. This I think is the source of Sikh vitality. It would not be wrong to say that the Sikh religion conveys through a single medium — the power of music — all the three facets of God. Their songs present the three-dimensional picture of God before the mind's eye — Truth, Beauty and Good. It is a religion that has beauty as its mother. Sikhism is the shine of a fully disciplined life on the countenance of saffron robed time. They are *jogis* who have not gone to forests. In their houses they have seen the dwelling of the *Nirankar Alepa*.

Love and the Five Senses

I have repeatedly referred to the central principle in Sikh philosophy—love. They have gone to the extent of identifying love with God. This love is however not that which is controlled by the five senses and *manah*. Herein comes a very delicate issue for discussion. It is regarding the nature of the ten *indriya*—the ten senses—and their ruling king, *manah*. (the wanton will).

In Samkhya philosophy a total dualism is maintained between *Prakriti* and *Purusha,* and *manah* and the ten senses have been relegated to the realm of *Prakriti*. They have been talked of in very derogatory terms in several Indian religions. Even the Gita likens them to wild horses. *Manah* has been called a monkey or a drunken elephant. All Indian systems are erroneously believed to have advocated that the senses and *manah* should be constantly suppressed otherwise they are sure to lead to disaster. The Sikh Gurus have put the idea with a difference. To them *Kudarat* (*Prakriti* or Nature) is the playful force of the Lord or His sporting spirit. It acts under His command. The Trinity is born of it. At no stage does it get loosened. It never goes beyond the control of the Lord. Even in its most reckless and defiant moods, it is only fulfilling His command. *Kudarat* is therefore a veil or illusion that the Lord has woven sportingly. A true Sikh is not suspicious of it nor has he to accept inhibitions or some special penance to avoid its destructive snare. He should rather learn to play this game in accordance with the will of God. The Gurus have maintained this position consistently from beginning to end. One special thing about Sikh philosophy is that it is free of contradictions.

According to the Gurus, one should not run the squirrel's rounds after the senses and the *manah*. But at the same time they do not agree that they should be subjected to any suppression. This would be the same as maintaining a dualism *ad infinitum*. But the duo, *Purusha* and *Prakriti,* do not last forever in the mind of the truth-seeker. They might last forever in the universe or in the mind of the scientist whose study is confined to the universe. The seeker of the ultimate truth comes out of this duality at some higher level.

After that level has been attained he cannot feel easy in his mind and heart if he insists on living with the idea of duality. There is only *Purakh* who is *Nirankar Alepa*. He is unrelated, unborn of any parent. He is neither lonely nor with others. His state cannot be described in relative terms. He transcends the theory of relativity. In his ultimate state *Kudarat* is none other than the *Akaal Purakh*. She is His sporting spirit.

According to the Gurus there is no need to quarrel with the senses and *manah*. Even as *Kudarat* is born of the Lord to fulfil His functions, so do *manah* and the senses grow from the individual soul to do its bidding. Since the individual soul is ordinarily ignorant or blind, the senses and *manah* behave wildly and wickedly. Their actions are only symptoms of the disease our soul is suffering from. If we suppress them, we only blind ourselves to a true diagnosis of the disease of the soul. The true way is, therefore, to strive for the evolution of the soul from sloth and ignorance to knowledge and love. When the soul flowers into love, the senses and *manah* instantly drop their wicked pursuits and become faithful servants of love. They are instruments of the active powers of the soul given for expressing it in this world of space and time. The Lord has made them in particular reference to this world. As this world is not built of pure elements, the Lord has given an impure and mixed nature to the senses, with the sole objective to equip them with a matching ability, so that they may bring victory to the soul in a world corrupted by a few with their cunning, cruelty and deceit.

A true seeker has nothing to fear from the senses. They are to him various forms of a faithful consort. The senses have a tendency to be coloured by the objects and events that a man comes across in life. The senses revel in imitation and self-befooling. These tricks do not befool a true seeker even as a wise spectator does not believe in the show of a magician.

Love and Anger

The Gurus seem to have realized that anger has a tendency to put worries in the heart of love. If we find everyone angry at our love, no matter how pure and full it is, worry overcomes love. Worry is a negative power that sets the intellect against itself. It puts our mental faculties to such thinking that is fatal and suicidal. A soul thus ridden by worries looks at itself with suspicion. It starts curbing those constituents of love that do not find approval in the eyes of those who are angry at it. They forget that love is a comprehensive emotion. To cut or curb some of its parts means its destruction. As a result, a life devoid of inspiration is left to us. It is flat and without the Divine fire. It is as good as dead.

The Gurus saw the faults to which the people had become victim. They wanted to teach their people the art of taking back their spiritual wealth of love. They did not agree with the saying: 'wisdom cannot be robbed'. It can be. Even the soul can be robbed. The wicked have subtler means of robbing the soul. You must know how to neutralise their deeds and maintain the purity and fullness of love. Out of the four perversions of love, love can be created again if you have the will and courage. Anger, worry, self-destruction and lack of inspiration and enthusiasm — these four perversions of love are to be seen with the eye of wisdom. Wisdom has the eye that sees within them the power to neutralise each other. Wisdom also knows how to activate this sleeping power. These perversions are ever keen to afflict the soul. If they afflict, the soul follows them and becomes their instrument. It is due to this possibility of perverting the soul that the Gurus had warned that even the soul could be robbed. There is no room for spiritual complacency in Sikhism.

Guru Teg Bahadur had sacrificed his life to protect the right of the Kashmiri Brahmins to live by their belief. The Mogul Emperor had denied them this freedom for he believed his belief was the only belief and the rest was blasphemy. Guru Teg Bahadur's self-sacrifice was born of the ideal of spiritual freedom for everyone. The importance of this right has not been expressed better than in a sentence of Voltaire: "I do not agree with anything that you say, but I will defend unto death your right to say it." Voltaire was a master of brilliant expressions. He was brilliant also in knowing that it was not necessary to stake life for ideals. Guru Teg Bahadur did not have the art of brilliant expressions, but he knew that an ideal needs sacrifice to overpower its opposite that is always found established in this world. He did not agree with the Kashmiri Brahmins' interpretation of the Upanishadic description of the soul as *'nitya shuddha buddha mukta svabhav'* (eternal, pure, enlightened and liberated). Those Brahmins interpreted it to mean that the soul would remain "eternally pure, enlightened and liberated" irrespective of what they did. Guru Teg Bahadur said that the word in the scripture was 'eternal' not 'eternally.' It was a noun, not an adjective. 'Eternal' made it a description of the ideal state of the soul, not of its actual state in every individual. 'Eternally' made it a guarantee that it could not be corrupted even if the individual indulged in bad karma. Guru Teg Bahadur said that they had become complacent and did not care that they had to purify their conduct to keep the soul in its ideal state. Deluded karma that did not care for purity of conduct and character had buried this ideal state of the soul. The soul buried under the load of bad karma was a soul in torpor. If the ideal state of a soul was in torpor that soul was as good as a robbed soul. The difference between Sikhism and Vedanta in the times of the Gurus was not of ideology, but of practicing and not practicing the ideology in daily life.

The wakeful soul does not get animated by the ten senses, and instead animates the sleeping power in them that neutralizes the perversions of love. Therefore Guru Tegh Bahadur did not react with grief, fear or any feeling of revenge when his dearest disciples were brutally murdered before him. His approach was both heroic and sublime. He did not take the agony of death to his soul. That would have been ignorance. That would have made the soul a home for parasites. He kept the soul unruffled. Now since an action aroused a reaction and he did not let his soul react, he had to make room for the appearance of the reaction, too, in the souls of the brutal murderers. The reaction of a bad karma had to be born somewhere. Guru Teg Bahadur thought that if the reaction, too, was born in the soul of the doer of bad karma, it would compel him to reform his karma. He succeeded in it due to the force of his right conviction. It is recorded that Aurangzeb lost the balance of his mind after getting the Guru killed. After the martyrdom he had a few sensational visions that completely shattered him. Guru Tegh Bahadur's refusal to let his love be disturbed by this sorrow proved very costly to the empire. Its roots opened. The reaction to this brutality was born there. Besides, it inspired the Sikhs to meet the anti-God in his own home and kingdom. They learnt the art of keeping spiritually detached even when they were whole-heartedly pursuing victory and glory. It was a new way to assert love that they had discovered under his leadership. They rekindled the dead embers of *nishkam karma*, i.e., disinterested action or action that was undisturbed by both fruitlessness and fruitfulness. They did not indulge in the self-defeating or self-deluding process of keeping away motives or desires from the expected fruits. They knew it was vain, confusing and weakening to act in this manner.

The ideal of detachment was attained in a different way. Not by cutting the bonds of fruits or motives from our minds and hearts, but by awakening in our souls the magic of love do we attain the ideal of detachment. Only a lover can be truly detached. One who lives for love cannot be fettered by karma, for love is neither a bondage nor release in the ordinary sense. It is beyond both. It is freedom that feels embraced from all sides, and yet it is embrace that does not feel like the embrace of some other person. Love is the highest experience of God beyond which the faculty of speech finds no scope for it and dumbfounded sees muteness as its next expression. Love is a complete synthesis of opposites. The true lovers get charged with another meaning due to the springs of love in their souls. A higher dawn spreads on the horizon of the soul. This light cannot be described. Only a young girl in love can experience it in her virgin body. It is a reward of purity. Love is given only to those whose hearts transcend opposites. To experience love one has to transcend the binding game of opposites that the human psyche plays. Indeed beyond this psychological play is the light that is love. That is why in *Japji* so much importance has been attached to *virginity*. It has been called a necessary medium to realize God. Virginity is not a virtue only in girls. It is a virtue to

be attained by men too. The Gurus talk of the virtue of virginity in
the soul that is essential to meet the *Waheguru*. The Sikh who has
chosen the path of love has to awaken the same fire of virginity in
his soul that nature kindles in the pure body of a loving girl in her
early youth. The *Japji* says:

> "Know ye that seeks God
> Purity of a virgin is the path to God."

Virginity is the state of alertness against both intrusion and
receptivity. At the same time, it is yearning and the awakening of
the spontaneous and innate moral sense. Unless a soul subjects
itself to the discipline of love, God does not touch it. Love is not
the act of loving. The act is an illusion. Making love is the
externalization, the expulsion, of the experience of love. Love is
the yearning, not the act, of love. In lost times, like the modern
times, people identify love with lovemaking. They do not identify
love with the yearning, pining and the ache of love. What they call
love is lust, not love. The virgin soul that yearns for love is love
itself. Love is ever new, ever fresh. The sweetest poet of Mithila,
Vidyapati, shot right through his heart by the arrow of love,
describes the state of the female in love in the following inimitable
way:

> *Sakhi ki puchasi anubhav mor*
> *Hot na preet anurag bakhaniye*
> *Til til nutan hoye*

> (You ask me to tell my experience — why?
> My friend I cannot, whatever I try
> It changes and turns new the moment I try)

Love identified with lovemaking transforms into a stale passion. It
ceases to have the quality of ever newness and ever freshness that
are essential signs of love. Love is a spiritual experience because it
involves the Divine whenever it happens to two persons. Were it
the same as lovemaking every mating beast would be a lover. Mixing
love with sex creates duality and self-consciousness. Love and
duality, love and self-consciousness cannot live together. To end
duality the soul must sacrifice itself to sexuality and get reborn of

it. Thus the soul returns from the experience of lovemaking to the yearning of love. Yearning is the reality of the soul. Its virginity is its reality, and virginity is yearning of love, not the craving for lovemaking. This is the message of the Gurus.

The Curse on the Beloved

Byron said that ill fate stamped all those whom he loved. Ill fate pursued them. He believed that there was a curse on his love.

The curse was not only on the love of Byron, but is on all love. It is on the love of God too. The martyrdom of saints and the tortures they faced illustrate it. Perhaps this is the reason why God does not make a human soul His beloved easily. He tests it and only when his love shows preparedness to pass through the ordeal of fate the Lord takes it as His beloved. It was not with any ease that the Gurus and Sikh saints became the beloved of God. They had to pass through the test of fire and torments.

The curse is apparently so. In reality it is no curse. It is only the last attempt of duality to stay as a shroud on the soul. It frightens with the curse so that the lover fears and gives up lifting duality's last veil. The Gurus knew it as the last veil of duality. They did not stay away from lifting it. They had no fear of its curse. It was like the curse of any drug-addict who frightens and curses those who prevent him from taking drugs because they love him and want to help him. The Gurus sacrificed their souls to the curse, and tearing it their souls got reborn of this last veil of duality.

The consciousness of all brave men of the West, like Byron, Nietzsche and Dostoevsky, has stoically suffered the curse, but they kept trying to lift the veil. Alas they could not succeed, and often they had to pay the very high price of sanity. In India the rishis knew such stoic persistence to be futile. They called it *the boon of Brahma*. Brahma's boon cannot be transgressed. According to the Indian mythology, Brahma created the universe. He has granted the boon of fruitful cursing to duality, because duality is the principle that has made creation possible, and Brahma does not want it to be transgressed by ordinary people. He knew that the rishis would transgress duality occasionally and very discreetly, only when it would be absolutely necessary for humanity's welfare. The method of self-sacrifice of the soul that the rishis had taught the Indians tears asunder the curse, and turns it into the mother of invincible love and oneness of two lovers, whom no power of earth and heaven can separate once God grants it recognition. Were all the powers to unite against it, they would wither like the yellow leaves of autumn, for God is the soldier that fights for a mortal's love, who has conquered duality.

Sikhism lays great emphasis on surrender to a true Guru. Surrender is not passive surrender in Sikhism. It is active self-sacrifice of the soul to the soul of the Guru. The Guru's soul does not grant it rebirth until it has learnt all that the teacher decides to teach it. It has a deep psychological meaning. The story of the Sikh lady saint Bhago is enough to illustrate this meaning. In her exalted devotion and pangs of love, she once tore her clothes and went half-naked to the forests crying for her Love. Guru Gobind Singh then gave her the attires of a man and under his influence she calmed down. Love in her discovered a comely road. Instead of becoming an object of contempt and social ridicule, she learnt to live like any other mortal, and still to live with a difference. The meaning and fire remained the same; only the form changed and became socially acceptable. It is significant to note that none of the Sikh saints adopted any unusual manner of life, impelled by the force of love. None of them became mad or eccentric like certain Sufis and Kalandars.

The problem of Bhago and its solution by Guru Gobind Singh epitomizes the entire Sikh approach to love. Bhago becomes mad out of love and Guru Gobind Singh gives her the clothes of a man and keeps her with him. The human soul is a female according to the Sikh faith, as I have said elsewhere, and God is the male who is to be wooed. The human soul wins Him by its chastity and total surrender. The Lord comes to its door. This is a moment of great significance as described by all great saints who have experienced it. It is awe-inspiring. Sometimes the saints have fainted the moment their Beloved Lord appeared before them. They fainted out of awe. The details of the union of the soul with God have not been described in the Sikh scriptures. However, it can be surmised from the few details provided by the saints of different faiths. This union between the soul and God is an active union from both sides. Even as the soul gets reborn from God, the soul, too, gives rebirth to God. The pangs of the soul that mothers God are far more than those of a mother at childbirth.

The soul that had been pining for the Lord suddenly changes at the very moment when its wish is getting fulfilled, because it finds its love for itself stronger than its love for God. How can the lover (soul) show her face to the true lover (God) with this lie in her heart. She is ashamed of her love for herself. It is staring in her eyes. It has surprised her suddenly at the moment when the lover had arrived after a long wait. She is overcome with the shame of being unworthy of what she sought. God is no foolish mortal lover with whom deception goes as well as faithfulness. In the first meeting of eyes God would see her falsehood. She does not want to fall in the eyes of God. What will He think of me? To be worthy of Him is now more important than to have Him. The priority has changed suddenly. She has no option but to run away from Him to hide somewhere in the deep and dark wood, until she can make her heart true and worthy of Him. The running away has another reason too. The soul cannot bear to produce the Lord. The birth pangs are unbearable even as the soul imagines it. It is not like the meeting of two bodies. In the love play between the soul and the Lord, the Lord gets inside the soul as the embryo that has to be instantly given birth. It will not be a conception in time. There is no entity like time in this meeting of lovers. The love play, the conception and the birth, all actions, take place instantly. And the worst is that in giving birth to the Lord the soul shall blow out. Whatever the soul had known to be the sum total of its being has to die. It is, therefore, not only the moment of union with the Lord but also the moment of the death of the soul. The soul at the end of its tether loses faith in God's word to Arjun, "I do not let the souls of my lovers perish."

When the Lord makes a soul His beloved, *Maya* takes up its wildest form to frustrate this love. The form is so terrifying that the strongest souls shiver like dry leaves. That is why God makes only the evolved soul His beloved. From others He expects yearning, devotion and surrender, so that their souls may be purged of all impurity; so that they may rise to a level of perfection where they cannot to be deluded or frightened by the extreme illusions of *Maya,* which is waiting to cast her last net of illusions that look no different than truth and can be cut only by the heart that has no lie, no deception and no fear. *Maya* takes on its extreme form before unflinching seekers of God and looks stronger than God. The last act of the union with God takes place now. When He responds to a beloved soul and reaches her door, *Maya* has His permission to take a form here that deludes even *pragya*, the highest faculty of the saint. *Maya* separates the two. The soul experiences that all its pangs and sincere devotion and its acceptance by God are unable to subdue the wicked wind that separates them. This is a moment that creates doubts, frustration and madness in the soul just at the moment of its union with God. The power that separates the soul from the Lord when He comes to its door is indeed the subtlest trap of *Maya*. Only that soul passes the final test that sacrifices Nirvana and the union itself, not out of fear or vanity, but out of supreme confidence in its love.

The *Chaturvyuh* (four-fold trap of *Maya*) takes entirely new shapes to confound the soul when the Lord comes to accept it as His beloved. Insult, defiance and an urge to run away from Him, to create a distance between Him and itself and a terrible force of insanity tearing the very soul—these are the four tendencies that have appeared so often in saints at the moment of their encounter with God. Bhago, also behaved unbecomingly and ran away to forests, thus creating a distance between herself and Guru Gobind Singh. Had the Guru not intervened, had he not used his illuminated love to reconcile her to the Lord, she would have been a prey to more baffling forms of *Maya*, as in the case of several saints who did not have such good luck as she had. The next form of *Maya* that confounds such saints has often been waywardness—an irresistible urge to waste the soul's love on some petty person, leaving aside God.

History is full of the record of lisping saints who stopped at the half-house. Their souls failed them and proved cowardly at the moment of their encounter with the Lord. They withdrew from Him. God could have helped their further flowering. But it threatened to be a very painful process. They ran away from it. Still they had yearned and burnt for the Lord till the final encounter. Their yearning did not go in vain. As a reward they got many spiritual powers, *riddhis* and *siddhis*.

A passing reference to India after independence may help in highlighting the injurious effect of lisping saints, since after leaving the track of disinterested quest of love they often turn vain and greedy. After independence such lisping saints and deserters have been leading India, by forging links of common interest with politicians, rich persons and bureaucrats. They have been showering their *riddhis* and *siddhis* on lesser beings only to sustain their imaginary awesome status in the eyes of the masses that flatter them for being more than what they are. Their advancement had come to a dead stop. They had no courage to get seriously involved in the quest of Truth or Love, for a single step onwards demanded the extinction of their ego and of the false status they had built for themselves. They had kept misleading the people, as the people had no ability to see through the hoax. With the help of their followers, who were in large numbers, they blocked the way to spiritual leadership of a few true seekers of Truth who could lead further the spirit of India from the ancient to modern times. They did so for they feared that if they allowed this march toward light their hollowness would get exposed and they would be thrown out of business. As a result true seekers of truth, beauty and good could not influence the minds of the people. After independence India's spiritual and cultural growth declined ironically. It was the time when it was most needed. After political freedom India would have gone for mental freedom. India's mental freedom, whenever it will gather momentum, will never be of the Western type because of her profound spiritual wealth and moral values. Imitating the

Western obsession with sexuality, as if it were the key to mental freedom and modernity, and the panacea of many human ills, has impressed the Indians. The results of this imitation are somewhat dismal and obvious. Not to see them requires blindness. In every field of humanities, like literature, philosophy, history, painting, sculpture, films, serials, media, religion and governance the net gain has been — inability to give expression to the peculiar suffering of modern Indians. Without the disinterested quest of truth and love no soul can empathize with another soul. None of the few Indians sincerely engaged in these fields has been allowed to take forward the arrested soul of India. Such people have been denied the facilities of communication, by those who control the media, often due to sheer pride, foolery or the ill effect of some past karma. A nation cannot be built on mere technology, economics, information and entertainment.

Man's soul may be in fetters, but it is never helpless. It has to will. It can get out of the slumber, no doubt, but it has to will to get out. It has to overpower the indolence that feels many times stronger than the soul whereas it is infinitely weaker. One has only to resolve to wake up so that God may help. Within a short period the awakened soul will find what it considered as heavy as a mountain was as light as a cloud. You cannot take the Indians one step ahead without helping their spirituality on its path of further evolution. Material development, without fulfilling modern India's need of the spiritual truth that can absorb it, and that can take away the corrupting power of prosperity, will be superficial and sentimental. We cannot keep burying this need under the political gimmick of equating all religions. Spirituality is not religion. It is the source from which religions take birth, but fail to promote spirituality since politics and money hijack them.

There is no Day of judgement in Sikhism. God does not judge and punish in Sikhism, just as in Hinduism. He loves, forgives and saves. The intervention of Guru Gobind Singh saved Bhago from the traps of *Maya*. It is interesting to see that not only in the case of Bhago but repeatedly this intervention has taken place in Sikh history. None of the Gurus took to the popular practice of religious pride. The last Guru had promised that wherever five true followers of the Gurus will assemble and remember him he will be the sixth man with them.

The four-fold trap of *Maya* is only to be seen, not to be recognised, for recognition makes it real. It is a play of illusion and should never be allowed to become real. The power to make it real is inside every soul. If the soul recognises it, it becomes real—it is as simple as this. The Gurus have, therefore, nowhere tried to describe *Maya* in detail for fear that weaker followers may take it as real. The traps of *Maya* are part of His play. They are not real. Those who keep alive the courage to meet the Lord get the light to recognize *Maya,* the trickster. They aim at taking rebirth from this terrible mother, as Hanuman took from the mother of snakes, Sursa. A love reborn from these wayside robbers alone gets acclimatised to earthly conditions. It fulfils its dream. It unites with the Lord.

Sikhism has successfully blown-out the myth that madness and eccentric behaviour are signs of true love. The Gurus have shown that madness is a baffling experience in love, not a part of it. Instead of being a higher state of love, it is a hijacker of love. They had faced and exposed the strongest forms of ignorance that pursue the seeker up to the summits to deviate. Calling madness a higher form of love and eccentricity a sign of genius is the sign of spiritual weakness. The Gurus have shown that the true lover and the true genius are neither mad nor eccentric. Lovers and geniuses that go mad are people that lack the spiritual courage not to be proud of their achievement. They have not performed the *Atmayagya* that makes them realize oneness with humanity. Without the spiritual courage that eliminates the pathos of distance none can walk over the razor's edge.

The four forms of *Maya* have nothing real about them. They are paper tigers. But it is not to be said; it is to be realized. Only a daring soul can realize it. Courage does not rise in the soul by any artifice. Sentimental words, praise and outer encouragements may excite the mind or the blood. They have no effect on the flowered soul. Only intimacy with Truth, God or Love gives the courage to the soul that does not fear ordinariness.

The Gurus' concept of love is simple. It says that the experience of love is a recording in time. But love is the soul, and there is neither time nor space in the soul. Time is an illusion for the soul. Therefore the recording of its experience of love also becomes an illusion, however true the love may be. The cruel world shatters only the recording of love, i.e. the image of love in the mirror of time. It cannot touch love, which is identical with the virgin soul. Only the yearning of love is an event that happens in the soul. Experience of love belongs to time, which is an illusion from the spiritual point of view.

According to the Gurus, only union with God is self-realization; nothing else is self-realization. And the soul unites with God only through constant yearning for love. The physical experience of love that a wife gets from her husband is an event in time, not in the soul. Her soul must sacrifice itself to this experience to get reborn as a virgin yearning for love. Otherwise time will intervene between her soul and God who is beyond time (*Akaal*). A lover who practices this discipline in earthly love truly unites with the earthly lover. It ultimately leads to union with God.

The lovers who exchange words like 'I love you' create duality between the soul and love. A soul that recognizes its love makes its love a subject of time. It degrades it, from immortality to mortality. The soul of such a lover goes to sleep, and time becomes his soul. Time is non-existent for the soul. Time's coming into existence for the soul is, simultaneously, the coming of a veil on the soul. The soul that stops yearning for love is identical with the sleeping soul.

Time is an intuition of the mind, not of the soul. Those who degrade love from yearning to experience, get trapped in the trick that time plays on such deluded souls. Time makes them yearn for the immortality of their experience of love. Experience of love cannot be immortal, because it belongs to time, and time cannot be immortal because it has a beginning and an end. They forget the yearning for love that is already immortal, since it is soul itself. Love is not action. It is the source from which action flows. Yearning for love in the soul is an action beyond time that does not bring fetters. Hence it is action that brings freedom from action. Self-sacrifice of the soul to its experience of love re-kindles its memory that it is itself love.

Lower immediacy precedes while higher immediacy succeeds intellectual knowledge in Bradley's philosophy. In Sikh philosophy, lower or fleeting love precedes while higher or everlasting love succeeds spiritual knowledge. The passionate unity that young couples feel without spiritual knowledge soon gets lost as the passion flowers. After spiritual knowledge love comes back to the couple never to wither. If spiritual knowledge is not crowned with immortal love, in spite of being as intense as in the virginal state, and as new, it is no spiritual knowledge. Spiritual knowledge does not sow seeds of discord between man and woman. It rather unites their souls never to part till eternity.

Who says the sweet pangs of first love never return to the lover? They return, the Sikh Gurus say, after he attains spiritual knowledge, and they return never to part.

4

The Unreal

*T*he unreal, according to Sikhism, is no creation of God. It is born of human ignorance, and of the untrained and unbridled will of many. The universe or nature is real. An individual's particular view of it is unreal. To see the thing as it is, one must first learn to surrender one's will to the will of God. All sins, lust and ignorance are born of the obstinacy on the part of the individual to assert his will. His will disturbs the psychological self that is the storehouse of all the powers given to him. These disturbed and excited powers create an unruly *haumey* by interweaving without knowing the Divine pattern that is the model to be imitated for such interweaving. Arbitrary interweaving creates *haumey,* which is the pride that overpowers and possesses the soul. It is the chimera created by the individual will. From it proceed a number of wrong ideas and twisted visions that completely upset the soul.

The unreal, according to Sikhism, is two-fold. It is *haumey,* i.e., ego, a false growth of our psychological powers. The other is *haumey's* vision, i.e., whatever it sees and thinks the world to be. It is this blinding power, born of it, which has been called *Maya* by the Gurus. It is a cloud of smoke. It is a wall of sand. It simply does not exist for the wise. It melts like ice before the rays of truth. But for one under the proud spell of *haumey* it is a private reality. Not only in the madhouses, in the open world as well, people enslaved by *haumey*, live in their private worlds. The private world is different in each case. This private world is real for that soul alone, and in fact more than real in his case, for he is completely under its control.

There is no communication between the private worlds of two such *haumey*-ridden persons. There are walls between such souls and neither recognises the other. Nor they recognize the *Waheguru*.

Love is the power that frees us from the network of *haumey*. The fisherman retires and the lonesome fish, the soul, is no longer lonely.

The Gurus have used all the traditional words for *Maya*. It is crafty. It is a fiend. But one should not confuse it with *Kudarat.*

All ignorance is born of ego. When the senses dominate the intellect, the result is ignorance. When *haumey* dominates the soul, lust, pride and anger are the results. The wise reverse this order. In them, *haumey* removes its veils from the soul, and the senses act at the command of the soul. This reversing is the same as a journey from darkness to light.

Haumey ceases to exist when the will is surrendered to God. The soul then sees Nature as she is in herself. It sees Nature, what Kant calls, as the thing-in-itself. *Haumey* produces ignorance that sees and befriends *Maya,* not Nature. It sometimes acts as a serpent that binds the soul and sometimes as the trickster that deludes it and makes it commit error after error. One gets involved in a frustrating play little knowing that he himself is its originator. "Only the true Guru can save the soul from it," says the *Granth Sahib.* "*Maya* is the mother of the five deadly sins."

The *manmukh* soul is dominated by the vagaries of the heart that has not yet been illumined by the light Divine. *Maya* governs such a heart and *Haumey* is its constant companion.

One very significant contribution of the Gurus is their unique way of psychological cleaning. Besides the spiritual soul, the individual has the psychological self. Though it is unreal in the spiritual sense, in practical life, people take it as more real than the real soul. It is a storehouse of unruly passions and wild forces. They can raise such storms in the soul that not a ray of its light remains visible. Unless the various faculties of mind and body are disciplined, the soul remains powerless to express itself. Its radiance gets clouded and a man departs from life without awakening his soul and making it conquer worldliness and *haumey*, unite with God, and spread the tranquillity and love born of this union. The soul cannot ignore the psychological self. Either it conquers it or gets ruled by it.

Haumey can be likened to the libido. Like the libido it appears to be larger and stronger than the soul. And yet it is not real. It is a dark creation made of shadows. It is, however, not the Absolute that the libido, as conceived by Jung, is. Unlike the libido of Jung, it is neither mysterious nor unpredictable. *Haumey* or libido, as conceived by the Gurus, disappears when the *Waheguru* appears in the heart. It cannot stay in a heart that is full of love. The following lines from *Japji* testify this observation about *haumey*:

> "It is indeed the truth, doubt it not
> Where Ram is, *haumey* dwells not
> Know thee Nanak the mark of the liberated
> He knows Ram and *haumey* he knows not."

The individual soul shares the powers of God on a small scale, but only if it is awake. Otherwise *haumey* uses the powers given to the soul by God. Ignorance becomes the stage manager to present the show created by delusions, ambitions and greed. *Haumey* builds with those powers a small island, and crowns itself as its despot. This isolates it from the Lord. Individual will makes it an isolated maniac lost in its island. Submission to the will of God gives the soul will-power that is steady and illuminated, while the will of the individual is blinded by desires. Will power is a gift from God to the soul that has submitted his will to God's will. It makes such a soul a soldier of Love. Active participation in the Lord is advocated in Sikhism. It is possible through an act of will. Here the Sikh Gurus differ from other teachers. Surrender to the will of God has been understood by several other systems to be the same as the destruction of personal will. Hence there has been no dearth of saints who have likened individual will to serpents that ought to be crushed by one that seeks God. How wrong this has been is evident from the clinical studies of the modern psychiatrists. Destruction of individual will does not mean the automatic appearance of the Divine will. The Gurus have talked of a positive way of dealing with this problem. You cannot be in communion with the will of God by destroying your individual will.

A higher effort and determination are required for this. Your individual will is the only link you have with the Divine will. The Gurus say, instead of destroying your will, teach it to become an instrument of the Divine will. The One transforms into many, not only at the spiritual and natural levels, but at all levels. The Gurus seem to be saying that this transformation is taking place at all times everywhere. Wherever human life is, there the One *Nirankar Alepa* is transforming into several faculties and powers, to equip the individual soul with sufficient instruments helpful in attaining liberation. The soul can liberate itself from the karmic bonds only with the help of karma that do not produce fetters. The Gurus do not believe that the soul can be liberated without doing karma. The way to bondage is deluded karma, done out of greed, anger, hatred, fear, envy, lust or revengeful passions etc. While the deluded karma binds the soul, selfless karma frees it. Thinking truthfully, compassion, love of humans and animals and unconditional love of God are examples of such karma that liberate.

The Gurus in their debates with the *siddhas* had hit hard at their belief that they could liberate their souls by avoiding all kinds of karma. The gurus said that even thinking and meditating that they did in any case were karma. They said that where there was life there was karma. No living being could avoid karma. Even sloth and indolence were karma, though of a senseless kind. God's power *Kudarat* (Nature) had transformed into many powers and faculties in the human personality to help man to do karma. At all the levels of the human personality, like thought, feeling and will, the One Reality was appearing in many forms. None could reach the One by destroying the many. The wise ones had learnt the spiritual art of rolling back the many into one, in their minds. To hear the call of the One amidst the calls of the many, man required sincere love. It was here, more than anywhere else, that man had learnt the importance of love. In the clamour of a thousand warring desires, it was love alone that gave you some clues to the Divine Will.

Those in whom love had not awakened had always let pass the Divine Will as one of the many selfish wills.

The Lord is playful. Love is required to understand his play, and also to play one's role cheerfully in his infinite play going on everywhere in the universe. Those who do not realize the central theme of all creation — Love — fall prey to *haumey* (ego) and ignorance. There are two paths in the heart of man. He who goes for asserting his individuality has not yet seen the home of the Lover *Waheguru*. Even after attaining the highest spiritual summits, the Gurus never gave any value to their flowered individualities. The soul gets clouded the moment it gives itself importance. All meaning and value of the souls is the Lord. The tenth Guru went so far as to curse those who thought of building a memorial to him.

Such was their humility that after knowing *Waheguru* as much as was possible for any man to know, Nanak said, "If I knew would I not describe Him." (*Japji*). Nanak draws attention here to a subtle distinction between ultimate knowledge and discursive knowledge. A flowered soul that has realized oneness with God cannot see Him as an object, and cannot describe him as an object. The soul that describes Him has only intellectually known Him, and has, therefore, not known Him, since He cannot be known without identifying oneself with Him, and on getting one with Him, He ceases to be an object of knowledge.

Is the World Incurably Sorrowful?

The Buddha had said that everywhere there was sorrow in this world. People forget that it was the sentiment of adolescent Buddha who had seen for the first time old age, sickness and death. It was the time when the first flush of youth had appeared on his cheeks. These cruel realities of life had been hidden from him all along. After attaining Nirvana when the Buddha repeated the same statement it was not a sentiment but wisdom. He was not shocked by the sorrow that he saw. Long watch over mortality had given him a vision that noticed happiness too. He saw now the transitory character of both happiness and sorrow in this world. Everything was in a flux. He said there was happiness too, but fleeting, for *'too soon do the flowers of spring wither.'*

The Gurus had seen sorrow ever since childhood. Therefore it did not disturb their adolescence so intensely. Besides, the Buddha was born in free India, while all the Gurus were born in India enslaved, conquered and humiliated by foreigners. Sorrow was not a new thing to them. Therefore, they did not paint the world in lurid colours. They gave no prominence to sorrow in the world. The theme of their song was different. They sang of political freedom, religious freedom and righteous rule. They also sang of love between people, and of the need of the imitation of God by the ruler in his actions, so that he never deviated from justice, nobility and kindness.

The world to the Gurus is a projection of *Kudarat.* To call it sorrowful is no depiction of its true character. No doubt life is full of sorrow and the soul does not like sorrow. Its sensitivity gets hurt at sorrow. It is true that sorrows come to life. But so do joys. The Gurus would say that if life appears only sorrowful to someone it is because he does not want to see the whole truth about it. The whole truth about the world is that it is the expression of the infinite joy of God. The perception of the soul is all-important, since the world has no character of its own.

It is a psychological fact that after the early blazes of youthful sufferings people get sober. They start wondering at the way God has been living at the centre of the universe since eternity, and yet remains joyous, not pensive. "Let the world not cling to your soul," the Gurus said, "Live in it like *Nirankar Alepa,* the uninvolved Lord of all things. He does not get coloured by anything even though He has ever dwelt in the centre of everything. To a large extent the world is what mankind makes of it. Instead of philosophising about existence, the Gurus decided that they would not let humanity live like beasts. They would not let outsiders give the life of mute animals to the people of India. They would not let humanity and women be humiliated. They would not let children be brutalized. They would not let man be enslaved. They would not let the ruler deprive people of their human rights.

The Gurus say, bring down the Divine order in this world. Bring *Ram Raj* on earth. The world is the medium of love. If it looks full of evil, it is because of the rulers' ignorance that does not let people live by human values. The human values are the same as the Divine values. We do not need a law book to learn human values, since they keep getting born afresh in every human heart. They have been the same ever since the birth of man, yet they are freshly born every moment in the human heart. What was given to man as *Kudarat* had been turned into *Maya,* by the rulers' misdeeds born of ignorance. The rulers must collectively shun cunning, cruelty, wickedness and selfishness. Then the hard outlines of this world will melt to let us work out a human scheme of existence. Even the truest form of the world is only a phantasm of *Waheguru.* They said that the rulers should not make life miserable for the people. At the same time they said that the learned and the visionary seek no bonds with the world. They only illumine it with the springs of love hidden in their hearts. The rulers should take their help to know the nature of disinterested truth, beauty and good.

We have not to expect truth from the world of *Maya* that man has created out of greed and lies and rulers have exploited mercilessly. They have exploited the people by applying the partisan laws of their faith on people of other faiths. We do not have to ignore it as incurably false and malicious. We have to control its forces and shape it into a useful medium to express the values of man. When love sings of those values they get written on every leaf and on the face of nature. Guru Gobind Singh asked them to learn from Nature and go 'back to nature.' Nature shows the Will of God. Let us be nearer the will of God even in ordinary matters of personal hygiene and living. The Sikh love of Nature is expressed in the practice of not shaving. The logic advanced by the modern man to shave for cleanliness seems to be a misunderstanding of hygiene from these standards. The Gurus said, let us learn to bear the gifts of God with grace, cleanliness and humility.

The Sikh criticism of Schopenhauer would be that he had tried to learn from his shadow more than from his soul. In seeing so much sorrow in the world, he had projected a shadow of his ignorance that was larger than his ignorance. Such bids could never help in knowing the truth and attaining Nirvana. Due to certain shocks he had received from the indiscreet behaviour of his mother early in life, he had retained a distorted view of woman. He remained prejudiced against woman all his life. One who nurtures a prejudice against half of mankind cannot see the truth of human life. To consider one's own vision as the whole of knowledge is an ancient form of ignorance. The Sikh believes that knowledge begins only with the kindling of the lamp of love in the heart. A heart that has not been illumined by love knows nothing, no matter how brilliant its thoughts may be. It is not in the brilliance of an idea that truth resides. It resides in its comprehensiveness. A soul that has awakened to the touch of love will not see sorrow in the world. It will see Divine melancholy. It will see disinterested and unmotivated sorrow that is delicate, like a rose drenched in dew. It will see dreams in a procession, none of which is truer than the other. A dream is only a dream, and must be seen as a dream, not as reality. A dream does not become truth for being longer or for causing more pain. Had Schopenhauer seen the whole of truth he would have looked at the spectacle of sorrow in the world with the compassionate eyes of the Bodhisattva painted in the frescos of Ajanta. He would not have accused woman or anybody for creating sorrow in the world. He would have seen that life was sorrowful because all its joys and even sorrows were transitory. Otherwise poets would not have wept for the transitory sorrow experienced in love in the past.

The Gurus' view is that what the people call 'the world' is a fabrication and a web woven out of the political, economic, religious and sexual desires of the people. It is not the world (*Kudarat*) that God had created. God's world was permeated with the joy that God had felt in creating it. Powerful people have superimposed their motivated and fabricated world over the world given by God to man, and have made it a sad spectacle. The Tenth Guru had finally given the clarion call to his knights to revive the world of God. It would of itself revert to God's joy if the layers of fabrications superimposed by people, whose might was their ignorance, were neutralized. The knights by sacrificing their souls to those fabrications could neutralize and thus liquidate them.

The people of every nation are free only to create this web called 'their world' out of these four desires in any way they like. But once they create it, Brahma, the creative spirit of God, enters it. Due to the entry of the spirit of God, this web turns into the ruler of the world of those people who had created it.

This web is present inside the intentines of every individual belonging to that nation.

The creative spirit of God (Brahma) is present in the intestines of every individual belonging to that nation in another subtle form too, called 'sanskar' that are a body of certain instinctive or habitual impulses. They get formed in the intestines of every individual of that nation. A nation is free to choose its 'sanskar', but after it has chosen its 'sanskar' God's creative spirit enters it, too, and becomes its ruler.

These two forms of Brahma (the creative spirit of God) remain hostile to each other. They integrate only for those individuals who sacrifice their souls to both, get reborn from both and ask each to self-sacrifice to the other. On integrating they strengthen the guts. Fears disappear from such guts, and they transform into stores of infinite courage and fearlessness.

The Discipline

The Sikh discipline is *Sahaj*. It literally means the easy way. Being the easy way does not mean that relaxation in morals is to be practised. It does not mean a life of Bacchanalian revelry. Nanak used the word *Sahaj* only to show that his path was the opposite of the ascetics'. He had a revealing dialogue with eighty-four *Siddhas* on the Golden Mountain. The dialogue, in fact, continued all his life with others and also with himself. Wherever he met the *Siddhas* or *Naths*, he did not hesitate to expose the hypocrisy of the creeds that practised isolation from society, indifference to the misery of the people and devotion only to the quest of individual Nirvana.

Sahaj is the term used by a variety of sects, sometimes as diverse as those that preach salvation through active indulgence in the pleasures and those that talk of a moral and disciplined life. Nanak used the term in the latter sense. *Sahaj* meant to him a simple, natural and spontaneous life. His was a non-ritualistic, devotional approach as against the mystical, intricate and power-oriented approach of the king and the tantriks. Being natural did not mean to him a life given to impulses and whims. It meant a life that spontaneously imitated the life of God. *Brahmacharya* that meant to the *Siddhas* complete distance from woman was complete union with woman to Nanak. *Brahmacharya* literally meant imitation of God's conduct, and God did not keep woman at a distance from Him. Nanak's path was *Sahaj* also because it was the path of the sensible householder who neither hated flesh nor felt attached to it, who did not see woman only as a delicious piece of flesh. It was

Sahaj again because it did not require any secret initiation. It was as simple as love that Nature initiated, not man's will. Nanak's path was the path of love. It did not care for information or knowledge. It cared only for knowledge that was born of love.

It is highly significant to note that Nanak has used the moon as the symbol of truth. He has used the phrase 'the moon of truth'. Not even once has he used the phrase 'the sun of truth.' In the Indian tradition mostly it is the sun that stands as the symbol of truth. *Nath Yogis* believed the moon to be the seat of *Amrit* (nectar). The moon and Amrit are associated with Shiva *(Someshwar)*. According to the Nath Yogis the sun is *Shakti*. The dharma of *Shakti* is to completely merge in Shiva. Shiva and *Shakti* are present in each individual. Since olden days emphasis had been on the sun, i.e., *Shakti*. It had been treated often as the face of truth even in the Vedas. This idea, in mundane life, often resulted in making *Shakti* irresponsible and arrogant, even forgetful of merging in Shiva. Guru Gorakh Nath, therefore, said, woman the symbol of *Shakti* is like a tigress that ought to be kept at a distance by a true seeker. *Shakti* was said to be out for the sport of burning the nectar.

Guru Nanak made full use of the wisdom that the teacher-disciple-teacher, the long chain of rishis in India of each school of thought, spread over thousands of years, had attained by pursuing the same truth that was partly empirical and partly beyond empirical knowledge. Whatever the teacher learnt in his disinterested contemplation of truth he passed on to the disciple, and the disciple began where the teacher had ended. It was truth not prejudice that was nurtured thus. The guarantee that it was truth was as good as the guarantee of the scientific community, since the truth in each case was born of disinterested contemplation. And whatever this disciple on becoming the teacher learnt passed on to his disciple, and so on.

Guru Nanak did not denounce women or *Shakti*. The *Siddhas* who outwardly denounced them, craved for them all the more. They were degenerating in his times into lusty hypocrites preaching celibacy. He only shifted the emphasis from the sun to the moon, thereby correcting a profound error. By this change of emphasis, the sun would cease to be scorching; *Shakti* would stop her arrogant and destructive role and would learn to serve *Amrita* (nectar of knowledge). Nanak thus reversed the process that had crept sometime in the later Vedic period when Varuna, the Lord of waters and *Amrita*, was dethroned, and Indra, the god shining like a thousand suns, was given the highest seat in the grand assembly of gods.

The moral discipline in Sikhism is also different from others though the aim is the same. It would appear that in India a double moral discipline had developed—one among the religious men and the other among common men. Sometimes the difference was merely of intensity. There were, however, certain *tantrik* and *Sahaj* systems in which the cult-discipline was completely the reverse of the layman's discipline. They thought that to kill desires was to awaken their latent power and to turn them more deadly.

It seems that the laypeople in medieval India did not believe in the moral discipline of religious and cult schools as practiced by the brotherhood of adepts. Whatever the masters taught remained confined to a small section of devoted disciples. The laypeople preferred moderation. Sikhism preached a moral discipline that was nearer the laypeople. The Gurus thus enriched their life, by infusing it with their wisdom. It saved them from disaster. Here was a religion that spoke of their lifestyle with respect, and taught in such simple and direct terms that they could understand.

What distinguishes Sikhism from other medieval religions is its positive and daring approach to anger, pride, desire, possessiveness and ignorance. From ancient days, Indian seers have been denouncing these passions as evil. The Jains, the Hindus, the Buddhists have been preaching a conduct that avoided these five deadly sins. The Gurus have also called them sins, but their approach has been not of avoidance but of conquest and rebirth from these forms of the terrible mother. A unique thing about Sikhism is that it has developed not only a monistic thought but also a monistic conduct. It is one thing to preach theoretically that God alone is truth, but to give a discipline to all human actions, based on this belief alone, requires spiritual boldness and an original vision.

There are several religions that preach that God alone exists. He alone is *Sat*. But if we examine their ethical systems, we find that they have a lurking fear of some force that is other than God, call it sin or evil, whatever you like. They have given it many names. They seem to be preaching that a virtuous man should avoid its temptations or his soul would get lost. Christianity and Islam have accepted this dark, anti-God, lurking force in life, as Satan. A basic dualism has thus crept in those systems. It is of God and the devil. Whatever attempts Christian and Muslim philosophers and theologians have made to re-establish monism, the fact remains that their practical life on all steps reflects belief in two supreme entities—one bright, luminous, kind, and loving; and the other dark, wicked, and cruel.

After having realized philosophically '*Ekam Satya*' (God alone is Truth) the Hindus have not accepted the existence of the devil. None of the Indian religions believes that Lucifer, Beelzebub or Satan is responsible for evil deeds. Dualism has been altogether removed from faith by believing that one of the powers of God is *Maya* and this power assumes evil forms only to awaken the soul so that it may develop knowledge that is sleeping in it. It does not do evil for the sake of evil.

A man's intelligence and love—the two cardinal forces of Divine birth—get lost in the mirage of *Maya*. *Maya* does not acquire only such forms that are lesser than Nature's. It often acquires forms better in appearance than Nature's. A simile is drawn from the fact that artificial diamonds glitter brighter than the real diamonds. An ignorant man is more likely to go for the artificial than for the real. The magical lamp of Aladdin was lesser in looks and could be exchanged for an ordinary lamp because of the latter's better shine. This trade has been going on in the world ever since man has existed. Man has been giving up real love for the blinding intensity of the false love. Ivan Turgenev has written a beautiful short novel *The Spring Torrents* on this theme. It has been the pleasure of God to endow such powers to *Maya* that she could take up shapes brighter than God himself. *Maya* could be called the terrible mother whom psychologists discovered in the last century. I will return to this subject later. Belief in the existence of the devil, responsible for the evil that man does, is a primitive way of shirking responsibility for ones karma.

The Hindus could not find a way to practice their monistic conduct after their defeats at the hands of the invaders, because the latter did not only preach their religion. They forced by all uncivilized and mean ways their belief on the Hindus. The Hindus hold man exclusively responsible for what he does. They maintain that God always gives a choice to man, and if he chooses evil it is out of his freewill. He cannot take shelter that he had been misled by the devil. Since for a millennium the Islamic Law has ruled India, the practical life of the Hindus has been greatly confused. This law is based on the principle of retribution. It is based on the power of revenge. It is not sympathetic to criminals. It is opposite of the modern reformatory law of the civilized world. They consider the criminals devil's disciples. The principle of reformation of the criminal cannot work in states where the theological belief rules that evil comes from association with the devil.

Indian religions believe that evil is born of the ignorance of the man concerned and ignorance can be removed by right knowledge. They firmly believe in the possibility in future of a society in which there would be no evil. In ancient times when India was free only the deluded or the ignorant indulged in crime. Many hard-core criminals like Valmiki and Angulimal gave up crime on getting education about truth. They simply lost the impetus to commit crime. The test of a true teacher lay in his ability to dissolve the darkness in the mind of the criminal that inspired him to do evil. Indian religions believe that human nature is not prone to commit crime. It is only ignorance, or delusion about Reality that incites crime.

The Hindus do not believe that there is any evil power on earth that works against God, and that incites man to sin against the will of God. *Maya* only tempts him to adopt the easy way of anger, lust, pride, greed and ignorance to get things done according to his will. It does not force him. The choice is always his. That is why all the villains of Indian mythology hold themselves entirely responsible for the wrong they do, and do not blame any evil force. This freedom of man finds no better expression than in a sermon of the Buddha preserved in the *Surangama Sutra*. The Buddha tells his disciples, "Give up evil, my disciples. It is possible to give up evil entirely, that is why I say give up evil, my disciples. Were it not possible to give up evil entirely, my disciples, I would not say, give up evil."

The Sikh Gurus also believed that the temptation of evil was only the hot furnace through which a true knight passes, without disintegrating, to build his character on the immoveable rock of dharma. If the Gurus never retaliated the evil done to them with evil it was because the evil way did not convince them. They had cleansed their primordial nature of evil. They were not incapable of doing evil, because no man is incapable of doing evil. They had not chosen evil to be their strength. It was from their primordial nature that good came out with as much force as evil came out of the artificially created evil nature of the enemy i.e. the invaders of India. Indian thought is based on belief in the absolute strength of good. It also believes in the eternal law that good cannot be conquered by evil. Ram never felt the need to retaliate evil with evil. The unconditional good of Ram proved mightier than the combined might of all the evil forces of the world and the underworld.

The fifth Guru said, "Evil is unreal. There is no evil." It was left to the Sikhs to try a new way to overpower evil in life. One of the ways was not to recognize evil intellectually, emotionally and spiritually. Non-recognition of evil helped in not spreading evil to the intellectual, emotional and spiritual worlds of the man who did not recognize it. It helped in confining the evil to the world of action. It did not let it enter the subtler worlds of thought, emotion and spiritual beliefs in which also a man lives while living in the world of action. There was no need to know evil to eradicate it. It was enough to know that evil was not innovative like good. It appeared in set patterns that were derived from deception, lies, cruelty and cunning. None of its instruments had the inventive skill of good.

The Gurus went a step ahead of the Hindus. They did not avoid negative passions. They had realized that in order to avoid anger, pride, avarice, lust and other forms of evil the soul had first to grant recognition to them. That made them existent and real, while Nature had made them merely formidable appearances not realities. They could appear to be greater or lesser than the real. They could never have the Divinely determined proportions that were required by a thing to be real. The Indian sages practicing spirituality had made it a rule that their souls did not recognize evil and did not contemplate it, since the soul was real, and had the Midas like touch to turn anything real by recognizing its existence. It may not turn real for all the souls, but it turns real for the souls that recognize it. The modern practice common among the community of nations of granting recognition to a newly created nation, and its remaining like non-existent until such recognition, seems to be born of this experience of the human soul. A negative way of recognizing an undesirable thing is to actively assert its non-recognition. The Hindus had fallen prey to the evil of recognizing evil negatively. It had engaged them in the counter-productive practice of constant self-cleansing that killed their aggressive instinct against those that imposed evil on them. The result was political slavery.

The Sikh Gurus avoided this error. Blaming *Maya* regularly had turned it almost into some sort of a devil for the Hindus. The common people feared *Maya*, since they did not have the philosophic knowledge that it was God's power, not a power against good, but a power that aimed at promoting good in oblique ways. The Gurus knew *Maya* to be the terrible mother against whom the soul had to learn a little more of truth to be victorious. The soul could not defeat *Maya* in cunning, deception and cruelty. None could cross her barriers that did not have the wit that won her heart. She was won by grace, wit, self-sacrifice and unflinching faith in Truth. She had the Divine boon that nobody could go beyond her barrier without answering her questions. All others who tried without exceptional virtues had to become her prisoners.

The only prototype of *Maya* in the western lore is Baba Yaga, the witch who is ever keen to eat some Russian hero, but cannot since the hero outwits her. On being defeated she turns into a helper of the hero in his mission. The Gurus knew *Maya* to be like Sursa, the mother of all deadly snakes. She would not brook any armed opposition. Like the Non-being of Fichte that acquires existence only when Being opposes it, Sursa became stronger with every opposition by a number of heroes, until she met the exceptional, virtuous and loving hero Hanuman. Stronger than any demon or ogre, his greatest virtue was his wit. Hanuman did not fight her on learning that she had the boon from Brahma that 'whoever comes in her direction shall be her morsel.' He asked her to open her mouth to eat him, and started growing bigger so that she had to open her mouth as wide as the earth and sky. Hanuman knew the *siddhi* of becoming bigger than the biggest and smaller than the smallest. As she started closing her mouth after taking him in, he became smaller than the smallest insect and flew out of her mouth. After coming out he bowed down to her with folded hands and said, "Mother I have acted according to the boon. I have paid my homage to Brahma and you both. Now let me go for I am going on a noble mission of Sri Ram."

His wit in fulfilling the boon and also saving his skin immensely pleased her, and she let him go. It is significant of the Indian view of evil that its ultimate aim is to serve God. It is not like the hopeless and perpetual opposition of the devil to God. Hanuman is neither afraid of Sursa nor contemptuous. He is not angry either. He does not argue with her. He does not surrender, nor does he try to kill her. All these four negative passions (violence, hatred, surrender and deception) are absent from his behaviour. The negative passions grant independent existence to evil. The Indian way to fight evil is first to know that it is a servant of good. Even evil that aims at fighting to drive the seeker of good to utter hopelessness cannot escape the will of God. It shall be doing all its deeds in a pattern that will finally result in the victory of good. Even the most innovative evil is not innovative enough to beat the innovative skill of good. All Indian philosophies and religions ask of man and woman to be sure that there is no infinity in evil and its destiny is to bring victory to good. One has to fight it, and yet one has to ensure that it remains non-being in spite of the battle. To grant it being is to turn it into an equal and opposite. The Indian tradition does not grant independent existence to evil. All evil beings pay homage to Shiva, because they are there to fulfil the mission of God, which is to create conditions that unfold the hidden courage of the souls of men and women, and teach them the need to abide always, in all circumstances, even against the vilest enemy, by truth, beauty and good, and never to employ any evil to eradicate evil.

This explains the Sikh concept of evil as non-existent. It is not real. It becomes real only for the ignorant that hate or fear it, or accept it, or feel angry at it. One has to approach it with a sportsman's spirit. He has to fight this opposite with all seriousness, with a purpose to win. But this fight should have neither hatred nor anger nor fear.

The Sikh ethics represents the Indian tradition in a typical way. It does not avoid anger, hatred, possessiveness, desire and pride. By avoiding also you establish them. The Gurus popularised an original way. They taught that the emphasis should be on the substance and not on the form. Substance is the real. Form belongs to the realm of the unreal. Anger, hatred, etc., are mere forms. They cease to be sins if you make them instruments of Divine light, i.e. Love. They realized that to avoid them was also to give them a separate existence, and that would be acting against the basic creed of monism. Only the positive emotions like love, friendship, good will and compassion are real. Anger, pride, hatred and fear etc., are emotions that are unreal, as they come from *nothing* and return to *nothing*. They are emotions that are ultimately non-existent. If they are utilized consciously as unreal emotions in the service of real emotions they do not join the emotions of the enemy who uses unreal emotions as if they are real. Knowledge of the distinction between the two different ways of using negative emotions is of crucial importance. It is not self-befooling. If you do not know that the negative emotions of anger, hatred, pride etc that the enemy is showing are unreal in the eyes of God you will make them real for yourself only when your ignorant soul recognizes them to be real. The right way to conquer them is to see them as slaves of love. Thus the negative emotions of the Gurus served their central emotion, love, and turned the negative emotions of the enemy also into servants of love. "Truth alone wins (*Satyameva Jayate*)" says the sage Vyas, who is worshipped as Vishnu (*Vyasasya Vishnurupaye Vishnusya Vyasarupaye*), "is a Divine law that cannot be violated in spite of all violence."

It was a positive and profoundly philosophic approach. The passion with which the West devoted itself to realism during the 20th century has taught it that it was misplaced enthusiasm that distorted reality too often. Realism fails to deliver the result if it does not realize that the Divine laws are all idealistic. It is only in the backdrop of Divine idealism that realism bears fruit. If pursued as an end in itself it goes wild and becomes the instrument of evil. The surrender of passions to love is not easy. It involves a cycle of psychological rebirths. The negative passions in their intensity tend to eat up the soul. The soul takes its rebirth from the eater only when it has undergone the discipline of *Atmayagya* that teaches how and when the eater is unreal whereas the eaten is real, and why the real cannot be eaten up and consumed by the unreal. *Atmayagya* teaches the Divine law that is in operation in this world as well as in other worlds. It says that the unreal eater shall have to open and die giving rebirth to the real if the soul knows this Divine law and asks for its operation. Knowledge of this law is what makes it operative. Unless you ask for its operation the Divine law does not operate, for God has given free will to humans. He has given the earth to humans to run it as they will. He rules it by the Divine law when some human sincerely prays for it. It is this catch in Divine laws that had convinced all the sages that knowledge and prayer were the most important things for living on earth in peace.

The Gurus nowhere ask their fiery knights to suppress their negative emotions. On the contrary they have given them bold expressions. Guru Gobind Singh has himself described his battles that illustrate this Divine law. He and his knights always remembered that their anger, wrath and other negative passions were justified only because they were in the service of Love. The negative passions are never independent for a Sikh. The Gurus always prayed to God to run the world according to the Divine laws since the human rulers had put aside humanity. There are several prayers of Guru Gobind Singh in which he asks God for specific favours. But they are not for Sikhs only. They are for all those who live by truth not selfishness.

The thing that distinguishes the Gurus is that their anger was not master of their souls, but slave that served human values. Their aim invariably was the triumph of Love. The Gurus, therefore, fulfil the human dream of the superman. Nietzsche's superman was not the servant of Love, and he hated human virtues. He was the anti-Christ. That was why Nietzsche's soul failed to be its master. He ran wild beyond good and evil. His superman was not the ideal of one who held Love as the highest truth. Nietzsche's superman had run out of God's jurisdiction. Though God is the creator of the entire universe, He has drawn boundaries beyond which there is nothing for man. The anti-Christ superman of Nietzsche drove him beyond that boundary, and he met insanity there. It was misplaced boldness from the point of view of the Gurus.

The Gurus too had said a full and unrestrained 'yea' to life. But it was a 'yea' that served Love. They knew that a mere 'yea' was meaningless unless it brought happiness to the soul. They wanted victory but not without God. That was why they could preach virtue while wielding steel fiercely in battle. Their greatness was in their living as ordinary men. They had ambition, anger, desire and pride, but the inner light in all these passions was Love. It had completely transformed the passions. Their saintliness was not in having destroyed anger, pride and other deadly sins. Their saintliness was in remaining thoroughly unaffected by these strong passions. Not for a single moment did they forget that they were mere soldiers of light and Love. They did the penance that pleased the *Waheguru* for they were such yogis in whose person even negative passions had learnt to serve Love. The proof that they were right is that those who ventured to employ negative passions without making them servants of Love in the twentieth century perished and could not keep their minds integrated. It was this kind of walk that the sages of Upanishads had called a walk on the razor's edge. The Gurus did not have to curb human frailties because they had taken to the more difficult task of making the Divine spark emerge through them. They had to master the art of trapping an elephant in a spider's web. They had learnt to make the frog dance in the very mouth of the snake.

'The Gurus had realized that God had made man a queer combination of light and shade, but the emotion called humanity that he has kept in his heart as the guiding principle of his life has only light and no shade at all. They believed, like the rishi of *Prashnopanishad*, that humanity that seemed fragile was the only power that could smash the rule of evil in this world. They had realized that humanity was the only warmth that assured man that God was living with him on earth. According to *Prashnopanishad*, after creation God had turned into an artist for a while. Inspired by some artistic impulse he had picked up sixteen things that he had already created. He played with them artistically, and created sixteen arts out of them. "These arts live in the heart of humanity that lives in the heart and guides man."(*Iha eva antah sharire Somya sa purusha yasmin etah shodash kalah prabhavantiti.*) Humanity was a miniature of the virtues of God. It was something that convinced the souls that God was living with them in this world. If it was not there the souls panicked. The actual words in *Prashnopanishad* are — *Kasmin aham utkrantah utkranto bhavishyami kasmin va pratishthite pratishtha syami iti* — "What is that which if not present in the world I would be out of it, and if it is in the world I would be inside it?" God had created in humanity a living image of his virtues. Though God already lived in the heart as Brahm, it was not enough, since Brahm was a presence that was beyond thought. It was so abstract that it did not create confidence in man to assure man's humanity and soul that God was with him and he was not alone. The soul needed a somewhat concrete image of God, and that image was made of the sixteen arts.

It is significant that the struggle of the Gurus was not non-violent like Gandhi's. Yet the violence of the Gurus had none of the ingredients of violence, like cunning, deception or cruelty that their enemy was employing against them. If someone fights a war that is imposed on him it cannot be called violence on his part. If he fights it entirely with the power of humanity and love it transcends both violence and non-violence. It turns into something sublime. It is sublime like the wars of the Goddess Durga against the demons. This is exactly what I am trying to say about the Sikh Gurus fight against bigotry.

What historians have called Crusades had been cold-blooded massacre by the Christians and the Muslims of each other. William of Tyre wrote in the history of the Crusades that all virtue had departed. Both sides called each other infidel. The ideals of the Crusaders were chastity, poverty and obedience, but they were thrown to winds. Often they fought for money or for reserving their seats in heaven, by killing innocent people in thousands, including women and children. Pope held the deal: 'Crusade and not reach hell in spite of your sins.' The Turks and Arabs, on the other side, held out similar promises to their crusaders. Each of the crusading community called itself the soldiers of God and the other side infidel. Pope Irvin, King Alexis, the Turk and Arab hordes, Nooraldin, Baldwin, Reynolds, Pope Gregory, Richard the lion heart, and King Louis perpetrated devilish atrocities against the other community. The Knights of the Temple who had sworn to remain poor came out of the Crusades the richest men of Europe. None of the two sides had realized that the true battle for God could only be the battle that would be fought to save human values and love.

Wherever people fought in the name of God and religion, the war turned out ultimately to be the war against human values and love. Amidst all these religious heroes of the medieval times the Gurus stand out as the only Knights of humanity and love. Never, not even once, they went out of the bounds of human values and love. It seems that all through their wars they were conscious that the enemy should not be made to feel the absence of God even for a second. They could have unsettled the enemy by paying back his cruelty, deception and cunning, but they did not. It seems to me that humanity remained even in the thick of the wars at the top of the minds of the Gurus. The Gurus faced wars and persecution, judicial and non-judicial murders of their followers, and extreme brutality of the rulers only with their humanity, without succumbing to the temptation of answering demonic deeds with demonic deeds. Even when the enemy directly attacked their humanity with the aim of outraging it, the Gurus were never provoked. Their commitment to humanity amidst extreme provocation is beyond human endurance. No word can describe their fight except '*sublime*'. Perhaps nothing could be a better gift to posterity from a great man than the piercing of this world's ruthless established order with no other power than love. It seems the Gurus had grasped the message of God in *Prashnopanishad* better than any other that those do not fight for God who fight for God. Only those fight for God who fight to protect humanity and love.

Human body is an epitome of creation. It is creation in miniature. To regulate and discipline it in such a way that its negative urges get completely controlled requires courtship with death. The penance of Guru Angad is a typical illustration of courtship with death. The Gurus did not go to the forest for it. They lived in their homes and through *Atmayagya*—performed in their hearts—had learnt the noblest lessons from death that Nachiketa had learnt from Yama. The Gurus believed that one got from God what one dared from death.

Though the Gurus were adepts in Yoga, they did not refer to the *Chakras* and *Kundalini* like the Yogis. They did not want their disciples to get involved in the yogic art of unfolding the lotuses in the *Chakras*. According to yoga there are seven closed lotuses of energy in the human body that need to be awakened in order to live the full life of a free and fearless man. Yogis were using their spiritual and physical energies to forcibly open those lotuses. Many of them had lost sanity in doing this. Instead of applying force the Gurus applied courage and found courage more effective to flower these centres of energy. Each of the Gurus could have said, "I have shaken my hands with Death, my friends, and have not seen any glint of enmity in its eyes."

Nanak showed that the Guru too was an ordinary being, with the only difference that he lived by the divine emotion of humanity in his heart, not by the wily man that everyone was, who lived by the instincts of the Homo sapiens. He preferred to live as an ordinary farmer, working in the fields with his two sons, facing doubts and disobedience from them like any ordinary father, only searching keenly for the one who would come to succeed him.

The saints have often felt awe at the sight of the Divine. Awe is decidedly a big and final hurdle in the final union. When the human soul strengthens its little vein of courage to the highest extent, then only the leap beyond is possible. Not ordinary fear, in the last lap of the spiritual journey a highly subtle form of fear, that is awe, has to be faced, and courted and broken through. The process is the same that C.G. Jung calls the impregnating of the terrible mother in order to take a rebirth from her. Then comes *vismad* or a feeling of wonder joy and praise that unites with Him.

The people often came to the Gurus for solutions to the riddles that the enemy had created with slogans and rumours. The enemy soldiers came as tornado to present a visual of what they believed themselves to be. They believed they were the Fate sent by their God to the Indians, who, according to them, were born infidel. The Gurus allayed the doubts of their disciples by saying that those that believed they were the tornado of Fate for others feared their own Fate, and only those souls that feared their own Fate exhibited their infidelity by killing the innocent children of God. The true believers in God lived by the emotion of humanity in their heart, which is the living God on earth. They exhorted their disciples by reminding them that they had learnt how to get reborn from death, and the way to get reborn from Fate was not different. They said only those that protected human values and love were believers in God. Those that prayed to God in heaven and killed innocent people on earth and degraded love by raping women were the unfaithful.

It was difficult for the ordinary folks to brave the fears that surrounded their daily lives. The fear of the blade and the bullet, of bloodthirstiness and bigotry coming from the king was enough to break the courage of a subject people. Guru Nanak taught them how to get reborn of such fears, since on getting reborn of it fear turned into awe of God and gave courage for doing noble karma. They learnt from the tenth Guru not to fear doing good deeds (*shubha karman te kabahu na daro*). The subtlest fear was awe, and awe was an indication that God was somewhere very near them.

Such talks kindled hope in those people. Nanak would spend a lot of time with them. He awakened them from timidity to keenness to face the final encounter. Often the people would take courage only by looking at his serene face—bathing in the effulgence of intimations of immortality. Such light that they had seen nowhere would give them hope and trust in the Guru. Thus talking to the people and allaying their fears Nanak had opened the secret door to their simple hearts. Intimate relations with the peasantry and listening to their tales of woe and joy helped Nanak to develop the compassionate eyes that seemed to have "kept watch over man's mortality" for ages. They reminded the people of the eyes of the Divine that nobody had seen. Gradually they became sure that though they had not seen God, yet if God had a human body with eyes, his eyes must not be different than the kindly eyes of Nanak. The number of those who developed complete faith in him grew very fast. He would often ask them in a lighter vein something that was of great importance. Will you be able to stand upright before the Lord? When the Master will come in a sixteen-horse-driven chariot, a storm of reverence and blinding awe will be there. If you fear the enemy who comes only as a tornado how will you be able to face one who shines with more brilliance than a thousand suns at a time? Even the eyes of the angels cannot meet his eyes. Who else will help the Master to alight if you get dazed by awe?" It was in many such ways, and with anecdotes and tales of wisdom that Nanak regaled the people and kept their spirits alive. Their relationship was not of master and disciples only, but primarily of members of a single family. He did not teach everyone the abstract philosophy of monism. He talked about polytheism and of God whom they imagined in human form. As all rivers find their way to the sea, he showed their thoughts, beliefs emotions and dreams the way to *Waheguru*.

Sikhism is a religion that believes in building truth from whatever is available today in the human heart. It does not trust the spirit of negation and polemic. Nothing natural is forbidden. Even the hairs that grow naturally are not to be shorn off. Better remain closer to Nature, or even *Maya* for the object is to outwit *Maya*. Singular fortitude and courage are required for such a game. You have to play the game of wits, and the player against you is the terrible mother. It is this sportsman spirit that did not let malice, fear or personal grudge rise in the souls of the Gurus and their listeners.

Still, all the time, they were learning the lesson that they had to win for truth every little battle at home, in the market place and before the Qazi (judge). The Qazis were Islamic judges, originally empowered to decide the disputes between Muslims. But in India they were given rights to decide all legal disputes of the Hindus too.

The lesson that Krishna had taught in Gita had been most diversely and wrongly interpreted. "Thou hast not to desire the fruit!" This command of the Lord had come to mean almost a murder of the motive behind an action. The people had developed faith in action that led to nothing, like gossiping. They believed action for the sake of action to be devoid of fetters. The desire for victory had been inhibited. The Rajputs would fight only because it automatically brought honour and was a mark of bravery, without ever making victory their goal. Devout Hindus wanted simply to do good deeds, carefully removing the traces of pious motives. Such intellectual exercises were confusing their minds.

Separating motive from karma was consuming a lot of the energy of the people. Mathematical subtraction or division between karma and motive were the methods that people were applying. It had created chaos inside the individuals and in the society. People simply did not know what to do and what not to do. Nanak thought over the problem differently. His views can be summarized as follows: "We are preparing fresh bondages of sloth and inertia for our souls in this mood. Not to have some desire from one's action can be understood. However to desire that karma should bear no fruits is demented talk. Besides, not to desire the fruit for oneself does not mean that one should shake off all fruits from the tree of karma. To act vigorously we need some goal. We can get rid of desire or for the fruit of Karma only if we accept fulfilment of *Purusharthas* as the objective of karma. Fulfilment of *Purusharthas* is not a motive or desire, but a valid alternative to both. Its fulfilment does not bring fetters to the soul."

Another problem that Nanak faced was the dissolution of the archetype that was dividing the energy of the people between ends and means. This habit had taken deep roots in the souls of the people since it had been in practice for more than a millennium. The energy had been divided mathematically by subtraction, and, by extreme purists, by division. Nanak was against uniting the two energies of the human mind by the methods of multiplication or addition. He found a natural method of unifying any number of the energies of the mind in *Viniyoga* that Markandeya Rishi had utilized in his book '*Durga Saptashati*'. His views in this regard can be summarized in the following words: "We should not unite the means and the ends mathematically, by addition or multiplication, since mathematical methods apply to matter, not to the integration of mental energies. Mathematics turns counterproductive when it comes to the integration of the human personality. Ends and means can be united for the good of humanity through *Viniyoga*, i.e., the power born of sacrifice. The spiritual sacrifice by the soul of itself to the end and the means, and the invocation of a similar mutual self-sacrifice between the end and the means have the power to merge the opposites in the common root. This is the gist of '*Viniyoga*'. It will root out the archetypal error—of applying mathematics to our mental energies—that has rooted itself in our minds. He that discovers the common root of ends and means through *Viniyoga* does not have to fear the bondage of motives."

It was a simple philosophy that very much agreed with common sense, and no wonder that throngs of people from all the four castes and the Muslim community fell at the feet of Guru Nanak to find the road that granted worldly glory and bliss. Markandeya Rishi had practiced this higher form of yoga called *Viniyoga*. Guru Gobind Singh translated Markandeya Rishi's book of worship, "*Durga Saptashati*" and the practice of *Viniyoga* became popular among the disciples of the Gurus. It is the secret of the popularity of '*Durga Saptashati*' among the Sikhs.

Like the *Tirthankaras* the Gurus said: "Control your soul and you have controlled everything." Do not bother about your desires, thoughts or motives. The source of them all is the soul. Sacrifice it to the Lord. It has become lazy by habit, like a python. It just wants rest and therefore adjusts with every situation. Do not let it sleep. Do not let it compromise. It has to awaken and it has to keep awake every hour and every minute. Sleep is for the body and the mind, not for the soul. Unless the soul has surrendered its pride, its beauty cannot awaken, which is the same as the Lord. Unless it has tasted the sweetness of God, it cannot realize how sweet morality is. Mere joy is blind. It gets lost in its own follies and the soul keeps wandering from one life to another. But once it has experienced the flicker of love by sacrificing itself to God, it gets into direct communion with the Lord and then all that it does or desires, no matter how petty or ordinary it is, becomes an offering to God. In His eternal fire, everything gets burnt, renewed and transformed. Even a bloody battle transforms into a sacred thing. It is self-sacrifice of the soul to God that unites the fraction with the whole, and yet retains the individuality of the fraction. Such ideas were needed to practice the subtle philosophic heritage of India, Nanak provided them.

It is important to note that the Gurus have nowhere given any extreme importance to *Satyam, Shivam, Sundaram*. Nonetheless this trio has been considered the finest flower of all philosophy.

Instead of *Satya* the emphasis of the Gurus has been on *Sat. Sat* means the existent, the Real. The popular way for Sikhs to greet each other is *Sat-Sri-Akaal* (the God beyond time is Real.) There lies underneath a deep psychological meaning in this choice of the Gurus. It would seem that the main cause of the downfall of the Hindus, as that of the Greeks, was their emphasis on *Satyam Shivam Sundaram*. They considered this trinity to be the most secular face of God. But a closer examination would show that God is present in the human soul in a more elementary form than this trinity; and this trinity, derives its sanctity from that elementary form i.e., *Sat* or God in us. God lives in us as *Sat,* as the Being. The ontological reality is here and now. It exists. We feel it as Love. Truth is what this essence i.e. Love speaks through us. Beauty is the shine it imparts to our face and body. Good is its self-expression in action without compromising with evil. Truth, Good and Beauty are *Asat* when placed against this elementary form *(Sat),* which is God or Love. Whatever is *Asat* or non-existent can be manipulated into other forms. Truth is *Asat* in the sense that it only expresses God, who alone truly and ultimately exists. Truth is what God speaks or does. The Gurus were aware of the danger of extreme secularism. Secularism transcends only a narrow religion. Extreme secularism is madly ambitious. It aspires to transcend even God. It feels shy of the company of God. Therefore, it is the same as Void (*Ashnaya,* Nemesis). Truth, beauty and good without their nucleus, i.e., God, take to extreme secularism, i.e., the extreme thirst that is deluge, self-liquidation, not self-realization. Love of truth, as practised by extreme secularism, can lead to void, but love of God cannot.

Whatever man has expressed belongs to the world of sounds, words and forms. Expression is projected into the world of *Asat,* i.e., the unreal. *Sat* is inside the soul. It cannot be identified with any of its expressions. Truth is an expression of *Sat* in words or some other form. We have to practice truth. We do not have to love truth. Love is only for God. We have to love only God, not truth.

Good men and truthful men have always been exploited by worldly beings. They were being exploited in the times of the Gurus too. The Gurus considered it also a sin against God to let truth, good and beauty be exploited and molested. When these three expressions of God become proud and try to replace God they become prone to exploitation.

Truth has a tendency to be exploited. Beauty and Good also have similar tendencies. Very often, beauty prefers to fall to the snares of fools, ignoring the true lover. A good ruler prefers to be exploited by courtiers and flatterers very often. One who speaks truth secretly likes to be hunted and persecuted. There have been human complications built down the centuries around this trinity. Truth, beauty and good, devoid of their nucleus i.e., God, can become instruments of *Asat*. *Sat* is God (*Waheguru*), and *Asat* is evil, i.e., infinite thirst (*Ashnaya*), which has no soul. It is mere thirst without the thirsty. Thirst without the thirsty can never be satiated. Therefore it can never bring satiation and joy, because it is only after the fulfilment of thirst that joy and peace can be experienced. Without the thirsty, i.e. the soul, thirst in man turns into the thirsty void.

The central core of every great movement has been that it had restored that facet of truth that was most relevant to its times. We cannot evaluate properly the sacrifice of the Gurus and the truth they preached out of the context of their times and its special turbulence that they had to face. I do not find any example in world history after the Mahabharata except the Sikh Movement when a militant uprising was totally devoted to love and human values, and its leaders had no ambition to glorify their own personalities, and had no selfish ends to pursue. It was totally devoid of wanton killings of citizens in the name of religion. It was self-restrained, and confined to defend the freedom of the citizen to live by his faith. To salute such leaders is to salute the free soul that is the essence of every man. We cannot honour them more than their deeds that have sanctified their names before God. But certainly we can purify our souls with the memory of the Gurus' selfless love and pursuit of human values entirely for the sake of humanity. The two Mothers, manifest Nature and unmanifest Nature, stand to bear witness before *Nirankar* the Absolute that surely they were born of both.

Truth, Beauty and Good are mere forms. God gives them meaning, direction and fulfilment, if the truthful, beautiful or good person recognizes God as his nucleus. Devoid of God, even truth, beauty and good mislead. The Gurus never gave up this stand.

If we emphasise any expression that is very near the Real and call it Real, we do not do it any favour, rather we consign it to doom. All the great pieces of art, literature and philosophy that were created by great men, and that looked very near the Real, got ultimately confused with the creations of God, since God's creations also appear in our world in which great men's creations appear. Truth, Beauty and Good created by God in our world are all transitory. They appear in human form or as some spectacle of cloud, sea, or mountains or some other thing due to the play of light and shade in the morning, evening or night. All the glorious creations of God, all the beautiful, truthful and good people that God creates die after a few years. Nothing lasts of the magnificent things that God creates. All wither away after some time. Compared to these creations of God, the creations of our greatest men are mere illusions. They are imitations of God's fleeting creations, intended to bring some good to the suffering mankind, some truth to man's degenerated and falsified values, or some beauty to his wealth-oriented and vulgarised ways of living. Yet they had to suffer in many ways. If nobody persecuted some such great man, he had no reason to consider himself lucky, for society offered him other kinds of sufferings that were equally painful. If his hide was not removed from his living body, as in the case of Mansoor, he was spared for other kinds of torture. Like Marx or Dickens, he had to suffer real or imaginary pangs of poverty, or deprivation of some other kind, or sheer lack of fulfilment all his life. If he escaped this, he had to suffer emotional agonies like Nietzsche, Byron, Tolstoy, Dostoevsky, Hemmingway, Stephen Zwig and Mayakovsky, to quote a few from an endless list.

One thing is common to all of the creations of great men— their form was so pure that it created the illusion of Reality. Beauty, Truth and Good are the forms. The more beautiful, true or good our actions are, the more is the danger of our mistaking them for Reality. Beauty, Truth and Good cannot be exploited or persecuted as long as they realize themselves to be mere forms. The world has a tendency to elevate them. It worships them. It gives them a treatment that befits only the Real. Under the pressure of public estimation, even the most careful person falls to the error of considering his true, beautiful or good work to be at least as valuable as its original that God had created. It is a very common delusion to which great artists, thinkers, scientists and literary men fall prey.

It is a lie of a very high level that helps fate to mark their creators to stamp. The price they have to pay is too great. They err unknowingly and still they have to pay heavily. Ignorance of the subtle art called life is no excuse. Ignorance of the Divine laws is all the more no excuse. God does not punish them. It is their subtle ignorance that punishes them. They lived mystified why they were being punished. Nothing helped them to discover the little error that they had committed and that had made them victims of doom.

Truth, Beauty and Good created by our greatest men look almost the same as the Real. Once they are identified with the Real, the play of *Maya* begins. As long as the artist sees the distinction, he also sees his creative power as God's especial gift, or as Nature entering his personality and imitating God. It is because his ignorance is dormant, not active. To abide by the true road means not to let our ignorance play with us. Ignorance lives in some measure with the wisest man too all his life, since his soul is imperfect. When the soul unites with *Waheguru*, only then ignorance completely disappears. The Sikh faith extends hope to man's imperfect soul. Only if the soul lives by its imperfect light, does not indulge in the fanciful play of ignorance, *Maya* gets no opportunity to trap it. The ordinary man is therefore asked by the Gurus to walk on the straight road. If he does so, one day he is sure to get completely liberated. As man grows old he has to be more careful not to fall prey to delusions and lies. The trials on this road are too many. *Maya* at work in some people after overpowering their minds excites them to provoke and hurt others so that it might spread its kingdom inside the hurt people too.

Good, beautiful and truthful people are often identified with God by deluded followers out of admiration, or by cunning people out of ulterior motives, while they are only creations of God. Identification of great creative people with God gives *haumey* entry in their personalities. It is in this way that *Kudarat* (Nature) gets converted into *Maya*. The moment *haumey* fills them their corruption or exploitation begins. Instead of remaining *Kudarati* (natural) they become showy or artificial creations of *Maya*. At the same time a vain urge grows in them to prove that they are Real and they exist. Instead of remaining themselves, they try to become proof of the myth that they are Real. When a good, beautiful or truthful person's emphasis is on God as the Real her/his good, beauty or truth appears to her/him as the proof of God's existence. When her/his good, beauty, truth start proving her/his unique existence they mislead and bring them to grief. Her/his virtues become instruments of darkness. Such deluded people become self-conscious, which cuts them off from God. God's light appears in man's truth, good and beauty as long as he is conscious only of God. If women/men become conscious of their greatness also along with God's their link with God snaps.

Haumey is self-consciousness. All ignorance begins here. Self-consciousness or *haumey* coils round the soul and imprisons its light. Sikh discipline requires a correction or rationalisation of self-consciousness. When the self realizes itself to be merely a form of God, self-consciousness ceases to be a binding force. It no more confounds or hides light. It starts serving the Lord. *Haumey* or self-consciousness, so rationalised, is entirely different from the blind *haumey*. Instead of obstructing the light, it works as its vehicle. The Sikh discipline does not envisage the total disappearance of self-consciousness. It does not vanish, but it can be tuned to truth, which practically amounts to its dissolution.

From the practical or earthly standpoint, reality is five-fold— *Waheguru*, Soul, *Gurbani, Bhakti (*love) and *Kudarat.* These realities too cease to be real at the highest level where *Waheguru* is the only Reality. This five-fold reality remains Real only so far it realizes itself to be mere five forms of God i.e. *Waheguru* Thus a discipline has been prescribed for the highest realities too that are conceivable by man's soul.

Individuality is retained in Sikhism in a unique way. The soul has not to claim it as a right. A total transformation of the mood is a must. It has to learn to leave it to the will of God whether he retains its individuality or not. The discipline prescribed for the soul is not to treat itself as Real before God. It has not to fear total dissolution in God. The Wonderful God has a unique way of preserving the individuality of the souls. By His own will, He retains their individuality. Except such deserving souls whose individuality he retains, all others get dissolved in Him.

There are degrees of truth, beauty and goodness, according to F.H. Bradley. He writes in his book *"Appearance and Reality"* that, judged from the standpoint of the Absolute (God), the highest truth known to man on earth ceases to be truth, the highest beauty conceived by him ceases to be beauty and the highest good that he does ceases to be good. The Sikh denial of giving the same importance to truth, beauty and good that they give to *Waheguru* can be understood better in the light of this theory of Bradley. It was no idle dream of Bradley either. Human experience shows that truth, beauty and good have a tendency to get corrupted at the highest stage because of their inherent urge to claim the status of God. They are nothing more than chimera if man does not overcome this inherent urge. Sikhism tries to correct this error of truth by asking it to consider itself nothing more than a form or shadow of *Waheguru*. More important than truth, according to Nanak, 'is a true life'; and true life means a life that realizes God alone to be Real.

Because of their inherent imperfection, truth, beauty and good have a tendency to replace God and become despotic. They are born of human experience and as such have the seed of self-destruction within them. All our experiences of the Divine have to be treated as distinct from the Divine and as mere forms of the Divine, otherwise they turn destructive.

If we take truth, beauty and good to be identical with God, they cease to serve their purpose and become lies. Instead of remaining *Kudarat* they become *Maya*. Instead of remaining what God expected of them, they become what human ignorance makes of them. They get filled with *haumey* and *Avidya* and lead to further bondages. To stretch them beyond them is to make them enemies of their own limited being.

Another point is also to be kept in mind. The Wonderful God (*Waheguru*) is all-inclusive and excludes nothing. What we call ugly and bad also have place in Him. The whole about Him cannot be expressed. If we insist on expressing Him wholly and truthfully, we find that we have reduced God to chaos, full of contradictions. As a result, instead of increasing faith, we shall create many more doubts. All known truth is therefore partly true. Those who have tried to express all the shades of God have misled mankind. "Truth, like the dancing queen Salome,' says Nietzsche, 'should never drop its seventh veil, for if it does, it immediately demands the head of the Messiah."

According to Sikh philosophy, truth cannot express the Real, for the Real is *Waheguru* who reconciles all contradictions whereas truth has its own limitations. Whenever truth tries to express the Real fully, it gets confused and shows Him as a bundle of contradictions. The character of a saint whose soul has gone nearer *Waheguru* and has become more like Him also cannot be fully described or understood in terms of truth.

Whenever truth tries to be comprehensive, it creates doubts. The reality about the life of the greatest known man if described truthfully would arouse suspicion instead of faith. It is because truth is an intellectual and imperfect form of God. It should not be used beyond consistency. If we take it beyond reason or consistency, it becomes an instrument of *Maya* or ignorance. No man will appreciate a saint if he tells him truly the whole of his character or being. He will see him as a bundle of contradictions. But if he experiences all his imperfections through love for him, he will understand him. Sikhism does not advise man to stretch truth up to reality. We have to know where to stop the search of truth and kindle the lamp of love. The true seekers are lovers. Truth is known only to the lover, only because he knows its limitation. He knows truth's limitations because he loves the Real, and because of his love he is nearer the Real.

History shows that whenever truth tried to express the whole of Reality, it aroused, on the one hand, suspicions and, on the other hand, a martyr's zeal in the man who possesses that truth. The world rejects him when he is alive, and then honours him posthumously. According to the Sikh Gurus, all such persons are forms of *Maya* that appear to waste and dissipate the power of truth. A true seeker has to guard against such exploitation of truth.

He does not identify truth with God. He treats it as a valuable form capable of removing quite a few veils from *Waheguru* but not all the veils, and he certainly does not go beyond that.

Beauty likewise reveals only a little of *Waheguru*. It should not be equated with Him, for then it becomes a servant of *Maya*. God includes ugliness, which beauty can never comprehend. Beauty identified with God becomes arrogant. It forgets *Waheguru* and stops bowing down to Him. It is only love that knows God to be more than beauty. He knows him to be ugly too and still bows to Him. He does not hate ugliness. He knows that ugliness reaches Him and gets dissolved in His beauty, and thus only enhances His beauty, and does not retain its separate identity.

Beauty, truth and good are fractions of God that are accessible to human experience. A true Sikh has to value them as the highest forms of God known to man. He has only to avoid the Greek error of identifying them with God. Identification with God changes these useful and elevating forms of God into instruments of ignorance and *haumey*. This is the discipline of consciousness, according to Sikhism. Unless we discipline consciousness it will take us to the self-consciousness that is *haumey*, instead of the self-consciousness that is self-realization. All consciousness should be trained in such a way that it leads to self-realization and not to self-consciousness that is *haumey*. This, in a nutshell, is the theme of spiritual discipline according to the Gurus. It is not enough to be conscious. Consciousness has to follow the laws of *Kudarat*. It has to evolve according to the laws of *Kudarat* (Nature); otherwise it locks the heart in the coil of the serpent called self-consciousness. Consciousness flowers only when it moves toward the consciousness of *Waheguru*. This serpent of self-consciousness which is pride that binds the heart in its coils was called *Vritrasur* by the Vedic seers.

Will

Will is another subject that is a vital part of Sikh discipline.
What He wills happens
What man wills goes with tides
Like torn petals that nothing binds

Nanak

Nanak prays:

> "I seek nothing for me
> Except one thing that I need
> The contentment that has the power
> To make thy will sweet."

The Sikhs believe that the world is the manifestation of God's will, and it is surrender to His will alone that frees man of its coils, and helps him swim across the tossing waves of *Maya*. God is playful. Two concepts of God, common between the Sikh Gurus and the Vedic rishis, are:

> (1) God is wonderful
> (2) God is playful

The Rig Veda says:
Sa kridati (My Lord plays).

When He wills creation, *Kudarat* springs from him and the colourful play of life begins. One of the beguiling items of this play is the individual will. The Divine will has projected itself in several individual wills, at war with each other. Man gets lost in a mishmash of wills. He wills something. His near and dear ones will something else. His enemies will still some other thing. A confusing and conflicting life is the result. Will contradicted produces anger, hatred and violence. Lust, greed, and gambling are off shoots of will. Cruelty, madness, and pride are the products of a victorious will. Thus, whatever befalls a man in pursuing his will is bondage or a snare. The wise get out of this spider's web by trying to know the will of God. They surrender all their actions to Him. Then the Divine Will becomes a raft for the wise to take them out of the play of wills.

> "I seek no heaven
> Hell frightens me not.
> Thy will is my dwelling
> All else is nought."
>
> *Kabir*

Will has been recognised since ancient times to be the cause of man's bondage. The ancient religions therefore taught the destruction of desires, motives and all other forms of will. Sikhism, the youngest religion, spoke differently. It is not enough, the Gurus said, to seek a course of individual deliverance when millions are tossing on the waves. It is escapism to seek individual salvation when those who love us suffer from delusion. We must strive for their salvation; if possible, for the salvation of the entire mankind. Millions of fish have been caught in the net of will. To cut the threads only for myself with the sharp sword of love is to leave other suffering souls to their misery. A brave hero has to choose, even as Yudhisthira chose, to suffer in hell with those who loved him and those who he loved, instead of seeking a lonely heaven for himself. For this the Gurus had discovered a way, not of escape from the will, but of using the net of will itself to fish out Nirvana.

They had realized that in the starry light of the psychological world, a change in the weaving pattern turns the net itself into a means of freedom. Instead of cutting down the net, let us search the spider from whose mouth this net has sprung. It is none other than *haumey*. This mystical spider is the child of human ignorance, a creation of lust and selfishness. It has woven a net to catch and destroy humanity. Replace this spider with Love. Enshrine Love in its place. Replace *haumey* by meditating on His Name. Realize Him as Love in your heart. Let your soul sacrifice itself to *Waheguru*, and request him to change *haumey* into love. Thus a new pattern of psychological forces and the wills of relatives, friends and enemies unfolds in the heart. This new pattern, born of Love, is the will of God. Let the forces in the world operate according to God's will. The world will be then a projection of *Kudarat*, not of *Maya*. When Nature reigns, human souls do not get subjected to inhuman sufferings and forced subjugation to evil. The Lord has not created such sufferings for those who abide by Him. He is merciful. The pains that He gives are meant only to kindle the fire of love in us. He gives pain only to bring back his lost children to the right road. All other sufferings issue from the spider *haumey*, the son of *Maya*. On the one hand, it destroys faith in God by giving inhuman tortures to man. On the other hand, it wastes the human soul in meaningless sorrows without letting it experience the sorrow of love that is always illumined by joy. The sorrow of love is never pure sorrow or sorrow for sorrow's sake. Our life gets wasted in the worries of bread-earning and political safety. The real aim of life does not begin and in the meantime death comes. To create a safe world for the ordinary man where the wicked will does not rule was the task the Gurus took upon them. To fulfil this objective, a great transformation took place within Sikhism. Earlier it believed in what Saint Farid said, "If anyone strikes you with his fist do not strike back". This hymn forms a part of *Guru Granth Sahib* to this day, for nothing has been removed or added to it. By the time Guru Gobind Singh appeared on the scene, the Sikh approach had changed. The times had changed, and experience had taught more secrets of the working of the will of the wicked people. Sikhism calls those people wicked who seek their fortunes by leaping the bounds of human values. Therefore there was no point in sticking to the old approach. The Tenth Guru translated *Durga Sapta Sati* from *Markandeya Purana*. He gave a new form to the worship of the goddess in "*Bhagauti ki war*" and "*Chandi Charitar*". Bhagauti did not mean only the ancient goddess of that name to him. It meant the sword too. The Guru retained the spirit of *Shakti-puja*. Interestingly, *Shakti-puja* was the religion of Shankaracharya, too, at the time of his birth. It suited the times of Guru Gobind Singh. Bhagauti represented the Will of God. Since ancient days, *Shakti* has been appearing as the practical Divine Power that snatches power from the wicked and aims at restoring the order of the world in accordance with the will of God.

One of the ways the Gurus had adopted to ensure the rule of God's will in the world was to expose the wickedness of the dominating worldly will. The worldly will had concealed itself under a noble and acceptable visage. They had to expose it so that the common folks stopped believing it. For this, two of the ten Sikh Gurus had to die at the hands of the tyrant. Their persecution, a disturbing fact of history, is a classical example of the travesty of justice in Mogul India. Not only the known bigots, even some of those who have earned the name of tolerant and enlightened monarchs, when seen in the rays of truth are revealed writhing and sizzling occasionally with bigotry. Nanak made no pretence or concealment of this fact. He wanted the people to wake up from the illusion that the rulers were practicing religious tolerance. His soul cried in anguish:

> "Way is there none
> Darkness surrounding
> Kings with a butcher's passion
> The bird of justice O Father
> Where hath it fled?
>
> Weep I in despair
> The moon of truth my eyes see not
> O the Times, Such times."

The dominating mood of the religious world of the foreign rulers was madness in those days. A true Guru had to tear down all beautiful veils from this vile face of religion so that painted beauty did not conceal its inherent ugliness. Nanak knew that this would arouse the will of the people for truth and justice. The people would know the real motives behind the religious and political powers that were playing with their lives. This would spontaneously release forces from the people's will that would fight such powers. He had no need to be secular. Religion was not a discipline he had to subject himself to. Like nature's urge to bloom, like the silent, gentle force that opens the bud from within to spread its shroud into a loveliness of many petals, dressed in green, Divine love had already flowered the bud of his individual self. He was ripe for truth. By accounting the truth of contemporary life he would not have spread religious hatred. He spoke of it alike to Hindus and Muslims. His aim was not to fire their baser passions, but to awaken the sleeping Divine love in their hearts, for, if awakened, it would recognise neither Hindus nor Muslims. In awakening it the people would become it. Their passions, thoughts, in fact, all their faculties would get recharged with a different meaning and motive.

As I have said earlier, one unique fact about Sikhism is that it does not teach suppression of baser passions. Only the light that illumines them has to be changed. When Raja Hari Chand discharged an arrow that pierced the buckle of his waist-belt, it kindled the anger of Guru Gobind Singh, as described by himself, to a big blaze. However, he did not use this anger for a base purpose, i.e., simply to retaliate, as in any ordinary combat between two enemies. Uppermost in his mind, even at that moment of fierce anger, was the passion to unite humanity and spread the light of love.

Lal Chand was a Khatri who knew no arts of battle. Seeing his enthusiasm, Guru Gobind Singh gave him a sword and shield and asked him to run into the warring pathans. Bhikan Khan cut a joke. He said "Here comes an Arora, just fresh after weighing flour and salt. Look the Guru has given him a sword!" Upon this Mir Khan pounced on him but Lal Chand made two of what was one Mir Khan. "I shall kill hawks with sparrows"—was the slogan of the Guru. This at once explodes the invaders' myth of martial races. "One in whom the love of God has awakened" said Guru Gobind Singh, "count him worth soldiers one hundred twenty five thousand."

Ancient India knew no such myth as that of the martial races. The Gurus exploded this myth imposed on the people of India by invading hordes of Arabs, Turks and Moguls. It had weakened the people of India. It had made a small section of them unduly vain of the accident of their birth. At the same time nearly ninety percent of them gradually forgot that it was their duty too that India remained free. It had already made it easy for the warlords of Arabia, Turkey and Iran to invade, kill all citizens of rich cities and loot India. There were certain tribes of these countries that lived by the profession of organizing and raiding soft targets. They were like the dacoits of Chambal Valley in India — people who did not like to work hard but wanted to live luxuriously, people whose moral consciousness was not evolved to the level of the civilized world, and people who by temperament were volatile and vain. Those people, like experienced raiders, would discount a large section of the Indian people who avoided violence, while planning raids on India. They called those people who would offer resistance Martial Races, since they were discriminated in their countries on grounds of races. In India people were discriminated on grounds of castes (originally professions), not on grounds of races, while the regions around India divided people on grounds of races. Even to this day the Indian people do not have the habit of dividing people on grounds of races. The idea of Martial Races became fashionable when the warlords on becoming rulers of India liked to employ those people that had offered resistance to them. They started getting a separate racial identity. It somehow fed their pride in those days since barbarian rulers called killing non-fighters bravery.

The Gurus saw through this error that had entered the consciousness of the Indian people and was harming them. They saw that the foreign occupiers had reduced the number of indigenous fighters to lesser then one tenth. The Gurus, therefore, exploded the myth of the Martial Races. They drew men from the scheduled castes and other sections that had not been classified as Martial Races by the warlords, and taught them to be worthy sparrows, destined to explode the hawk of martial races. This was the restoration of human equality above artificial distinctions. They showed to the Indian people that racism was nonsense and a nuisance. They proved to them that any Indian belonging to any profession or caste could be a soldier to defend the motherland.

With Guru Gobind Singh a revolutionary change came in the eating habits of the Sikhs. The Sikh remained vegetarians during the leadership of nine Gurus. During the command of the tenth Guru many of them became non-vegetarians. Few know, however, the cause of this transformation. The cause was simple. Somehow the myth had spread among the soldiers of Guru Gobind Singh that the people of the tribe of Pathan ate one full goat each and therefore had great strength. The Guru realized that his Sikhs, who had assembled from several non-warring castes, were developing a complex. Therefore he allowed them to eat meat.

The Rishis, *Tirthankaras* and the Buddha had realized non-violence of a very subtle order that was born of compassion and the philosophy of karma and rebirth. Their brotherhood extended to the animals too. The religious consciousness of the people of India had grown along the line that a man could be reborn as an animal in his next birth if he indulged in karma born of ignorance, and an animal could be reborn as a human for a reverse reason. They did not deny the possibility of the sprouting of some knowledge in the soul of an animal. Some animals like elephants and some fish like dolphins have been found by scientists to be having fairly evolved brains that could develop intelligence. However, the Indian philosophy holds that knowledge is a function of the soul, and the brain is only an instrument of it. It believes that evil karma fetters the ability of the soul to know. The evil karma fetters dissolve due to learning and acquiring knowledge. Even good and beautiful karma have the ability to dissolve the fetters that check the soul from expressing its latent light. The Indian philosophy also believes that every karma-fetter is temporary and dissolves automatically after its time span. The time span of certain karmic fetters may end suddenly while that soul is still in animal incarnation. In that case the animal's soul may experience the sprouting of knowledge in it. Knowledge grows as a direct result of the dissolution of the fetters of the soul. The Indian thought does not accept that the animals, humans, the demons and the gods have different souls. It believes that all living beings, from the ant to gods, share the same soul. A mean ant can get reborn as a human or a god due to the dissolution of the fetters of its karma.

Sikhism also believes in this philosophy of karma, rebirth and the same souls transmigrating to the animal, human and other species. This philosophy is common to all Indian religions. The objection to meat eating among the Indians is, therefore, not born of inhibitions. It is born of compassion and knowledge. They are profoundly aware that they share the same life cycle. An animal that one is about to eat could have been his brother, son or some dear one in some past birth. It invokes genuine emotions of fellowship in them with animals. It is another matter that due to economic and other reasons people often ignore their compassion. Yet what Walt Whitman said out of a unique self-realization can echo as its own emotions and thoughts in any Indian heart. It is what the soul of the Indian knows. Due to living under the rule of foreign people who considered it unmanly to share such compassion for animals, some Indians had started blaming vegetarianism as the cause of their physical weakness. They did not check it with the Jat people of India who were strict vegetarians and yet proved to be more than equal to the people who raided India. Many other Indians converted to other religions that religiously practised meat eating to keep their identity distinct, lacked the courage to live by their inherent compassion for animals.

Guru Gobind Singh, even after permitting meat eating, never advocated wanton killing of animals as a way of strengthening the human body and hardening the heart. His message can be best understood from the practice prevalent among Sikhs in modern times. Many of them are vegetarians, while many others are champions of wild life protection.

It could be said, therefore, that the Sikh violence was in spirit a practical form of non-violence. It would be erroneous to say that violence has any attraction for a true Sikh. The latter Gurus were forced to take to violence by the insensitivity of the Moguls to their need of freedom to follow their religion and their need to be treated as citizens equal to the Muslims.

"A life devoid of love is a flower blooming in wilderness."

A people who sing thus cannot be fairly charged with any adherence to violence. The music that is sung in the Gurdwaras is tender, sweet and serene. They sing profound philosophic songs of the Gurus and other enlightened saints and poets. They sing above all of love. Love is the core and the pillar of their faith. The Sikh is profoundly non-violent because love is the highest spiritual goal of his life, and love is the finest form of non-violence.

The Sikh discipline is to be seen as nothing but a practical way of saving humanity at a time when a whirlwind of hatred, carnage and dehumanisation had arrested the natural flow of Indian life. Proselytising fury with the backing of the Government had tossed the minds of certain preachers off balance. They did not consider people belonging to Indian religions as people who deserved human rights. They thought human rights were not born with human beings. They rather thought that it was their right to give human rights to the indigenous people or not. Besides they considered it an insult to their religion if the Indian religions were given equal status. Even the learned among them quoted their scriptures and claimed that their religion did not permit them to allow others to practice their respective religions. There were still others that were fired by the mission of unifying all the people of India by converting them. Yet there were many Muslims in medieval India who practised, like the Indians, the highest ideals of love, non-violence and chivalry with non-violence. They have become part of the blowing winds of India, her peculiar greenery and the songs of love and self-bestowing virtues. Amir Khusro, Raskhan, Rahim, Jayasi, Nazir, Mir and Ghalib are only a few of them.

The Gurus found it impossible to live honourably as the subject of rulers with irrational attitude. They were born in a country where reason, equality and humanism had been held as the ideals of worldly people too since the time when the Western nations that are the modern champions of reason did not know reason enough to tell what made an action or a man higher than another. Life was not peaceful with the Gurus as it was with the Vedic forefathers who had subdued the enemies and could talk of the perfect conduct. They had a philosophy that did not approve retirement to forest if the ruler was harsh so that Nirvana could be attained. They did not like the path of the recluses both Vedic and Shraman (the Jains and the Buddhists). They wanted to live a family life and yet a life that was not in contradiction with the ultimate goal of life. They believed that the ultimate goal of Nirvana could be attained by doing one's duties disinterestedly to the nation, family and the society. They believed sincerely that their Motherland needed them. They were not prepared to leave her alone to herself. Besides they had judged fairly from the prevalent atmosphere that if some of the Indians did not combat, the invaders were bent upon eradicating their culture, philosophy and lifestyle. Their works of art were being destroyed and their places of worship were being desecrated. Sikhism was a religion that had taken a revolutionary stand in searching salvation within society and its conditioning forces. It aimed at perfection but not in isolation. They played the game of eternity on the chessboard of the social, political and historical forces with the invaders.

The Sikh discipline is simple in appearance but deep in essence. By controlling will, by subduing wild passions with the force of true love and by adopting the *Sahaj* road of a sincere householder, rather than the thorny path of a recluse, it aimed at entering the portals of eternity. No religious leader had taken the job so exclusively and seriously as the Sikh Gurus of showing the householders how they could cultivate and trade better, bring up their children as good citizens of the state, and how they could claim certain basic rights, and how, in spite of so much worldly involvement, they could enter the portals of Nirvana earlier than the average recluse. No religion had extended so much hope to the lay householder.

Extreme tolerance had split the senses and the intellect of the Hindus into two. Half of their sensuous and intellectual energies were spent on prejudices against the occupiers while the remaining half was wasted on contemplating their sorrows as slaves. The Gurus took upon them the task of bridging the split of their energies, by exercising the ancient disciplines of Viniyoga and Atmayagya.

Revolt against Their Times

*T*he Gurus were in total revolt against their times. The social order as well as the spiritual discipline had lost the track of the practical truth. The visionaries of India had taught two types of truth – *parmarthik* (absolute) and *vyavaharik* (practical). Vyas and Valmiki of the Vedic lineage, Nagarjuna and Kundakundacharya of the Buddhist and Jain lineage had taught people the distinction between the two paths, the recluse's and the householder's, that led to the same summit. The foreign occupiers had blurred this distinction by praising only the other worldly (*parmarthik*) path of the religions of India. They had found doing so strategically useful to them for it made the Indians disinterested in what they did to India and the Indians. Though the occupiers said that they were forbidden to praise any other religion for any reason, self-interest compelled them to this deviation. It alerted the Sikh Gurus. They felt that the occupiers would have loved it if tired of the yoke of their draconian laws and bigotry they too had quietly retired to forests in the quest of Nirvana. Many medieval Indian saints and lovers were only too keen to oblige them. The Sikh Gurus had seen something sinister behind this royal expectation.

The people of India had withdrawn from social realities and politics. Their attitude is crystallized in a famous couplet of Tulsidas: 'Let there be any king, we lose nothing.' Their temples were being demolished and their faith was being laughed at. To match inhuman provocation inhuman tolerance was breeding in the Indians. They were leaving everything to the aggressor. Their libido was fast withdrawing. Indian life had taken to regression.

Whatever roads a regressed libido seeks had already appeared in the Indian life. The *tantriks* and *kapaliks* had developed fearsome rituals out of a regressed libido.

The grand philosophies of India had been swallowed by the black magic of the invaders, who needed nothing more than a religion that had assured them that heaven was theirs for the sheer fact that they had converted to it. They had extinguished rather than quenched their philosophic thirst, since it had been found disappointing. Philosophy had told them they might be going to hell for the inhuman enthusiasm they had shown under the scheme 'proselytise and get a palace reserved in heaven.' It is a Divine reminder of his error that when the ruler stretches too far on the road of bigotry, in his own family certain fine flowers of the opposite kind get born. The Mogul family was no exception to it. They produced one of the finest examples of religious tolerance, cultural excellence and philosophic abilities in prince Dara Shikoh. He translated the Upanishads in Persian. A copy of the German translation of his Persian book reached Schopenhauer, and thus the journey of Indian thought in the Western hemisphere began.

The joys of courageous living with facts had withered altogether. The spirit of Chandragupt, Chanakya and Kharvel that had driven the Greek invaders out had completely died. The fire of Yashodharman that had burnt the fury of Mihirakul, and Toraman, the Huns – at a time when the Huns had nearly liquidated the mighty Roman and the Persian Empires – had long been extinguished. Instead of fighting against injustice, it was now allowing it to prevail.

This gave rise to several perversions in the life force of the Indians. Cold hatred, passivity, revengeful indifference, fear, constant brooding, and mystical living had developed into the archetypal character of the people.

The Gurus took upon themselves the task of freeing the people of these archetypes. The psyche of the Indian people had become full of treacherous maelstroms. They were suffering from a number of spiritual diseases because of the unfortunate decision to regress.

The Gurus, therefore, made it their first objective to expose the hidden fear and falsehood under the time-honoured practices. Guru Nanak made unsparing and direct attacks on the *Siddhas* who thought that theirs was a noble road leading to God. On the contrary, he said, it was fear with a misleading mask. He condemned their grand and awesome ritualism outright as hypocrisy. He said that it was nothing but the ardour of lost souls. The Divine lives in love and not in the manners of worship or mystical practices. To the too tolerant Indians they said that what they considered to be the virtue of tolerance was in fact the sin of skirting the truth. Tolerance stretched beyond human limits turns man into a slavish monster. (Shakespeare in Caliban, in The Tempest, has portrayed the complex personality of a slavish-monster). Non-violence was not withdrawal from action against violence. They said true non-violence was aggressive self-sacrifice. The truly non-violent would rather die for the honour of his Motherland than waste his life in cold hatred of the tyrant. They taught a new way of dying to the Indians: 'if the tyrant is too powerful we must still not submit, and if we have to die, let us die without hatred or fear. The real enemies are hatred, fear, indifference and regression. Let us fight and die cheerfully. This will give us a spiritual rebirth in our new generations and in the very soul of the tyrant. His ego shall be torn to pieces, for this is the price he shall have to pay for killing true men. The tyrannical foreign ruler will lose heart and man will prevail over the monster.'

They said that the attitude of a people toward women was the true measure of their psychological freedom. Woman, who was once a companion in the spiritual journey, had come to be known as a positive hindrance and an immediate danger to spiritual life. The Gurus read something deeper in this changed attitude of their people. It was an outer symptom of cowardice. The degenerated attitude to women was a mockery of the spirit of India, her fine culture and philosophy.

The attitude of the Gurus toward woman is in total contrast to the attitude of medieval Indians. They completely revolted against the medieval view regarding women. They called it a view born of ignorance and perversion. They called for a healthier life force, for without it, the boldness that was needed to accept truth was impossible to attain. They said, "Truth is a child of love and courage."

In order to understand the revolt of the Gurus against their age, their attitude toward woman deserves a deeper study. It will help us in understanding their relationship with their times correctly. I would also like to discuss the approach of Nanak and other Gurus to history. In writing history they took up an entirely original road. It had never been there in the Indian heritage. It was not there in their times though it was very popular with the foreign rulers of India who were colouring history with their fantasies. Since there were no Indian historians the Gurus realized that 'whatever the Moguls will get written in history about their glories and virtues and about the enslaved Indian people will be bombast of megalomania.' They knew that if they did not write the truth, whatever the Moguls would write would be called truth by future historians. They did not like that paid chroniclers should get a free hand to humiliate the Indian people with historical lies. Therefore while others confined to describe contemporary times in poetry, Guru Gobind Singh took to writing history in the Mogul style, which was an improvised version of Herodotus' style of writing history.

Approach to History

Among the last pieces of advice Guru Gobind Singh gave to his disciples was: 'Read the history of your Gurus from the time of Guru Nanak.'

The Gurus were ardent worshippers of God who is beyond time, and *Kudarat,* whom time affects not. Time and space are merely His plays. His *Maya* projects them like two beautiful carpets to arrange His several gifts of creation. The Vedic seers and Shankaracharya had also not given any power to time over God. Yet the Gurus diverted from the Indian tradition in a major way. Unlike the Hindu thinkers, they did not hold chronology in contempt. It appears that the Hindu mind had begun with a very noble plan of writing history in the form of *Purana.* The *Purana* culture of writing history interpreted every temporal event in the light whether it had been utilized to attain the ideal of the true human life or not. It looked at history as the struggle of a people to assert truth, beauty and good, as they understood it, through their actions. Truth was eternal and timeless, while life was temporal. Temporal life had to be made an expression of the eternal truth, moral values and aesthetic consciousness of the people. Some of the finest examples of writing history in the *Purana* style were the *Ramayana* and the *Mahabharata*. This discipline of writing history as *Purana* went on well until the self-acquisitive culture had come to India through the foreign invader-rulers.

The repeated defeats of the Indians were a great opportunity to the *Purana* writers to critically examine the causes of their failures frankly, and to suggest the way to make their values triumphant again. But the *Purana* writers showed extreme reluctance to account for their defeats. They did not realize that Mother India had been enslaved and the prime concern of the historian should be to find out how she could be freed. On the contrary they gave up writing history altogether. They had taken to the courtly habit of the historians of the invader-rulers to praise their princes ignoring the compulsions of truth. History had degenerated to elevating the kings of states that patronized the historian. They ignored that the first and foremost concern of the historian was to record the facts without colouring them. The result was that the best pieces of history during medieval days were Chandbardai's *Prithviraj Raso* and Kalhan's *Rajtarangini*, which do not come up to the current standard of objectivity.

Gradually history writing, due to the flattering style of the paid chroniclers, had come to be derided as a means of self-glorification. Theoretically the historians remained wedded to the ancient ideal of glorifying the wisdom of God, expectations from human beings, and of the Divine plan behind giving humans a home on this lonely planet called Earth. They still believed that through all historical events and deeds, and behind all historical forces, the people should be taught to discover the will of God. But on the practical side, the medieval historians lacked the comprehensive vision of Valmiki and Vyas that could have recorded the events correctly and projected the universal spirit working to express itself through them. As a result there is no history of medieval India written by Indian historians born in those times. Perhaps people had become too complacent to see their faults and too timid to criticize their medieval heroes.

Common people preferred to retain in memory the temporal events and heroes. Thus the information that was denied to them by not writing an accurate history took the form of myths and fantasies in the memory of laypeople. History was still there, but in a distorted form. It was neither representing the Lord and His will nor was it serving as a reliable record of those times. Rather it was playing with the memory of the people. As a huge serpent, myth took birth from the collective memory and coiled the soul of the Indians. This serpent's poison further laid the spirit of India to a sweet slumber. Somebody has described the medieval Indians as a people who once got them bitten by a serpent and are ever since in search of immortality without flushing out the poison.

The Gurus pointed at this degeneration of the people as they pointed at many others. They realized that refusal to write the history of one's people was one of the surest ways of blinding them. It was human to want to know about their past. If we do not inform the people about their past, they will fall on imagination and build myths. They will also lose the track of historical forces. They will cease to learn from errors and will keep on repeating the same errors. The people's march to light, sweetness and joy will get arrested. Their life force, finding the natural flow resisted, will take to exaggerations and hysterical expressions. The irony of India was that though the Indians did not write their history, they still had history, much distorted by envious and greedy invaders. And the invaders' lies were demoralizing the people.

It should not be wrong to say that most of our evil customs and practices have grown out of this self-blinding ignorance of historical forces during the medieval times.

However, some authentic details about the times and lives of Sikh Gurus are available. They have recorded the plight of the people in their days in plain and simple words. They did not spare their own ranks and have made no secrets about the lives and deeds of their followers. It is candidly written how the *masands* had started harassing the people so that the tenth Guru had to punish them. It is also written how the mother of Guru Gobind Singh did not like the *langar* or institution of the community kitchen. She ordered its closure once, to the great annoyance of the Guru. There are on record even such amusing and much revealing anecdotes as the quarrel that broke out during the visit of Guru Gobind Singh to Chittor between the Rajputs and the Sikhs because the latter had taken some goats without paying for them. One reads interesting details of the arrival of Guru Angad at the house of Guru Nanak and the service he rendered at the latter's fields. At places miracles are interwoven. For instance, when Guru Nanak says that Angad's new clothes are not soiled because of working in his fields, the mud on his clothes transforms into saffron. Similarly, it is on record that immediately after his death Guru Gobind Singh was seen by a hermit going on his bay-horse. He had smiled and told the hermit that he was on a hunting excursion. It turned out to be an information that aroused the emotions of his knights, as it reminded them of the promise he had made on his death bed "wherever five true Sikhs will assemble I shall be with them".

To say that it was not scientific history is to say nothing since there never has been any scientific history. History cannot exclude love and faith. The Sikhs wrote history of the kind that the early Christian saints wrote, the history of Christ written with love and faith, but without hatred for others and without misinformation.

Miracles recorded to glorify God's prophets and messengers serve the need of a community of believers, without prejudice to others. The believers do not ask others to take them. Such miracles bring the Guru close to the followers who feel distressed by his departure. They do not want others to take such miracles as part of their theology. It would be only discourtesy to the love and memory of their great men to put a question here like, do miracles really happen? Narrations of miracles that serve love are different from narrations of miracles that make the mind slave to superstitions.

No history of medieval India presents so authentic an account of the people as the Sikh books. The spirit of a paid workman often mars the Mogul historians' accounts. It also glorifies many misdeeds and distorts events. To pursue the simple narration of the times in Sikh books is to feel those days. It touches an adult nearly like his diary of his boyhood days. The liveliness and artlessness of the narration draws an intimate picture of the life in those days. Guru Gobind Singh's style of writing history was a departure from the *Purana-style* of writing history, invented by Vyas. Vyas would identify his soul with Truth and then narrate the events objectively. Due to identification with Truth, events would automatically take an order that revealed the triumph of Truth. In the times of the Gurus the collective quest of Truth of the Indian people had been disrupted due to foreign invasions. Much that was *anargal* (confusing) was happening that could not be given meaning in the *Purana-style*, and yet it was a truth of practical life and could not be ignored. Therefore Guru Gobind Singh adopted the Herodotus-style of writing history that had been imitated by Al Baruni and Farishta, the Arab historians, and was now the style of the Mogul chroniclers. However, he retained the spirit of Vyas and adhered to truth. Guru Gobind Singh's allegiance to truth makes the Sikh history a more reliable account of the history of those days than what was being written in the Mogul court. The Sikh history makes one feel the pulse of those times and also the horror that was pervading the cities and villages. People come out of those pages as living beings with all the traits that are available to this day in the Indians. It is difficult to find elsewhere a more earthly and realistic account of the character of the medieval Indian people. One can see clearly the historical, religious and social forces in the events presented.

The concept of God in the writings of the Gurus seems to be the same as that of the *Ishopanisad* — *Isha vasyamidam sarvam yatkincha jagatyam jagat* (Whatever is there in this universe, sensitive or insensitive, is pervaded by God from all sides, inside and outside.) God is not only transcendental He is immanent too.

Only he can truly know the Timeless God *Akaal Purakh* who has experienced Him as the truth that pervades time. He who is beyond space and time is also within space and time. To call God only transcendental could be only an intellectual argument for intellect's sake.

Henri Bergson calls memory a psychological form of time. The Vedas say that time entwines living beings in its coils. The Jains say time is also a name of the soul. One of their scriptures called *Samaysaar* (the Essence of Time) is in fact a treatise about the soul. Memory, *prarabdh-karma* (fate), *punya karma* (good deeds) are all manifestations of time. The Gurus believed that the human soul was bound in the coils of time. To get released from it one must learn the art of straightening the coils. Time coils the soul only as long as we insist on interpreting events to prove prejudices, superstitions or partial truths. The man who goes for the whole of truth gets freed of the coils of time. Time gives up its serpent form in his case. The force of Reality i.e. Love straightens it for him who goes for the whole of truth. One gets released from the prison cell of time. Such a person is fit to take a journey beyond time and to experience the truth that is *Akaal*. Time is the prison house of the human soul and a correct understanding of it, which includes a correct recording of history, frees from it. One who would try to reach the Timeless without paying to time whatever is due to it would land in nothingness.

The Sikh history is not aimed at giving only an account of the glories and exploits of the Gurus. It candidly records their woes and sorrows and also the defeats and the treacheries they were subjected to. The recording has been to a great extent impartial. As a result, truth, as it had become, as it should not have become, as the forces of ignorance had made it, rises from those pages. India is not yet fully rid of those *anargal* (confusing) forces. Those mutilations and evils are still very powerful in our society. The Gurus exposed their roots naked to the annoyance of many. They made the roots of those evils bare so that those who were considered brave might test themselves. The Gurus said that truth did not consist in forgetting the shameless and cowardly acts committed by the rulers against the people. The ashes of the wronged ancestors had mixed quietly in ashes and their souls had gone to the celestial kingdom of the true King *Waheguru.* But the seeds of the injustice they had suffered at the hands of the rulers are lying on the soil. They needed to be burnt so that they did not produce their likes. The way to burn them was not revenge. The doer of injustice and his progeny must be made to realize that evil does more evil to him that employs it. The Mogul king wanted them to take his communal and dastardly acts as acts of Fate that could not be undone and must be ruefully endured, so that the Gurus might get thoroughly frustrated in their mission. Their mission was the restoration of the rule of practical truth i.e. dharma. The Gurus did not take them as acts of Fate. They participated in those events and turned them into voluntary acts of self-sacrifice in which the Sikh martyrs allotted the role of the butcher to the king. Indeed they were acts of martyrdom. Martyrdom is not getting killed deliberately for a noble cause. It consists of pursuing the objective whole-heartedly and not minding if life is the price one has to pay for it. The lawless and cowardly death sentence executed against Guru Arjun and Guru Tegh Bahadur, and the live burial in a wall of the adolescent sons of Guru Gobind Singh were not pre-meditated acts of martyrdom. It was the price that those brave men paid willingly since time had demanded those wages for working henceforth for their freedom.

Great must have been the love in the souls of the Gurus, because their action in return of cruel and insulting acts perpetrated against them did not emanate from wrath, hatred or feelings of revenge. No such negative passion was allowed to reign over their souls. The Gurus believed that an action was justified only when it was born of love and compassion. They fought not to avenge the massacre but to carry on the torch of freedom further, without getting arrested by grief or disappointment born of the act of the king. Thus they ensured dispassionately that such monstrosities did not go without proper reply from humanity. They fought not to express their anger but to show that their long arms were given to protect the ancient children of God—human dignity, human values and love.

Toynbee had made it clear that no history could be written without some motive behind it. All history is exposition of some idea of the historian. Gibbon's history of the Romans, and Spangler's history of western civilization are studies from particular points of view. The historical facts are given an order under the force of that motive. Even narrations of facts in the newspapers are motivated. Communists call themselves scientific historians. Marx's motivated interpretation of history to prove materialism as the absolute truth is a proof of their lie. The Indians had decided that if motive has to be there, let it be the motive of Truth. *Purana* were interpretation of facts from the point of view of Truth. Vyas's slogan was: Truth alone triumphs (*Satyameva Jayate*). The interpretation of facts in the *Purana* did not justify a particular people or religion. It justified Truth both theoretical and practical. Dharma was practical Truth common to all the people irrespective of their religions. Dharma was the name that the Indians gave to practical Truth. Dharma was not religion, but the touchstone that proved the falsehood or truth of all sorts of religions.

Modern historians are coming to the same conclusion to which the ancient Indians had come. History is no longer considered a useful study if it is a mere recording of the exploits of some ambitious individuals. It was inferior work relegated to paid chroniclers. Much above that a true historian today is supposed to see the march of humanity beneath the individual scores. History is the record of the struggle of man's soul to reach the practical Truth. Mathew Arnold has called practical truth culture. The visionaries of India had added only one word more to culture — Nirvana. Practical Truth cultures the life force of man during his journey on earth and brings uncompromising freedom i.e., Nirvana to life beyond the grave.

Every historian picks up events to suit his narrative. But the events already come coloured to him, because it is the nature of imagination to get dissolved in facts. Whatever facts a people preserve in their memory get automatically coloured by their imagination and memory. Memory has its own colours and so has imagination. However dispassionate we may be, the very placing of a thing or person in memory or imagination somewhat transforms that person or thing. These are basic characteristics of our faculties. Call them human frailties if you like. Sages like Vyas had called them inner realities that must meet outer realities through *Viniyoga*, for the resultant of the *Viniyoga* of these two realities is practical Truth. Man can imbibe it and get rid of the colouring of events by memory and imagination. Instead of wishing the faculties given by Nature to be other than what Nature had made them, the Indians had discovered the way in *Viniyoga* to make the natural faculties reliable instruments of truth.

Hence the task of interpreting history was left to the sages, who were disinterested watchers of the human drama of mortality, dreams and ambitions. They had no fear of worldly losses and no desire for worldly gains. Instead of the sages fearing the kings, the kings feared them because of their ability to see the truth with the help of the same imperfect faculties given by Nature. Those men of truth had trained their vision so that after seeing correctly the present truth they might foretell the practical truth that was likely to unfold in the human drama. Their duty was to project the Truth hidden in events and deeds and warn the kings and the people if they had deviated.

Later came the age of downfall and defeats when the people out of individual ambitions stopped paying attention to their forewarnings. They retired to the caves in the mountains from their hermitages that were near the cities. The deluded kings, having forgotten Mother India, had taken to building their individual States. Much bad blood had developed between them, and they had started plotting against each other. As a result they got defeated at the hands of warlords and greedy invaders who had their minds set on a single aim of surviving on the fruits of others' labour. Visionaries who could guide them through the haze of unhappy facts were to be found nowhere. The Indian people were no longer kept informed of the direction they had to take to walk toward Truth. The racial mariners had lost their compass. As if lost after shipwreck on a frosty cold night, the people had started moving helter-skelter in panic. They had forgotten the discipline that had taken them to

Truth at the dawn of their civilization. Guru Nanak appeared amidst them when they had already spent more than half a dozen centuries in a state of stupor caused by the darkness of foreign domination. He saw the collective consciousness resigned and blinded, like a serpent lulled in its coils. In frantic attempts, it forced its hood here and there to no avail. It was smarting against wounds inflicted by gangs of brigands from across the barriers that were hell bent on exploiting the opportunity created by the loss of their compass by the Indian mariners. Malicious eyes and thirsty greedy tongues and blades were wounding their collective consciousness, and with each wound it was madding more and more. All the noble virtues that it had developed after sacrificing millions of brave men and women on the path of disinterested quest of truth were turning into negative forces because of its self-withdrawal. Higher achievements in a mental state of depression had turned against them. In this mood of self-withdrawal, the ideal of *ahimsa* had become death instinct and love had turned into a beggar, for they are virtues only in brave souls that aggressively seek Truth.

Nanak and after him all the nine Gurus took upon themselves the task of interpreting to the people their history in a way that they might grasp its truth and power. The people knew their history but did not know that it was anything more than sweet lullabies. They were asked to remember the atrocities they had been subjected to and the causes thereof. They were not to swallow humiliation and injustice. They were to remember the great men who had stood for human values and Truth; and not to imitate the foreign rulers who had equated their private beliefs with the practical truth of humanity. The Gurus took upon themselves the task of sharpening their memory and awakening their courage to face the truth. The fanatic approach of the rulers was exposed and challenged. They were told that it brought no good to man. It only strengthened forces of tyranny and ignorance against the common humanity of all humans. It is the characteristic of deluded minds to get violent on being exposed to truth. The attacks of the rulers turned all the more violent. It was for the souls of the Gurus to protect the people against the outrage of their humanity. To let the humanity of any person outraged was the greatest sin that the soul could commit, according to the Gurus. They protected humanity that still lived in people's heart. Each Guru was an awakened soul and no lesser were their knights.

The Gurus were secular leaders of a religious movement. They were secular because they hated no faith and no man on grounds of religion, race and colour. They were secular because they did not proselytise. Yet they were religious in the highest sense of the word, because they were leaders of a religious movement to which conversion was politics not religion; to which religion was the self-sacrifice of the soul for the protection of tender humanity that had not grown beyond childhood, since wild people had been killing it during its infancy.

Secularism did not mean to the Gurus a spirit of fighting shy of Truth because it looked intimate to their soul. Secularism did not mean to them tolerance of the humbug of the rulers of calling themselves faithful and the people infidel. The Gurus said that there was no unique faith that alone deserved survival. Secularism did not mean to the Gurus blindness to forced conversion and outrageous behaviour with women. Secularism to them consisted rather in not getting provoked by the enemy's misdeeds into wild passions of revenge. Secularism was in not raising a blind passion to match blind passion. Secularism consisted in knowing that such actions were unworthy of men. No matter who did them, they were totally incapable of furthering humanity's cause. It was of no avail to take revenge for them. At the same time to ignore them was to go against Truth. The task before the Gurus was to give a suitable reply to atrocity and meanness without resorting to atrocity and meanness.

The entire Sikh legend is an exposition of the power of faith in Love. Even the Moguls who detested it could not consign it to the class of unbelievable miracles, only fondly remembered by a closed and deluded group of people. It was itself a miracle that out of faith in the delicate emotion of love had grown an indomitable will that was proving stronger than their own will that, they said, was born of spiritual powers. And without affecting the tenderness of love, this indomitable will struck terror in the heart of the mightiest empire of its time. None of the ten Gurus showed any cruelty or indelicacy. Their battles were the battles of love, for the sake of love, and were fought by lovers. On one side were believers in love, and on the other believers in theocracy. The latter had combined their spirituality with cruelty of the worst kind. The power of faith in the fragile emotion of love, exhibited in their actions by the Gurus, was simply astonishing. Not even once did they retaliate cruelties of the enemy, who did not only kill the saint-soldiers, but killed in the style of butchers. To bury alive inside walls, to pierce every limb with burning rods and to kill children before their parents were not sufficient punishment, in the eyes of the rulers, to those who had asked for no more than the right to live in honour as citizens of the State.

It was a sublime attempt to fight militarily the forces of evil without losing the human soul. Much as I look to the history of mankind, I find no parallel to this great upsurge of the Sikhs. The point of beauty in it was its adherence to human virtues. Their blade did not serve dark passions of fury, wrath and hatred. First those passions were to be subjected to the delicate emotion of love. Imbued with this new meaning, they were let loose. Then there remained nothing in them to be afraid of. They did not lead them away from the human aim. Love's tyranny elicited praise even from the enemy. The enemy learnt that in spite of its tenderness, love was no weakling. Love was not the sentimentality of gloomy hearts. Love had the support of God to be victorious. The wicked had conspired to popularize the myth that the fate of love was sealed with despair, sorrow and failure. The Gurus asked: "If love is God and if the earth is his creation, how can love fail on earth? It is a lie propagated by those who cannot love and want the kingdom of earth."

The following four kinds of obscenities have always terrorized love by imitating tornadoes: (1) First of these obscenities is Fate, what the Moguls called Kismet. It is an obscenity because it outrages the modesty of the heart. It robs the heart of grace. Without grace the tender ray of love loses its link with God. It is this link that keeps it strong with God's strength, in spite of its tenderness. If the heart resists the tornado it hardens, and loses the link with God due to hardening. (2) The outraged or hardened heart develops the obscenity to betray everyone. The power to betray love enters the heart, as a twister, only after it has been outraged or betrayed. Such a person betrays every one: the parents, the teacher, friends and the lover. (3) The third obscenity that enters the heart as a twister is meanness with money. Such hearts can see no divinity in the world. (4) The fourth obscenity swirls through the closed petals of the heart that feel like a lotus. It separates the petals and lodges in place of the beloved a mad and possessive nude in it and closes it for the rest of life. All the motions of this nude excite the heart as a delicate and silken copy of a tornado. It compels the heart to spend itself over lusting. To a heart devoted to lusting with this fabulous nude in the heart love becomes a stranger that once lived in its neighbourhood. Such a heart is as much devoted to this nude icon as a true lover to his lady.

The rishis had taught the soul of the person ravaged by the four tornadoes to come to the rescue of the heart. If the soul makes self-sacrifices to all these four experiences and performs *Atmayagya* the four tornadoes shift to the soul and leave the heart. The heart recollects itself and gets closed to all tornadoes. It becomes a virgin again and the memory of the tornadoes vanishes from it. Such a soul liquidates the tornadoes forever. It is in this way that the true disciple of the Gurus quietens the tornadoes that rob the best power of man, the power to love. In his heart the tender ray of love returns that links it to the *Waheguru* again.

Some cunning people who wanted to rule over mankind had created the myth that the fate (*kismet*) of love was failure and tears. They had separated the three – love, faith in God and self-sacrifice of the soul. Originally the three are integrated in every heart. God must be integrating them through *Viniyoga*, because it is *Viniyoga* that revives their lost integration. If separated and then united by any method other than *Viniyoga* their infinite strength does not return. The popular saying that love is a Divine power that does not succeed in this world, and gets rewarded only in the other, is a myth. The Gurus exploded this medieval myth. They gave the slogan— 'Love is sent to this world to be successful. It is the greatest presence of God in this world.' Never before did a band of philosophers sing Truth so sweetly and as soldiers ousted wickedness so delicately. The Gurus had vowed and proved that they would not let any power other than love rule their inner and outer world.

You have some of the finest examples of the soldiers of light in the history of the Sikhs. Their rise looked like the fierce waves in the ocean to those that did not trust love, yet even as the ocean does not break its bounds so did the Gurus never break the rhythm of love. For they knew love was the rhythm that came from God, and any addition by man in it turned it into pride (*haumey*). One could not punish others for then the lover turns into the police of love and ceases to be the lover. One could not show to others how important he was for love, for than it turned into ego. The soul had continually to sacrifice itself to love for if it did not it ate out love. The moment the soul forgot that love was not its property but a wild, poor and nameless flower that had grown in it, it withered and disappeared. It was not anything like the soul's cultivated spiritual powers. It was like a wild growth not of the spiritual genre. It was nothing to be proud of. It had not grown due to spiritual cultivation. It was neither the cause nor effect of anything physical, psychological or spiritual. It was beside everything that the soul knew to be valuable. Love was: "A violet by a mossy stone half hidden from the eye." It was none of the valuable things known to the soul. It was God himself. The soul had to sacrifice itself, everything that it was, to it. It was the moment of the soul when it became twice born. It was the moment to lose its pride of divine pedigree and to be like the divine. It was the moment to get over the distinction of the valuable and the ordinary.

In spite of the high tides of passion for freedom in their hearts, never once the Gurus did cross the bounds that cannot be specified. Those bounds have not been described by any lover. They never showed any passion to become rulers. Their aim was only to install Love as the ruler on earth. This attempt of the Sikh Gurus has not been properly evaluated. When history finds someone of the vision of Vyas, he will surely give a proper place to this Sikh pledge. He will call it the same that drove Krishna to love the milkmaids, forgetting the celestial goddesses. The Divine could enter the hearts of the milkmaids only after getting dispossessed of all his divine qualities. God had said, "I walk behind the milkmaids so that the dust their walk raises may fall on my head." Further He says, "Nothing fascinates me. Nothing can bind me. Nothing can contain me. But where this love is I come to get bound and fettered." And love does not know how to bind. Love does not know that it is so important to God, and rare too that He cannot create it for Himself. The Gurus had gone beyond the spirituality of the saints that felt itself greater than the delicate emotion of love. Love was the soul of spirituality. All spiritual powers had first to get disenchanted of their own enchanting spell to transform into the delicate emotion of love. Spirituality has first to acquire the ability to tolerate without staggering to see God look so insignificant in comparison to glorious royalty, and unrewarding too, having nothing to give, so powerless and helpless. The soul that sacrifices to such a Lord alone knows what it got. It has not been described in the scriptures.

It seems that the religious consciousness of man has developed into philosophies mainly in two areas of earth, the Middle East and India. In both places it grew on opposite lines. The religious consciousness in Middle East produced three major religions – Judaism, Christianity and Islam. These religions in the long run transformed spiritual power into political power. In India no religion came even near the idea of converting spiritual power into political power, not even Sikhism, in spite of its active interest in the political situation of India. Even religions like Jainism and Buddhism, which did not believe in a Creator, kept spiritual power separate from political power. The religions of Indian origin have checked the ambition of the political men from assuming Divine power and vice versa. They have also kept alive the idea of the equality of all religions and also of all living beings. It is significant in this context that the tenth Guru had abolished the institution of the Guru and had made the love songs contained in the Granth Sahib the absolute authority. It completely removed the possibility of the political power replacing love.

In the religions born in the Middle East the spiritual power had changed into the political power. These two religious consciousnesses of humanity need to be integrated through *Viniyoga* in order to realize why they are two, why not one. Religious consciousness has to be one if it has nothing up the sleeves. The identification of the spiritual and political powers in the Middle East had led to a struggle between the three religions for supremacy, each religion calling the other blasphemy. It had removed God from power. The excuse that each has a different God is a cover up for this coup. Even in admitting people to heaven God depends on the recommendations of the leading men of their religions. Some leading religious men make promises that only politicians make, like – you will get heaven if you simply get converted. Passion for proselytising is the same passion that politicians use to win elections.

Perhaps political power was the only thing that man could create without God. Spirituality could not be created without God or Truth. Though they have filled political power with spiritual ideals, it has been useless, since politics heeds no spiritual counselling. If it heeded certain religions sometimes, it was not because of trust in them, but because it found it convenient to ride certain religions. Modern man finds himself helpless before spirituality that looks like political power. The reason is as simple as this - political power pursues no end except itself. Once you convert spirituality into political power you cannot stop getting confused.

God is needed to check the madness of political power. Man wants to live by human virtues - love, compassion, kindness, liberty, fraternity and equality - that he has discovered to be as much essential for his happiness as food and shelter. He has discovered their essentiality, after suffering much at the hands of the insane political power, during the two millenniums after God's disappearance from governance. Man has known that political power only kills human virtues. He has also known that only God promotes them. Man's existence on this lonely planet called Mother Earth has been miserable, ever since political power has substituted spirituality. Politics cannot be trusted the job to enshrine human virtues in administration, by which alone humans can to be governed. It is only because political power, being a substitute for spirituality, simply cannot serve what it substitutes. Even democracy that claims to be the promoter of human virtues does not promote them. Not because it has no will, but because it simply cannot. Even religious leaders have given up their aim that used to be living the selfless life of the saints on earth. Many of them have shifted to capturing political and economical powers. Even the 'Templar Knights', who had sworn to remain poor to serve humanity selflessly, forgot humanity within ten years, and became the richest people in Europe. The history of holy men in the West after crucifying Christ has been of winning kingdoms and converting people with the power of the State.

It is a miracle that, in this vitiated global atmosphere, the Gurus entered politics as servants of God. Their God was the God of all living beings, not the God who favoured some religion and needed political power to be popular. They refused to identify political power with spirituality. They told the kings that spirituality was not the subject of governance, and conversion could not be a subject of the State, nor of any organized brotherhood. To convert people to one's faith was not a subject of political rights. They said that spirituality was not aware of any rights. It was concerned only about enshrining human virtues as the ideal of political power. They said political power was the servant of spirituality, not its substitute. In the views of the Gurus the very idea of a brotherhood of proselytisers was a political idea, aimed at corrupting spirituality.

The Gurus had seen that political power, whether secular or religious, shattered humanity that God had lodged in every human heart. Shattered humanity had transformed into pairs of opposite impulses, like living in fear or becoming fearsome; living in greed or becoming poor; living in lust or turning frigid. Both the alternatives in these pairs encouraged and perpetuated each other. They gave no room to humanity to stage a comeback. The Gurus' had found humanity to be the most delicate emotion that could not survive without the support of the soul of man. The politics of each of the ten Gurus, therefore, had only one objective – to be the lone knight of humanity, like Krishna.

The Gurus had realized that when the soul became humanity's true friend, and took on itself humanity's worries and problems, as if they were its own worries and problems, only then humanity could live by its delicate emotions. Humanity's emotions are earthly images of God's virtues. Otherwise, it shatters into pairs of opposite impulses. They had found humanity delicate like a flower that scatters by the slightest shock, but becomes King of earth if the soul becomes its best friend. In ancient times the ideal friendship of the soul and humanity had once freed the earth of political greed. Krishna was the soul then and Arjun humanity. The Gurus said that what provided meaning and purpose to the delicate emotions of humanity was the emotion of emotions, the emotion of love.

Two millenniums ago prophets of the Middle East were all prophets of Judaism. According to the Hebrew Bible, the prophets after Moses had declared that God had disappeared and hidden his face from man. No man or woman saw God as Moses had. In the books of Joshua and Judges (Bible) God's presence is already greatly diminished. In the Hebrew Bible God step-by-step withdraws himself. In the book of Esther God is not mentioned. The hiding of the Divine face is only half of the story. The other half is a shift in the controller of human destiny from spiritual power to political power. In the medieval times for the first time in her history, India had started suffering from this malady that had been brought by the invaders from the Middle East.

The transformation of spiritual power that earlier governed human affairs into political power had begun when people told Moses, "Let God not speak with us, lest we die." However the actual transformation began when Abraham confronted God after God had informed him of his decision to destroy the people of Sodom and Gomorrah because of their sin. Abraham questioned the wisdom of God's decision. He asked, "Will you also destroy the righteous with the wicked?" He argued further, "Far be it from you to do a thing like this?" (Bible 18:23-25). Abraham pursued negotiations with God on this issue. At this stage the religious consciousness in Middle East started changing colours from awe, wonder and total trust to political settlements. The political voice in God's story started growing louder. This rebellious attitude changed the religious attitude in the Middle East gradually from total submission to the wisdom of God to amendments in God's decisions through negotiations and recommendations. Prophets later on started telling people that they would recommend their cases for seats in heaven to God if they converted to their paths. They started believing that God in spite of his supreme wisdom needed some political advice before granting migration to heaven. This elevation of politicians almost to the level of God has resulted in confrontation of man with God ever since.

The modesty of unconditional love of God had been outraged. In place of unconditional love of God consciousness shifted in the Middle East to unconditional love of the prophets because they negotiated terms diplomatically with God and ultimately brought total political authority to man. The arrogance of man reached new heights when Abraham's servant asked the invisible God Yahweh to "practice fidelity with my lord Abraham." And God did what he wanted. The religious consciousness of Middle East took it as a sign of the triumph and independence of God. It did not see that God did not even ask him whether he had been given the power by his master to talk to God in the manner he talked. It was not because God became weaker before the growing power of man. It was because God enters the world of man on man's terms. The more the prophets of man wanted him away the further he receded from man's world. Not only God, the Indian scriptures say, even angels keep away from the world of man if they are insulted.

The struggle with God over power reached its climax when Jacob fought with God (32:25-33). God did not prevail on him not because He could not but because He would not if there is no reverence in man for Him. God only asked Jacob to let Him go. Jacob refused to comply unless God blessed him. Thus Western religious consciousness entered a dangerous phase when God was not free even to bless or not out of his free will. Granting free will to man came to mean denying free will to God. These episodes only show a growing disrespect to God. Jacob is shown to have been alternately deceived and cared for by his sons. It should have served as a warning to man that what he did to God his children would do to him. But man's arrogance looked at it otherwise. Increase in man's power vis-à-vis God was seen as man's triumph. No better proof can be found for the dictum of the sages that "bad times reverse the intellect." R E Friedman rejoices in his book *The Disappearance of God* that Moses' conduct was "a leap that increased human status relative to God." To say the least, it was a misfortune. It would neither arouse surprise nor contempt in Nanak. It would only arouse his common sense to step aside from a happening that portended ruin. Friedman is jubilant that "Joshua had exceeded even Moses in tipping the Divine-human balance." Nanak would say, like any of his rishi predecessor, that reverence, love and self-sacrifice of the soul to God are the only ways to have a relationship with Him. Nanak would warn that the fact that no harm came to Moses and Joshua only shows that God does not take revenge, and the greatest tragedy is His disappearance from the life of man.

Yahweh (God) told Samuel, "they have rejected me from ruling over them." (1 Samuel 8:4-7). Friedman, too, admits the growing concentration on "political authority." As time went on governors replaced the kings. This change ousted God completely from the human scene. At least the kings derived their authority from God, but the governors were human authorities that derived their power from another human authority, not from God. The only sane voice comes from the psalms that lament "God's disappearance as a more terrifying condition than Divine punishment." But it is not effective. Further on the relationship itself disappears. "It does not appear to be so much a matter of God's 'transcending' history as simply disappearing." (Friedman) And "Yahweh regretted that he had made humans in the earth." (Genesis 6:6). This development has been taken rather strangely by the Western genius. Nietzsche simply found fault with God. He says that the Bible began with a mistake on God's part. Mark Twain has similar thoughts: "If the Lord did not want humans to be rebellions, why did He create them in His image?" Yahweh says, "Return to me, and I shall return to you." (Zech 1:3; Mal 3:6-7). But man does not pay any attention. The 20th century's Western philosophical and literary legacy is rather full of suggestions that God is dead. Irreverence to elders is only a fallout of this attitude to God. Reverence is not slavery, and irreverence is not freedom. Freedom is in the feeling of it, not in defiance.

The feeling of Divine absence has contributed to producing depravity, fear and distrust between humans. As I imagine the Gurus in the 20th century West I hear their sutra for the remedy of the Western sickness – 'coming of age does not give man the ability of God to enable him to officiate in place of God. Even all the combined wisdom of angels cannot officiate for God. God is irreplaceable. Responsibility loses meaning and vigour the moment God disappears from human life. It becomes a dead word without the moral impetus that comes only from God's absolute wisdom and authority. It is a delusion of the Western man that God wants to train man in his profession, because it is no profession but uniqueness. The awe of God is the actual motivation for love. To take away the wonder that God is is to take away morality from man.

The Sikh Gurus' struggle becomes globally significant in this context. They had served the Western religious consciousness indirectly, by checking the Mogul political power from becoming the source of proselytising. The result of the Gurus' disinterested pursuit of truth has been that the intellectuals in India were not faced with the terrifying views that God had died. Being nearest to us in time among our illustrious forefathers, the Gurus have helped us, and that is why we Indians do not face the problem of an absence of universal moral values.

The soul that gives up the emotion of love to get spiritual power has no respite from the revolving wheel of power, from spiritual power to psychological to physical (military) to political and, to repeat the same cycle, to spiritual and so on. The only hour of glory of the political power is when it cleans the nation of the earlier power. The glorious hour in India of Islamic political power was when it cleaned India of indigenous rulers, of the British power when it cleaned India of the Islamic power, of the Indian politicians when they cleaned India of the British. The glorious hour of a political party in a democracy is when it cleans the nation of the party in power. Political power has been a mirage in the desert of human unhappiness. It gives no happiness. It rejoices itself its cleaning and the nation simply watches stunned. The political power feels glorious in its hour of cleansing, and is thus like the power that cleans the bowels and that power belongs to the demon Nirriti in Indian mythology. It seems to have become the same for the Middle Eastern religious consciousness too. It had been snatched from God and has been busy only cleansing nations so far of their belief in the delicate emotion of love as the acme of spiritual power. The other powers, the spiritual, psychological and physical (military), also rejoice their victories, giving no happiness to the soul.

The Gurus tell the soul, 'in order to feel happy get reborn of the lure of these four powers, for happiness does not lie in power. It lies in the delicate emotion of love.'

Women

During medieval days even learned Indians had been contaminated by the low status the conquerors of India had given their women. The conquerors believed woman to be a half-wit compared to the full-wit, man. Either the Indians had forgotten or defeat and humiliation had made them sceptical of the wisdom of the ancient sages. The sages had accorded woman a unique status. They had said that until some woman voluntarily and happily shares her life with him, no man could fulfil his life. During medieval times when the invaders ruled over India that same woman came to be regarded as a positive hindrance to man's spiritual growth. They had come to look upon her as embodiment of ignorance. Shankaracharya had called them 'the gateway of hell'. Tulsidas had classed them with the cattle and the uncultivated. It pained the Gurus to see woman in degradation. The Gurus' told the people, God became two, man and woman, for the sake of a beautiful play called love. One soul is there in two bodies of beautiful clay. It is not a riddle. It is the truth that you have to realize.

In ancient India even demons aspired for the love of woman. They abducted them hoping devilishly that the abducted women might start loving them. There is not a single case in ancient India when a demon had raped a woman. The belief was common that woman helped God realization in a sweeter way. Sages of rare spiritual vision, like Agasta, Marichi, Jaimini and Vashistha had taken spouses for love. To the Indians God had never been a hard and unsparing master who wanted man's love and attention all for himself. He told spouses to love sincerely 'and that will be your love to me. You both have different minds. Do not judge each other since my mind is half hidden in woman and half in man. How can half of my mind judge the other half? It is like a letter torn vertically, each sentence is torn in between. Unless you integrate the two minds through *Viniyoga*, you cannot know what truth is.'

The Indians forgot practicing *Viniyoga* during the medieval days of India's slavery. Yoga was the way to unite like minds, while *Viniyoga* was the way to unite unlike minds. The medieval foreign rulers had a different approach to woman. They did not like to fall in love for that meant giving women an equal status. The very idea of it was unbearable. To this day they proudly claim that religion forbids them equality with women. Scared by their disrespect for woman, the parents in India stopped sending girls to schools. The two main sources that could keep woman at par with man — education and participation in society — were cut off from woman. She thus lost her strength and got caught in the whirlpool of ignorance, superstitions and fears.

The Gurus asked for the creation of natural conditions for her. Nanak said,

Why consign to evil and abuse woman
She the first teacher of kings and great men
Who raises them from child to man

Asa Rag

The Sikh Gurus allowed woman free, uninhibited and equal participation in the spiritual as well as social life. If some men protested that women were ignorant, the Gurus said let them express their ignorance. When Nanak put Angad, a guest, to work in his field, his wife rebuked him for such unbecoming behaviour with a guest. It is significant that Nanak did not speak to her harshly. He said that there was no mud on his clothes. It is said that the mud turned saffron. Angad became the second Guru of Sikhs. Nanak had not chosen his son to succeed him and had given preference to Angad.

Sikhism is a practical religion and has nowhere disregarded facts. It recognises that woman can speak out of ignorance, but so can man. It protests against the suppression of her voice. If she has been made a depository of ignorance, this is collective ignorance, not feminine ignorance. Why add fear to folly by suppressing her voice? Throughout there have been efforts in Sikh history to raise woman to her ancient spiritual heights. She is trained to care for love and not for herself. The learned Gurus showed extreme humility to learn from women. They had inherited their vision of women from the ancient learned men, and it was this vision of the rishis that India needed in their times. It was woman's kind outlook and innate sense of oneness with all life that was most needed when hearts had been frozen and speech muted.

The Gurus have advocated for deep intimacy and love between man and woman, not only for domestic happiness, but also for spiritual realization of truth. "O couple dear, vain it is to live as two, for the opportunity given to you in human life is rare!" thus sang the third Guru in *Sahi-raag,* "You are one soul in two, one soul, bodies two, out of love, and to share love."

The true life of a couple is to live the individualities of man and woman and to live above it too, for life's fulfilment and soul's fulfilment are attained together. Their souls are not two individualities but the same lamp of consciousness in two. It is the same consciousness that remains obstructed by their respective masculine and feminine natures. The masculine and the feminine are not their real identities, for whatever consciousness they have is borrowed from the soul that is the same in both. This borrowed consciousness in each tends to be proud and insensitive to what is going on in each other's mind. They can know each other's mind only if their souls occasionally cast aside their masculine and feminine shells, and use their power of empathy to experience what emotions the other has.

Let me illustrate application of *Viniyoga* from an example of family discord. Take the example of a husband who before going to office tells his wife that he would take her for outing in the evening. In the day he gets involved in official worries and gets a chastising from the boss for neglect. He comes back home sullen, with a cross temper, expecting love, care and understanding from his wife. The wife is sore that he has completely forgotten his word to take her on an outing. And instead of explaining he is cross too. She sees chauvinism and heartlessness. She has been feeling lonely and her hopes of revival were pinned on the outing. She serves him tea and later on food with a mournful face to show her protest. All the time he is unhappy with her behaviour and complaining in his heart to himself that he gets the same atmosphere at home and in the office.

The first step of *Viniyoga* is to accept that each person is closed like the monad of Leibnitz. He/she perceives only his/her emotions. He has no perception of the other. Their psychological shell, i.e. their respective masculinity and femininity, prevent each from empathizing the emotions of the other. Living in their psychological selves they have forgotten that they have souls too. What their masculinity or femininity cannot do their souls can. If they activate their souls the same faculties of their minds will start empathizing the emotions of each other. The way to activate the soul is very simple. One has only to make an autosuggestion to the soul to sacrifice itself to both the masculinity and the femininity that are coming in each other's way to empathize, and to get reborn of both. Now the soul can command the shells too to sacrifice unto each other and get reborn. It will make them aware of each other's feelings. Instantly a new channel of communication will open and they will start empathizing with the other. Empathy will draw the husband closer to her. He will learn that what he was seeing as her pride and insensitivity are in fact feelings of loneliness and neglect. And the wife will also know that it was not male chauvinism.

The barriers break in a moment. Such is the power of *Viniyoga*. This integration is all that *Viniyoga* is. *Viniyoga* is the art of living in two dissimilar personalities, which is the basic qualification and purpose of marrying. To marry is at once to become two from being one, and the art of discovering the way to make the two selves one again. Nature creates such complications lest man and woman forget that the real purpose of marriage is the realization of the truth that two opposite bodies have been occupied by one soul. Those who realize it find marriage a grand opportunity to fulfil, at the same time, the passions of life and the aspirations of the soul for light, and more light. This in brief is *Viniyoga*. This illustration shows that the art of bringing two heterogeneous personalities like man and woman to unity *is Viniyoga*, not yoga. I must divert a little to explain a very important point of the Gurus' philosophy that has not been explained hitherto.

The Sikh was expected by the Gurus to practice another discipline of *Viniyoga* too. Each had to realize the three loves — love of the spouse, love of the Guru and love of the *Waheguru* at the same time. How could it be possible without *Viniyoga*, for in each of these three the Lord had placed a different expectation? This discipline of *Viniyoga* is a way to break through the hard core of *haumey* (the ego). It appears to me that the Gurus have shown a very bold and practical way to couples. The love for the spouse is intimate and behind the curtain of shyness due to its sexual intimacy. The love for the Guru is without sex and yet intimate, for it requires *Viniyoga* with the enlightened soul of the Guru of the shrouded soul of the disciple. The love for the *Waheguru* grows out of these two loves as the bud grows out of the stem and the flower out of the bud. It is the same love that spends its passion with the spouse to become lighter and intrinsically thirsty due to the fire for another kind of union, the union of the lesser light of the soul with the fully enlightened soul of the Guru. This love takes away all the fears of the journey upwards. The Guru has seen all the subtle turns, labyrinths, mysterious caverns, valleys, mountains and the dark and deep woods on the upward journey. He promises to be the companion all along the way. He/she has only to remember the Guru and he would be there to help him/her, no matter how many centuries intervene between the disciple and any of the ten Gurus. The Guru shows the way and shares the trials and tribulations with the disciple. Now courage unfolds in the latter to go close to the awesome light and pure radiance of the *Waheguru* that surpasses the brilliance of a cluster of a thousand suns, and yet is not scorching but delicate like the caressing touch of the mother to a newborn babe. The *Guru Granth Sahib* records this teaching in the following beautiful song:

> She who loves the only husband, the Eternal Husband
> Is blessed in sky, on the winds and on land
> She fulfils her husband in truth to the end
> She who loves the Guru, wounded by *Waheguru's* rays
> Loves none else but the Eternal, the only Husband.

The love between a man and a woman has not to be seen as the lowest in the hierarchy of love. There is no hierarchy of love in Sikhism, as there is no hierarchy between the stem, the bud and the flower, though each of the succeeding is more fascinating and fuller. If there is gradation in the mind of the seeker he cannot experience any of the three in joyous abundance and unrestrained exuberance. The secret of self-fulfilment lies in pursuing each of these three loves to their zenith, for at the zenith all the three turn out to be variants of the union with the only lover *Waheguru*. Ramananda's song in the Holy Book talks of awakening the same love between an earthly couple that exists between the Absolute in the male form of Vishnu and the Absolute in the female form of Laxmi. Parmanand in his song, also compiled in the Holy Book, speaks of the love between the milkmaids *(Gopis)* and Krishna — a love in which the

Lord turns into many copies of Krishna to love each *Gopi* exclusively. It is earthly love no doubt, but a love that transcends the difference between the celestial love of the same couple in Golokdham (heaven) and their earthly love in Vrindaban (earth). Such unification of earth and heaven without forgetting their distinctions is possible only through mastery of the art of *Viniyoga*. Kabir had also idealised true love between man and woman. It was for the Gurus, however, to say that true love between couples is love in which the bodies and the souls unite to be one. Such love, the Gurus say, requires the purity of a virgin. It is not explained whether it hints at non-indulgent love, or indulgence that does not produce karmic fetters. It is, however, clear that the union of such enlightened couples is, simultaneously, a renewal of the virginity of the soul. It is believed that since the realized soul offers itself indulgence in spite of being full and abundant, such disinterested indulgence is an act of beauty that creates no fetters, and renews the chastity of their souls.

It is a known historical fact that all the Gurus lived with their families. To renounce the life of a householder and become a recluse was meaningless in their view. Guru Angad attained enlightenment while living as a guest in the house of the Jat girl Nihali. None of the Gurus went to the forest in search of enlightenment. They felt that the forces that led the human soul astray were ignorance (and fear, envy, revenge, hatred and other variations of ignorance) pride, lust, anger and greed. These deadly forces, they said, were available in homes as much as in forests. The real thing is the unfolding of the knowledge in the soul that alone can conquer these five deadly foes of man. This also means the awakening of the love that cannot be misguided, intrigued or frightened by them. It is not mere spiritual strength that leads to salvation. One who wants liberation needs to strengthen the delicate emotion of love without depriving love of its delicacy while strengthening it.

The Gurus talk of love as a delicate emotion that has more strength than all the armies of the world. Yet it remains a delicate emotion all through, even when it conquers all physical, psychological and spiritual powers. The delicate emotion of love gets lost during spiritual self-purification and spiritual enlightenment. However, one should not forget that the test of spiritual enlightenment lies in the rebirth of the delicate emotion of love from the spiritual powers. If this rebirth does not take place all spiritual talk is nonsense, since in that case spiritual growth has been a wild growth, not the growth that takes to God. The Gurus were aware that the spiritual world is not all pure and good. It has the same evil along with good that one experiences in the psychological and the physical worlds. Those spiritualists who believe that their being spiritual is enough guarantee of being on the right path are self-complacent. They are unaware of the precipices and steep falls that are a speciality of the spiritual world, and that take straight to the deepest dungeons of hell. The spiritual man who does not develop the ability to get rid of spiritual cruelty, spiritual pride, spiritual ingratitude, spiritual violence and spiritual stupidity gets lost in a darker haze of evil than an absolutely ignorant man.

The love that the Gurus talk of is similar to the love that is full of an exquisite pain that stirs the soul, the heart and the body of a virgin. The love of a saint and of a virgin are similar in every aspect, except that the saint experiences it after attaining the peaks of spiritual enlightenment, while the virgin experiences it before experiencing spiritual enlightenment. It is different from the intellectual love of God that Spinoza talks of. It is also different from what the Pope and the Muslim Imams and Muftis describe as the spiritual love of God. The spiritual power is higher than all other powers in the Sikh Guru's view too. But they are quite clear that love is a delicate emotion that transcends spiritual strength and knowledge. They are against identifying love with spirituality, since spirituality is only illumination and power, albeit the highest illumination and power. God i.e. Love to them is the ultimate Reality that is neither strength nor knowledge, rather from which strength and knowledge flow like water from the white joy of the snowy peaks. The saint has to embrace and sleep in the arms of winter, and not turn blue, to experience the love that the virgin experiences without the saint's penance and rigour. The pride of saintly penance, self-denial and rigours prevent the saint from accepting that his love is the same as that of the virgin in love. He, therefore, gives a new name to his love. He calls it spiritual love. He is unaware that it is an error born of pride, and it will prevent him from uniting in love with God. Love is beyond physical, psychological and spiritual distinctions. It is beyond all kinds of powers and weaknesses. To identify love and spiritual power is to turn spiritual power arrogant and cruel. The Gurus say that spiritual cruelty is worse than other forms of cruelty. It is the root of religious hatred and the superiority complex that religion gives, and turns a stupid man more stupid than the stupidity he was born with.

The Gurus say all spiritual powers are not conducive to Nirvana. Spiritual pursuit can bring knowledge to the soul, but cannot flower this knowledge into wisdom. Without love mere knowledge does not attract the attention of God. Unless God gets interested spiritual knowledge serves only to keep the personality clean outside and inside, like a well-dusted room, but it would remain empty, howling like winds even when the wind is low. Even Vyas had suffered this extreme agony caused by spiritual knowledge that failed to produce the love that a virgin feels. It is this exquisite pain of the pining virgin that has the magic to flower spiritual knowledge into wisdom. The spiritual power is as much capable of leading astray as any other power. To be spiritual is no guarantee of being near God. One could have a thoroughly spiritualised *haumey* (ego). Spiritualised *haumey* cannot take to God, as fish cannot learn flying. It can take only to a deeper hell.

The Gurus have tried to build a road for couples, and have asked them to walk on it fearlessly but lovingly. They have said that without doing anything more than loving truly they could meet the *Waheguru*. It is for this reason that Sikhism is a very revolutionary religion, since most religions call the natural love between a man and a woman as nothing more than a prelude to procreation. The scientist supports those religions rather vehemently by calling love no more than the mating calls of beasts. The Gurus said, contrary to it, the mating could only be the beginning. If love is sincere it comes from the soul, and what comes from the soul would not stop until the souls mated, and the mating of the soul is the most difficult exercise of spirituality. Mating of the souls is the same as two souls turning into one. This jump from dualism to monism is the same as the jump from bondage to Nirvana.

Brahma the God who had created the first couple, Manu and Shatrupa, had told them that they were two halves of his body, and they had the freedom to take the creation further or to end it before its time. Procreation was of course a duty, for the sake of continuing the human race. But what after they had produced children? Above every biological and social function they had to discover the lost home of their souls. It was in discovering it that the entire distance between sorrow and joy would be covered. There could not be any joy without love between them. They could have only pleasure without love. Mere pleasure was something that would soon tire them out. It would soon turn monotonous. It was only love among their emotions that never went stale and that changed every moment into a new wonder. Therefore, love was the secret of their Nirvana, their happiness and their progress on earth. As the population would increase new problems would arise. Unless they applied jointly their wits their children would make their lives worse than being dead. Hence so much emphasis in Sikhism on service of the people, on political correctness and love. The Sikh religion is not narrow in any way and it does not teach bigotry or building a closed society. The Sikhs are prone to building a better society and fighting disruptive forces rather than destroying what exists for the pleasure of destruction. They are a people who keep weapons as marks of their religion since they were born in turbulent times, and had to survive against forces that were out to wipe them out. Yet, unlike most of those who take pride in calling themselves martial races but have ended up becoming paid mercenaries that rejoice in killing innocent citizens, the Sikhs live as hard working and honest normal citizens in whichever country they have settled in, finding venues in all departments of social living: music, science, art, governance, politics, and military. Their love of earth is such that they have been travelling and settling in far off places and making those lands fertile and their services efficient by their labour. They are jovial, friendly and brave, ready to sacrifice their lives for love and friendship. Betrayal is not in their blood. It is rather astounding that, for a short duration though, such brave people could be manipulated and misled to raise arms against their own people by those who had always treated them as their worst enemies. It is a proof of the sincerity of the teachings of the Gurus that ultimately they could see through the evil plan of the enemy. The flame of true love kindled by their Gurus helped them to pierce, ultimately, this worst darkness of their history.

It is significant to note that Guru Gobind Singh was already wedded to Jito when the hand of Sundari was offered to him. The Guru accepted her because her father wanted to ensure that she got a husband who could help her soul to experience the love that was above the worldly love. This episode illustrates the basic tenet of the Sikh faith that the union of man and woman is the best instrument of enlightenment and Nirvana. Guru Gobind Singh married a third women, Mata Sahib Kaur. Mata Sundari had attained such purity and intensity of the love of a virgin, which is the ideal of Sikhism, that after the Nirvana of Guru Gobind Singh his generals entrusted her the leadership of the community and the army that had grown very large, fierce and indomitable. It was only the express command of the Guru—that the institution of the Guru should not be continued after him and the *Granth Sahib*, the Holy Book, should be given the status of the Guru for all times to come—that perhaps prevented it. Had this command not been there, Sikhism might have experienced a brilliant happening that equalled men and women in every respect by installing Mata Sundari as the next Guru.

The third Guru, Amar Das, composed several songs that elaborate the Sikh approach to women. A great emphasis has been laid on the faithfulness of a wife to her husband. The spouse is her ornament and beauty, both. If she is not true to him, there is no happiness for her, neither here nor hereafter.

"She who is devoid of virtue," says the third Guru, "and who is attached to a second lover, or is shared by two lovers, shall not find the season of love (*sawan*) sweet to her, for sweet is the virtue of fidelity and sweeter is her steadfast love for one man." At another place he says, "The beloved God adorns good wives." It is the same idea that has been expressed in the *Mahabharata, Karpur Manjari, Markandeya Purana* and almost every important scripture of India. It has been long trusted as the views of rishis, who were both men and women, revered for their disinterested views. The great scholar of the Indian lore, philosophy, aesthetics, religion, art and culture, Ananda Coomaraswamy has elaborated this common aspect of all Indian religions in his essay *'Status of Indian woman'* included in his brilliant book on Indian culture *"The Dance Of Siva."*

The Gurus' view is that woman is a store of several mysterious powers of Nature. That is why she has been called since ancient times *Shakti* (power). Her mysterious powers unfold at the time of her first lovemaking. In her first lovemaking she offers her mysterious powers to her first lover and unites her entire being with him. Man does not have those mysterious powers of Nature. Those powers are as intriguing as mysterious. If she loves two men, her mysterious powers get confused - with whom to unite? Confusion enrages them and they turn hostile to the woman. They confuse the energies of her mind and body with both lust and self-punishment for it. She turns into a chimera to herself and an enigma to others. That is why all wise men in India advised women not to indulge in wantonness out of revenge or for any reason, even if her husband is lecherous. Wantonness adds to the evil karma of both, but woman gets doubly punished since it disturbs the very chemistry of her body. It makes her heart a cavern where unknown voices wail. It is all because Nature goes against a wanton woman. It is not male chauvinism, as some sexologists, incapable of seeing beyond the haze of sex, say.

Like the rishis, the Gurus had full faith that woman can attain Nirvana by merely loving and serving her husband. However, her love and service should be born of knowledge. It should be voluntary. They condemn the husband who forces obedience and service on her. There was a vast difference between the invaders' and the Indian views on this issue. While the Indians said obedience has to come from freewill and knowledge, the invaders claimed that their religion allowed them to use force against women and force them in every possible way to obey their husbands. The rulers were prejudiced against the Gurus for their prohibition of force against women. They feared that the Gurus' view was encouraging lasciviousness in Mogul women. They had concocted a charge against Guru Teg Bahadur based on this fear.

The Gurus exploded the myth that the Indians had a tragic and hopeless destiny that the invader-rulers had popularised among the Indians. The invaders had popularised the myth that the Indians had lost India to them because God had sealed their destiny, as they did not believe in God, and were infidel. The Gurus said that there could not be a lie that was more naked than this. They told the invaders that millenniums ago, when the invaders were lost in their wild, primitive and God forsaken dreams, the Indians had been worshipping God and living entirely by God's wisdom and will. This had annoyed the Mogul rulers and they had singled out the Sikhs for torture. They perpetrated all kinds of cruelties on them to break their spirit but could not. It was because they had the best specimen of humanity as their leaders during the years of their struggle against the Moguls.

The Moguls said that the life of the Indians had to be tragic for being infidel, and after death they were destined to go to the deepest hell from which there was no hope of redemption. The Gurus told them plainly that it was not worthy of being human to become the spokesmen of God. They asked the rulers to stop the persecution of the Indians. The rulers had branded the speech of the pundits—who had only challenged their false propaganda—blasphemies against Islam. They had got them inhumanly tortured and killed. They had created an astonishing legal system in which Hinduism and other Indian religions could be abused in any manner, and their temples and idols could be destroyed in any numbers, with absolute impunity. But if they spoke in protest they were given death sentences that were executed horribly to create terror. The aim was to inhibit their free spirit. This policy had succeeded since many Hindus had lost the courage to protest. For several centuries the illiterate people were continually made to hear that they were infidel.

Guru Nanak was horrified to see that if a people were denied the freedom to protest against the lies that the rulers perpetrated against them they lost the will to live by truth. The life instinct was so strong that if a people were given to choose between living by truth and getting persecuted and killed, or living peacefully without telling the truth, they would choose the latter.

Nanak was horrified to see all tongues muted and inhibited against truth. None of the great men of medieval times – Jaidev (1170), Trilochan (1267), Namdev (1270), Ramananda (1299), Ravidas (1384), Kabir (1398), Surdas (1478) and Dhanna (1415) – had spoken of the evil that the invaders had piled on the Indian masses. They had diverted their attention from the contemporary horrors and had concentrated on singing only of the timeless God. It shows the intensity of the fear that had been created by the invaders to paralyse the wits of the people. Even the outspoken Kabir did not have the courage to condemn the royal lies. He criticized superficially certain aspects in a light vein that only entertained.

Guru Nanak was born in 1469 AD and Guru Gobind Singh in 1666 AD. In between these 197 years were born the ten Gurus who stood for the freedom of speech. Their freedom was confined to defence against the royalties' lies. They never attacked the royal faith in retaliation. Yet they had to pay a very heavy price for this courage. Two of the Gurus were beheaded. All the evils that come with the denial of the freedom of speech had seeped in the Indian character. The four obscenities discussed earlier had taken firm roots in their character. The present rush in India to imitate only the obscenities of Western life in the name of the freedom of speech is only a pretext to give expression to the obscenities that seeped in their character during the medieval times. They are copying the worst part of the Western Culture now when it is on the decline. It is an irony that when the Western culture was at its zenith the Indians detested it, and now when it does not want to be copied the Indians are copying it. The Indians of the ancient epics are no more there, and abuse by perverted invaders for nearly a millennium has confused their character by the constant provocation they provided during their theocratic rule. Even the Indians are not aware of the degrading changes that have taken place in their character, because the perversion has sunk in their unconscious. This decadence can be helpful in developing a greater character than our ancient ancestors only if our souls resolve to get reborn of our unconscious. Merely expressing them will never drain them out.

According to yoga, every human has a finite personality (*sthula sharira*) and an infinite personality (*sukshama sharira*). The two personalities were turned hostile to each other, by the cunning mechanism of the invaders. This hostility is at the root of the corruption and obscenity that have erupted after independence. The cure lies in *Atmayagya* and *Viniyoga*. These two ancient disciplines can cure us of this hostility between our finite and infinite personalities, and of the personality split caused by this hostility.

The finite personality consists of the body, its habits, character, social and financial status, age, colour, height etc. The infinite personality consists of the following four constituents: (1) The serpent energy sleeping at the root of the spine, called *kundalini*, that looks infinite due to its many times greater energy than our physical energy. What the medieval yogis called its awakening was nothing more than its extreme intolerance of the sexuality of our finite personality. *Kundalini* has turned only into a moral police made of the nine-tenth of the energy spared after the creation of the finite personality. The Gurus were aware of its hostility to even normal sexual activity. It was because the invaders believed in the theory of the original sin that holds sexuality responsible for the expulsion of Adam and Eve from the heaven. They had forced their conscious intolerance of sex on the Indians too. Therefore the Gurus never asked for the awakening of *Kundalini*, and questioned the medieval yogis who were devoting a great part of their time to awakening it.

All the energy released at the time of the creation of the body does not get utilized, and nearly nine tenth is left out. Many yogis saw it in their vision as a serpent lying coiled at the root of the spine. This energy angered by what it calls the sexual excesses of our body rushes to report to its Lord, the mind, that has been personified as a miniature of Mahadev (God) lodged in every individual as his mind. (2) The mind, a superstructure of mental energies, over and above the brain too looks infinite. It feels like an infinitely vast and deep cloud of mental energies. It is too simple and unsuspecting and believes in the report of the *kundalini*. It punishes the body by making the society hostile to the individual. It is his own mind that unsettles the finite personality of an individual. Foreign invasions only carry out the sentence that the collective mind of a people passes against themselves. The sentence that the mind passes are always unjust, since they are passed on the reporting of *kundalini* that is a puritan and that has no sympathy for the body and its normal pleasures.

The Gurus wanted to free the Indians of the hostility between their finite and infinite personalities. This hostility was the result of the four obscenities that a theocratic rule had forced down the Indian personality. Therefore the Gurus stood for a married life, and said that it was perfectly compatible with the quest of Nirvana. (3) The mistaken union of the *Kundalini* and the mind creates a fate for the body that traps it in a compulsive karmic play of the four obscenities. It makes the society unsympathetic and aggressive to every individual who wants to live a normal and uninhibited life. It makes the individual a compulsive betrayer of everybody, as if to compensate the unjust punishment that society gives him. It also turns the individual mean about money and property. The body feels for its money and property as if they are its limbs. The body turns too lazy to love any other body. Its love veers round some obscene nude born of some experience or sheer fantasy. (4) The society develops the same hostile attitude to the individual that his mind has toward it.

It is a tragic play staged by the infinite personality of an individual for the entertainment of the soul. Tragically enough it uses his finite personality as the hero, whom it destroys, even as a tornado throws to shreds a town. It is inhuman and it is in our hands to turn it human through *Atmayagya* and *Viniyoga*. If the soul sacrifices itself to this play, instead of getting entertained, and gets reborn of it, all these four negative powers of the infinite personality turn into positive powers that help the finite personality to go forward toward a better future. It is in man's hand to have the fate he likes – this is the ultimate message of the Gurus. They were optimists and they never trusted bleak premonitions. They had perhaps envisioned this cruel play of the infinite personality of man that ruins his finite personality so callously, only because of a medieval archetype. The Gurus emphasized the knowledge of history, philosophy, music and warfare. These four disciplines when properly exercised can pull man out of this archetype.

Western Culture in its modern decadent form considers pursuit of abnormal and outrageous 'sexuality' holier than God. It is more concerned about feeding its perversions out of fear than out of any knowledge. It fears that if men and women did not satisfy its perversions they will lose sanity and become home to many mysterious diseases. This fear has come to India too, through their imitation of the decadent phase of the Western Culture. Modern man is a hedonist who parades himself in nude to prove that he is an intellectual. Little does he know that a dying star sucks in its black hole all the weaker stars around it. The Western Culture has lost its vitality ever since it took seriously the Faustian gospel: "No progress is possible without the collaboration of the devil." (Goethe: Faust). Freud turned this gospel into a scientific truth by giving it psychological depth. It is now the gospel of weak sexologists who are a class of people that could not come out of the reeling shock administered by Freud.

Attempts have been made to show that women have been given a subservient role in the Sikh scriptures. Such critics do not understand what the Gurus meant when they said that the highest good of a woman lies in service to her husband. Further analysis will show that it is a very narrow reading and it rather totally distorts the spirit of the Granth Sahib.

We should read the above guidance to women with the following utterance of Guru Amar Das:

> There is one and only one male
> In this beautiful world that God made

All those called males and females
All alike are his loving females.

The refrain of the Sikh hymns referring to woman is mostly of a spiritual nature. It would appear that the word 'woman' in them mostly stands for the human soul and the word 'husband' for God. Several songs in the *Granth Sahib* show that the same discipline has been prescribed for man and woman.

A small probe will show that the Gurus have prescribed three loves for a woman: one is God; another is Guru; and the third, her earthly husband. The three loves can be integrated through *Viniyoga*. She has to love a husband who reconciles her with the Guru and the Lord. If it is not so she is not obliged to waste her life for the worldly love of an earthly husband. It would be wrong to infer that a woman attains salvation by sincerely serving a worldly husband. Unless her love for him is reconciled with her love for God and the Guru, she cannot experience bliss. Not only that man goes astray by indulging in the snares of a worldly wife, a woman too gets lost by serving the thoughtless whims of a worldly and shallow husband. Where all are females it would be pointless to subject half of them to the other half. Even men are females. The souls of men and women, both, have equally to anoint with noble thoughts and love and dress up beautifully in the sweet shyness of a virgin, putting on the jewels of virtues to woo the Eternal Spouse. They are all His beloved. It is within this larger objective that an earthly pair has to adjust itself. If their mutual love is taking them away from the Divine spark, they have to abandon it without a second thought, for it must be the creation of *Maya*. One has to distinguish between the many kinds of love. Love is a many splendoured thing, but only when it unites with the *Waheguru*.

At another place, the scripture says, "She who serveth the Male and destroyeth *haumey* (ego), verily, by the word, becomes a male herself."

This line is of great significance. It opens another side of the issue. The female is to flower into the male. This is again not a biological metamorphosis. The language of the holy book has the soul as its object, not the body. The soul given to man is female. By its ardent love for God, it partakes His nature. From passive, it becomes active. It participates in His functions, and, as Guru Gobind Singh did, it even goes to help the Lord in re-writing the destiny of the people. The sorrowful tear tainted story of the oppressed Indian was transformed into a saga of glory and valour because some of them had become male by the fire of their virgin souls.

The ardent love of Guru Amar Das for God, the only male, went so far that he did not hesitate to address himself and others as if they were all females:

> "Come my sisters, I sing my secret to you
> I am a sacrifice to the Great Sister, The Guru
> He taught me to find my Beloved, and the art to woo."

Sikhism is spirituality that has conquered its pride to recognize the delicate emotion of love as its finest flowering. There is no compromise on this issue at any stage. It is indeed a miracle that they could make even spirit so earthly and concrete that, instead of taking them to the void, it taught them to dwell on earth and make it a little capital of God with no other power but the emotion of love. There is no difference between true spiritual love and the emotion of love in Sikhism. The Gurus showed that spiritual love that conquers its pride of being spiritual is the same as the delicate emotion of love.

Men and women as biological entities have their rightful place in the Sikh religion. However, it is the soul within that alone matters and it is feminine in both. The only task before both is to come closer in such a way that the pride of each gets cast off as tattered and outworn clothes. As it happens, a new soul awakens in both, and both attain a state of union where, to use an Upanishadic phrase, so often used by the incomparable doyen Ananda Coomaraswamy, 'each is both'.

"They are not husband and wife," says Guru Amar Das, "who live together and share their lives. Rather, they are husband and wife who have one soul in two bodies, and are one in all states, sitting, sleeping, or away from each other."

Sikhism accepts the phenomena of total merger, total union between man and woman. This is possible only by the awakening of a subtler soul in both, before which their individual souls feel like outworn clothes. This subtler soul is the Loving Soul, the Wonderful Soul, which unites with the *Waheguru*. When it awakens the attainments of the individual souls look like products of ignorance and their individualities mere pride. A couple's united ascent has been thus described as a process of the many returning to the One.

Man and woman have to awaken the love that pierces them through and through and kills their narrow selves. "Only those," says the *Granth Sahib*, "that while alive are dead, understand God's ways. Nanak, who dies such death lives for ever."

It is this kind of death to which the magnificent Buddha refers when he talks of the 'dying out of the lamp.' It is this philosophic death to which *Tirthankara* Adinath and several *Nirgrantha munis* have made repeated references. It is the same that was known to Plato and Christ. Sikhism has accepted the word Nirvana in its traditional meaning. It is to them the same as it was to Vardhaman Mahavir and Gautam the Buddha. It is dying out. But dying out of what? Of *haumey*, the ego, the narrow self. It is only after the death of this narrow self that the true self awakens. The same light that first appears shrouded and dubious reappears in the brave heart as a clear and luminescent flame. For this, one has to shake hands with death. It is not death of the body. It is death of the psyche, and finally of the soul, a much difficult thing. It is only the fearless that can attain it. A man and woman dead in this manner, re-awaken as a single luminescent flame of love. This flame partakes the joys of the *Waheguru*. It is this that a true Sikh is to aim at.

The attempt everywhere of the Gurus is to inspire the ordinary details of life with a new meaning. Until truth shines and beauty illuminates, man cannot be free of the bewitching play of shadows.

I would dwell upon one more point in this context. Guru Amar Das says:

"She fears and she loves
Her ornaments are fear and love
The Guru favours her
And God lives with her."

Apparently it should be puzzling to read the advocacy of fear in a creed totally devoted to fearlessness. But on seeing a little deeper, the anomaly fades. Fear is the inheritance of man from an insecure and wild ancestor. This gift comes to him unwanted. Woman is more susceptible to it because of several dangers to her body and beauty. Her very being is animated with fear, for though man has learnt to clothe himself and to live in palaces, his original appetites have the same savage bluntness, and woman, for the crowds, has not risen to be anything more than a feast or recreation. The Gurus have only enlarged upon this available fact. It was not their tradition to ignore facts. Fear was a gift to man. How to get rid of it? By making an offering of it to the Lord Himself. From Him all passions spring. The passion of fear had sprung from Him on the demands of the primitive men, our ancestors. The Gurus taught women the art to offer fear to God. To fear Him is the same as to get rid of fear. He is illumination and wisdom. He is kindness and Love. Such a Being can never exploit another's fear. Better we direct this faculty of fear to Him. If we do not do so, fear shall still be there, sleeping in the unconscious recesses of our soul. Any tyrant will reawaken it to suit his purpose. The passion of fear is not to be left alone. Anything that we have is bound to express itself, whether we will it or not. Better we will it, and will it with knowledge, to offer it back to God, for thus we make it subservient to wisdom. Its destructiveness gets checked. When offered back to God it disappears forever. Whatever undesirable emotion we offer to God goes to *Yogmaya*, God's mysterious power that controls *Maya*.

To fear God is a necessary step of spirituality. It is a process of taking rebirth from the agonizing past. It is coming out of the womb of time. It is an entry from time to the timeless, from *Kaal* to *Akaal*.

It is a very practical and sure approach to utilize our weakest points in a way that they too form our strength. The carvers of human destiny have always chosen this course. Fear is the weakest side of man. It does not disappear by merely resolving not to fear. All present day cruelties and cynicism are nothing but mutilations of fear on being suppressed. Modern psychology has established that the lib movement among women, the new wave of black magic, the hysterical modern music and forms of amusement, and the four above discussed obscenities of our society are all expressions of some deep-seated fear. All our sciences, civilizations and humanities have not been able to remove the pangs of fear. We do not wear it openly, for it looks undignified, and therefore it lives in us in concealment and has developed the art of disguise to an amazing extent. No wonder that the Gurus did not teach the suppression of fear, as was the common custom. On the contrary, they asked to expose the fears constructively and harmlessly. For this they taught to fear God actively, with the belief that it was the surest way of overcoming fear.

The mute emotions of a dishonoured and enslaved woman often create unconscious feelings of shame and humiliation in her child. This creates the 'pathos of distance' between the mother and the child. Her cheerfulness and sorrow both arouse contempt in him, since he suspects them to be connected with her master. As he grows the estrangement starts expressing itself in frequent outburst of anger on both sides. Communication breaks down, and the son develops a preference for dubious ways of earning money and indulging in pleasures. This change occurs in his spiritual life too.

This state of affairs had come to be between Mother India and her brave sons before the advent of the Gurus. India had been a cultural unit for thousands of years. But those brave sons in the times of the first Guru had forgotten the face of Mother India out of shame. The Rajputs in Rajasthan, the Punjabis in Punjab, the Marathas, and the southern people had all lost the ingrained sense of belonging to the same Mother. Mother India was no longer the pious goddess whose hair spread over the white neck of the Himalayas and whose lotus feet did the ocean wash. She had been dishonoured and enslaved. All her glory was shed. Therefore, her sons preferred to be called by the names of their provinces or cities, rather than as Indians. This break of communion between Mother India and her sons had its worst effect on women. They carried the tales of the woes and joys of Mother India in their songs and muted emotions, finding no response in man. It seemed as if men, in their pride, did not want to remember their dishonoured Mother.

This has been the strongest reason why in medieval India communion had broken down between the women and the brave, virtuous and learned men. Women were being considered the companions of the courtiers, the sex-obsessed and the foolish men, who had no higher goals to pursue. It was the same woman who had been a companion of man in his highest pursuits in ancient days. She was such an inseparable companion in all the higher pursuits of man that a *Yagya* by Raja Ram without Sita was considered incomplete. Yagyavalka had made his two wives, Maitreyi and Gargi, constant companions of his philosophic adventures. Pandavas had made Kunti and Draupadi regular counsellors in dharma and their wars against Kauravas. The best philosophers and rishis and warriors had been often guided or inspired by women. Such was the faith in woman and her virtuous being that Ram staked everything to protect the honour of his wife and the brave Pandavas forgot everything except the vow to revenge the little act of dishonour that had been done to their wife. They accepted Draupadi's provocative speech to avenge the wrong done to her by Duhshashan as a wise piece coming from woman's nature.

During the medieval days no such faith was left in women. Thousands of them had started burning themselves to prove their chastity after the death of their husbands, and to win back a place of honour in the memory of their people. The greatest yogi of his time Gorakh Nath said woman was a tigress who should be kept away. Many yogis learnt the art to keep her away from the wisest animal elephant that keeps the tigress away. Whether Shankaracharya, the greatest intellectual of medieval days, had denounced them outright or not, people believed that he did. Woman came to be considered as a positive hindrance in higher pursuits. The philosophers, poets and warriors were no longer interested in the freedom of India. They had left Mother India, and as a natural sequence, also women, to their confusion, sorrow and folly. They were in search of a heaven away from them. Their philosophy therefore grew wings and became more and more abstract. The fine synthesis of this world with the other was lost. The warriors did not think of the honour of India. They were busy with petty quarrels and personal glorification. The aggressive spirit of Chandragupt Maurya, King Kharvel of Kalinga and the Guptas was lost. Clever men were stealing away their individual fates from the doomed destiny of Mother India. They did not want to share her dishonour. They did not want to fight and strive for the restoration of her honour, for the whole affair seemed very humiliating. The best among them became, therefore, impractical dreamers, while the ordinary men, oblivious of the huge task, got busy with the worries, ordeals and pleasures of life.

The Gurus broke this torpor. They came forward to share the grief and dishonour of Mother India. In the ordinary events they saw the glow of her tears and sufferings. With William Blake they could have said:

'The caterpillar on the leaf,
Reminds me of my mother's grief.'

The tormented soul of Nanak recorded the woes of his time. His heart was outraged at the shame heaped and the cruelties perpetrated. The Gurus refused to consider women as hindrances in the spiritual journey. Like ancient rishis, from Nanak onwards, they lived with their women, sharing their lives and enriching their vision with the world of women close to them. Spiritual pride was not their main. They pleaded for woman since woman was Mother India and the Indian people to them. They did everything possible for her freedom and honour. Guru Tegh Bahadur did everything to persuade Aurangzeb to give the Indian people their rightful freedom of faith back. Finally when nothing worked, they brandished the steel and made a clarion call to the sons of India to snatch freedom from cruel hands, and if some cruel destiny created by the enemy blocked their way, to roll its head from the Himalayas into the

Chenab to roll onwards to the Arabian Sea. There was no shame for them to fight for Mother India and to show that they belonged to a dishonoured Mother.

Power

The concept of power in Sikhism has a very unique spiritual significance. It was not only a matter of wielding weapons. The concept of power grew very slowly. It was invented by necessity. The fifth Guru asked the Sikhs to be powerful. Their determination to use power to regain the freedom of India remained rudimentary for a long time. It was only the tenth Guru who gave the institution of *khanda di pahul* or baptism of the sword.

After Shankaracharya, the Hindu mind had started undervaluing all mundane things. They had misinterpreted the profound philosophy of *Maya*, propounded by Shankaracharya. It was too subtle to be understood by average thinkers. Ved Vyas and Valmiki had taught the people to give due importance to physical strength. But somehow they believed that Shankaracharya's philosophy had taught them that power was illusion. It was a case of misunderstanding. Due to this misunderstanding the Absolute got relegated to pure abstraction. God had been disconnected from life – so intense was their fervour for purity, and disgust for their profaned life. The Gurus told them an entirely different thing. They said that physical power and weapons were spirituality in earthly guise. They kept only one condition. It was that power would be used to further the cause of love. No violence for the sake of violence, he warned the Sikh. No emulation of the Moguls frenzied by power. This was the same as the spiritualization of power. Strength was a manifestation of God, which had been given up by noble men only because it had been abused by the wicked people for inhuman objectives. The teaching of the Gurus was that it was further detrimental to human interests to give up power. They said, bring power back to the service of humanity. We have not to surrender the means only because they have been abused. We have not to give up utensils only because some people had taken wine in them. The road of retreat is not for the Sikh, said the Gurus. The Gurus baptized the sword in the name of God.

Power is not only a political means to the Gurus. The fervour with which Guru Gobind Singh has composed his hymns in praise of *Chandi* and *Bhagauti* shows that he is definitely seeing some spiritual meaning in power. If we realize that the Sikhs began with the spiritual quest, and only conditions compelled them to take to arms, it will become easier to realize that power is dark (*tamasik*) spirituality to them. They have rejected the medieval Hindu thesis that power was the opposite of spirituality. In the true monistic tradition they have maintained that it is spirituality itself that on being hit by wickedness turns into power *(Shakti)*. Power is God turned matter. Matter craving for its original form i.e. God turned into (*Shakti*) i.e., Power.

Psychological researches of the twentieth century have more than established the transformation of physical and psychological energies into each other. Ayurveda, the medical system of India, has been saying since ancient times that the spiritual and psychological and physical ailments have their roots in the provoked unfolding of the soul due to inhuman and subhuman behaviour of some people in society. Ayurveda thus establishes the intrinsic unity between the three energies of man.

The Gurus saw that the invaders had evolved their spiritual seed into forces of plunder, terror, cold hatred, cruelty and hardened egoism. They did not run away from this abuse of the spiritual seed. They said wrongly unfolded spirituality could be returned into the spiritual seed wherefrom it had to be unfolded again. This time the unfolding should not be in reaction. It should not be born of provocation. It should be born of thinking truthfully. It should be born of a cool and calculated spiritual deliberation. It should not be born of fantastic and unrealistic ideas like the idea of eradication of evil. 'Instead of such negative objectives choose the positive objective of fighting for love. We shall fight a comprehensive battle that will serve humanity, instead of terrorizing it.' The idea of self-sacrifice of the soul struck them as the only way to do this. It was not a matter only of checking their own spiritual seed from unfolding into corrupt forces. The whole nation was rocking on turbulent tossing on such waves. The spiritual seed of millions of men had taken to wrong flowering, due to unconscious imitation of the wrong flowering of the spiritual seed of the invaders. This malady had to be checked and reversed; otherwise this error would become part of the personality of the Indians too. If the spiritual seed got corrupted the spiritual enlightenment of the people would turn into spiritual darkness. India would then lose her culture that had taken several millenniums to build into a life force – a life force that was a spontaneous physical parallel of India's spiritual attainment. The Gurus said that India's life force was unique: it was spiritual without imitating spirituality. It had taken the great Indians millenniums of living spiritually, intellectually and emotionally by truth, beauty and good to grow spiritual qualities as impulses in their life force. The life force being common in all human beings, even ordinary Indians had inherited the highest human values through the common life force.

Guru Arjun and Guru Teg Bahadur had decided to sacrifice their lives after long and cool deliberation. Their sacrifices were exercises of *Viniyoga* that could make spiritual power appear in the form of the fragile sprouts of life. Those fragile sprouts of life had the character of the immortal soul though they were mortal. Both knew that their sacrifices would open new windows in the people's psyche that had been shut by fear and tyranny. Their aim was to break the inhuman pattern that the spiritual and psychological powers of the enemy had taken. The sprouts of life that had the character of the soul provided a vision of life to the people that equalled immortality. It was to work as the ideal that the spiritual and psychological powers could serve. It remained beyond the grasp of all the invaders of India, because it could not be known without practicing it. The catch was that any outsider who had practiced it once could not leave it. After knowing it no man could stoop low enough to exploit it for perverted pleasure. Its ability to synchronize the mortal life and the immortal soul was too valuable, and he could not leave it for any mundane gain.

The Sikh Gurus provided a catharsis to the Indians in medieval days. It was unparalleled since it purged their muscles, blood and minds of the hellish life force that had come riding the invaders. The invaders were riding horses and the hellish life force was riding the invaders as if they were its horses. That was why they acted like fiends even after victory, as if their aim was not only victory but also mutilation of humanity. The invaders had hoped to transfer the riders that were riding their selves—the hellish life force—to the selves of the Indians. The invaders had learnt from long association with hellish forces that if they only do to the Indians what the hellish life force had done to them the Indians will go mad with anger. They also knew anger to be a great conductor of evil. They hoped that the hellish life force would then find the freshly angered Indians very attractive for riding and would shift their seats to the selves of the Indians.

But the invaders' dream of transferring those hellish creatures to Indian bodies could not be realized. They remained riding the back of the invaders all their lives. The invaders did not know that even hell had its rules, and one of its rules was that its hellish creatures liked to keep the company of those who had invoked them The Gurus knew this rule. They asked the Indians not to do four things to the invaders. 'Do not hate them. Do not be angry with them. Do not love them, only sacrifice your souls to them. Do not be surprised if they do inhuman things to you for they can do nothing more than the macaberesque.' The Gurus taught their countrymen and women not to give up the ancient vow taken by our ancestors to fight only in the company of truth, God and love. They said that the enemy had grafted spirituality from outside in his soul. Spirituality has not grown from his soul. Therefore do not take his spirituality seriously.

Viniyoga

Unconditional love has been the goal in India of all great men and women. It has been the goal not only of lovers, but of men of action too, like the warriors, Arjun, Ram and Guru Gobind Singh.

It might sound to some readers too idealistic a goal, practically impossible to attain.

Let us examine a bit, whether it is practicable or not. Fear has been the opposite that has often chilled the ardour even of lovers. Let us see how fear does it and whether it can be defeated by love alone, without the help of any other power.

Love is extremely sensitive to pain, not only to one's own, but of others' too. If the lover does not fear dying, the tyrant believes, kidnapping his beloved will pluck all courage out of him. Let us imagine a beloved who loves her lover truly, who does not intend to love anyone else, yet who does not want to die for love, because she is too innocent to comprehend how dying can serve loving. We begin the story after she has been kidnapped and forcibly married to the villain.

She gives up loving her true lover externally to avoid the sword of the tyrant husband. Though her love is true she does not have the experience to realize how her dying can fulfil her love. She wants to live and still hopes to meet her lover some day by chance or luck. She is optimistic that everything will again be as it used to be, and the bleak facts will fade out from life. She still loves her true lover in her heart. Her love has transported her consciousness to the dreamy world of love so much that the sad fact of her forced marriage has become unreal in her consciousness. Constant torture to make her accept the cruel facts of her life as reality break her one day, and she gets filled by the incongruity of being the wife of another man while she loves her original lover. It causes shame to her. Shame is a form of fear in her case since she has not committed any sin. Only circumstances created by others have made her situation sinful. All fear is ultimately the fear of losing what is dearest to one. The beloved under examination now faces two fears – (1) the fear of being killed by her enraged husband, or of being stoned to death by the community; (2) and, if they are forgiving, the fear of being looked upon as a women who is devoid of honour.

A person facing these two fears, however strong, cannot retain sanity, since the power of the heart and the mind are limited. (3)

Her mind loses concentration due to these two fears constantly hanging over her. Fear multiples in her case. In addition to the above two fears, she develops the fear of losing sanity. Loss of sanity makes love itself meaningless, since an insane person cannot experience the beauty, pain and joy of love. Without these experiences, the pursuit of love becomes senseless. (4) The will power devoted to love of such a person dissipates with the fear of insanity and goes wild. Will power loses its concentration and direction. (5) The result of this fourfold attack of fear shakes her nerves, and fills them with such cold winds as leave no fire of love alive. It does not leave even some amber of love to smoulder, burn or smoke without flame.

The tyrants have been sure of success against the strongest lovers, because of having these five fears at their service, which seem to be strong enough to extinguish love.

The Gurus practiced *Viniyoga,* which all true lovers of India had been practicing since times immemorial. The minds, hearts and nervous systems of those who practice *Viniyoga* do not waste their powers over resisting fears. They rather resort to the opposite of resistance. They welcome fears and leave them to the soul. The soul in *Viniyoga* sacrifices itself to the fears aggressively, with the objective to get reborn of them. The soul does not let fears reach the faculties of the mind and the body. It intercepts fears and, instead of combating, sacrifices itself to them. To make fears the very mother that gives the soul rebirth is to overcome fears. Fears then turn into the terrible mother of the soul. After giving rebirth to the soul the terrible mother starts looking fondly at the soul as its own child. Instead of frustrating, it starts advancing the cause of the soul.

This is the path of aggressive self-sacrifice that had been taken by the Sikh Gurus, the Buddha, the rishis and the *Tirthankaras.* This is the path to immortal love, absolute love (*Kevalprem),* and unconditional love. *Viniyoga* is turning fear meaningless and unproductive. It results in the re-assimilation of the negative power of fear in *nothing* from which it had sprung. It leaves the tyrant powerless against love. He can no longer frighten the lover. *Viniyoga* turns the very tide of fear toward the tyrant. The tide of fear that had been directed toward the lover now turns to frighten and derange the tyrant. It happened so in the case of Aurangzeb. When the fears raised by Aurangzeb to extinguish the Guru's love, honour and life failed to frighten the Guru, and the Guru sacrificed his life quietly without fear or fanfare, the tide of fear turned to its source - the Emperor Aurangzeb. For long hours of days and nights he would keep lying in delirium, raving like a mad man and confessing his bigotry and crimes time and again.

Viniyoga is not obstinate, determined and adamant loving. The lover practicing *Viniyoga* does not ignore the hostile attitude of those who hate love. He is only careful that his emotion of tender love does not get affected with hatred. For it his soul takes all the hatred on itself. He keeps the hatred of those that hate his love and his love as two separate powers, and his soul sacrifices itself to both. In spite of the qualitative distinction between love and hatred, his soul looks at both the emotions equally. Both belong to the category of emotions. Emotion is their common point. The lover emphasizes only this common point. He only remains aware of their difference without emphasizing it. When the soul does not attach any sentimental value to love, the tender emotion of love loses all its pride. *Viniyoga* snaps the relationship of cause and effect that had been existing between his love and their hatred. By losing pride love intensifies and turns into the unconditional love of the soul. It turns into something like the light of the sun that does not get affected whether you worship it or spit at it. The aim of Guru Teg Bahadur while practicing *Viniyoga* was not to convert Aurangzeb's heart from hatred to love. He knew Aurangzeb was adamant on hating him fanatically. The Guru was leaving now everything to *Waheguru* - his own unconditional love and the hatred of Aurangzeb. The practitioner of *Viniyoga* knows that God is only Love. The emotion of hatred comes from *nothing*. Hatred does not belong to God. It is a power that comes to man's soul due to the soul's power of ignorance. Ignorance and *nothing* combine to create hatred. The principle *ex nihilo nihil fit* means 'nothing comes out of nothing'. Hatred is 'nothing' that comes out of *nothing*.

The play between human ignorance and *nothing* is not a subject that man should pursue, since the more a soul knows it, the more it becomes a private reality to that soul. This privatisation of reality gradually isolates and takes one away from God into labyrinths that are illusory creations of ignorance and *nothing* but look real to the deluded soul. The tyrant's deluded soul goes away from God, no matter whether it takes the name of God five times a day or ten. The Guru by developing his love into unconditional love had detached it from the hatred that Aurangzeb's mind was offering him. He had snapped the link of cause and effect between the two. The Guru's aim was fulfilled, whether he lived or had to sacrifice his life since his love had transformed from conditional to unconditional. In *Viniyoga* the soul, the mind, the heart, the nervous system or any part of the personality of the lover does not fight fear. While all other parts of the lover remain passive, his soul aggressively sacrifices itself to fear.

The soul does not attack fear for whatever the soul attacks gets promoted and becomes a spiritual power. Since the soul is immortal, whatever it tries to annihilate, quite contrarily, turns immortal. It is something like all things exposed to nuclear emission become radioactive. Instead of attacking, the soul that practices *Viniyoga* sacrifices itself to the power that opposes it. Guru Teg Bahadur took a practical step to liquidate the opposition. His soul, instead of deciding itself who of the two was right, he or Aurangzeb, left the decision to God. His soul did this by sacrificing itself to both his love and the hatred of Aurangzeb, as two emotions, without attaching any adjective to either. He left the decision to God knowing that God never supports hatred. He involved God in his affair by sacrificing his soul. Whoever sacrifices his soul involves God in his affair – it is a spiritual law that few know.

God does not hate, Guru Teg Bahadur's love got the power of God and did the miracle. In a few years the emperor was shattered. He wrote to his son Azam, "I myself am forlorn and destitute, and misery is my ultimate lot.' To another son he writes, "I know not to what punishment I shall be doomed."

The self-sacrifice of the soul calls for no elaborate practice. It needs no ritual or technicality. It consists of a simple address by the individual to his soul to sacrifice itself to whatever thwarts its progress. The Indians were interested in using the purity and wisdom of the soul in daily life. The soul is bound by a Divine law to obey the individual whenever he asks it to sacrifice itself. This is enough for the seeker who wants to make a practical use of the soul. Sacrifice grants the soul entry inside the complex system of fears. This entry earns the right for the soul to command all the fears to make self-sacrifices to each other. If it is not done, fears unite and multiply.

The practitioners of *Viniyoga* do not argue with those who question the very existence of the soul. Such agnostics stop questioning once they experience the fruit of *Viniyoga*. *Viniyoga* is a simple cure to personality disorder. The seeker discovers the truth that the soul is the greatest power on earth. There is no way the fears can disobey the soul that has earned the right to enter them through self-sacrifice.

Multiplication of fears is also not to be dreaded. On multiplying the many fears get compelled by the power of *Viniyoga* to neutralize each other. Guru Gobind Singh epitomizes the practice of *Viniyoga* in the following song:

> Not mine, thy will may prevail O Lord of all Truth
> I seek your nature that abides by nothing but Truth
> My prayer is granted in your holy word that I hold
> 'Truth melts when love's soldier sacrifices his soul.'
> Your heart melts, love oozes out of Ultimate Truth!
> Lover's mortal fears dissolve in your Eternal Truth

Glossary

Atmayagya: *Atmayagya* is the ancient Indian way of overcoming the obstacles in life. The secret of this spiritual exercise lies in the truth that whatever physical, psychological or neural malady or obstacle my soul recognizes as a power working against the flowering of my personality turns spiritual, simply by getting recognition from my soul. On getting thus spiritualized it becomes nearly impossible to get rid of the obstacle, since the soul contaminates it with the radiation of its own infinity. As a result, though the obstacle is finite, and though it is within the power of the soul to liquidate it, the soul fails to liquidate the obstacle and gets puzzled and overpowered. There is no way known to man other than *Atmayagya* to get detached from the obstacle, and to merge it within Nothing from which it had grown to create a delusion of its infinity.

The only way to get rid of the obstacles – which are of two kinds, outer obstacles and inner delusions - is the soul's self sacrifice to them, and the soul's command to them to give it rebirth. These two actions of the soul are called *Atmayagya*. The soul loses nothing from its self-sacrifice, since it is immortal and cannot be consumed by whatever it sacrifices itself to. Rather self-sacrifice wins the authority for the soul to command the obstacles to give it rebirth. The obstacle turns docile only when it is forced through *Atmayagya* to perform this function of a mother of giving rebirth to the soul. This self-sacrifice invokes the infinite courage of the soul, and helps it to get rid of all the obstacles that are carried over from the soul's one incarnation to another, as karmic bonds.

Obstacles generally appear in groups of four. The soul, after sacrificing itself to all the four, commands them to make similar self-sacrifices unto each other. The seeker must utilize the spiritual law that makes it a categorical imperative for the obstacles to obey the command of that soul which sacrifices itself to them. When the four obstacles make self-sacrifices unto each other, they lose the power to bind the soul with their fetters. They get reduced to nothingness, and instead of binding they help the soul experience its infinite freedom.

Atmayagya keeps all the psychological obstacles and powers of one's personality within the psychological limits. It also keeps all its physical obstacles and powers within physical limits. The fascination of seeing these powers falsely magnified as spiritual powers is one of the greatest fetter that deprives the soul of its intrinsic freedom, that is also joy, knowledge, love, and liberation, all these and much more.

The rishis practiced *Atmayagya* constantly. It was an inevitable exercise for the soul that cared to remain awake and unpolluted. It was somehow forgotten during the medieval days of the slavery of India – i.e. during the dark night of India's soul. Sooner or later the Indians will again resume practicing *Atmayagya*, because there is no other remedy for their peculiar malady. As soon as the Indians will start practicing *Atmayagya*, halted and baffled humanity will find its path to true progress.

Atmayagya is of special significance to Sikhism, since Sikhism does not believe in suppressing or killing negative emotions, like anger, ignorance, sexual desire, pride and greed. The Gurus had warned their disciples against the error of taking their negative emotions always as misdeeds of the soul. In a country enslaved by some inimical foreign power, the negative emotions of the people generally turn out to be merely reactions of their souls to the excesses of the foreign rule and to the preponderance of evil in the inhuman behavior of the rulers with the local people. Suppression of these reactions would have deprived the Indian people of the signs of the deep harm that political slavery was causing them. The Gurus, therefore, taught their disciples to keep the reactions alive, and yet not to let them get spiritualized. The danger of getting them spiritualized was only too great, since the foreign rulers had spiritualized their own negative emotions. Furthermore, the foreign rulers valued their spiritualized negative emotions as if they were their special spiritual virtues. The Gurus, therefore, asked their disciples to sacrifice their souls to negative emotions so that they lived only as physical and psychological reactions and indicators of the evils of slavery. They were keen that their reactions to slavery did not get spiritualized.

Chakravyuha: *Chakravyuha* is the whirlpool created by the combined activity of more than one obstacle in the spiritual, neural and psychological energies. In modern psychology these whirlpools have been called complexes (for example the inferiority, complex, and the Oedipal complex).

Dharam-Khand: Sikh cosmology calls this world in which man gets born *Dharam-Khand.* Sikhism calls it *Dharam-Khand* since only dharma helps man to live in its worldly mire as a lotus. Those who do not live by dharma

soon find their wits soiled and their common sense lost. Their nervous
system suffers enormous stress, and life turns into a maze to them. Those
who live by dharma find *Kudarat* on their side. All the divine and natural
powers support them in countless visible and invisible ways.

Granth Sahib: *Granth Sahib* is the bible of the Sikhs. It is a collection of
songs, scripted and rendered into music (*ragas*) by the ten Gurus and a
few other liberated souls, irrespective of caste, creed or religion. The only
criterion for inclusion of a song in the holy *Granth Sahib* has been the
purity, spontaneity and the exquisite pain of true love.

Gyankhand: The universe is as much a psychological reality as a physical
reality, i.e. a material Thing-in-Itself. As a psychological reality,
experienced within by every body, it is an evolving reality for the seeker
and a static trap for the wayward person. The secret of evolving lies in the
pursuit of dharma. The nearest equivalent of dharma is the law of nature,
as it is enshrined in the heart of man. One who lives by dharma, though
lives in this world, yet finds his heart blossoming in a higher world. He
starts living mentally in the higher world called *Gyankhand*. Here his mind
develops naturally the power of meditation. He also develops a taste for
truth and true knowledge. This psychological transformation creates a
lasting atmosphere in the seeker's heart. It is an atmosphere that is
conducive to true knowledge of visible and invisible things. This
psychological world experienced by the seeker within his heart is called
Gyankhand. Here the unwavering mind of the seeker meditates on the
nature of Truth and Reality. His mind develops the beauty of brevity and
economizes on its energy, without fostering any external restraint.

It is in Gyankhand that the psychological self gets liberated of its
complexes. Here the psychological self gets merged in God, and the lover
becomes inseparable from her Eternal Beloved. At the same time, it is a
corresponding subtler world too, an outer reality, to which the soul of the
true seeker ascends. It is the union of the soul with *Waheguru*, but this
union is realized by the soul through the medium of the psychological
self, which is only its shadow. It is union through the mediation of Nature,
i.e. the four aspects of the *Antahakaran*, (i.e. the intellect, the I-ness, the
will to unite and the primordial mind/*chitta*). The *chitta* in its original
form has been described as *shanta*, *ghor* and *mudha*. These three qualities
of the *chitta* can be translated into English as tranquility, profundity without
content, and innocence, respectively. Only a *chitta* that has retained these
original qualities of it is capable of catching the glimpse of the *Waheguru*.
These original qualities of the *chitta* are often missing in the *chitta* of the

people of the world. It is because of the impact of the corrupted *chitta* of others. This impact raises the storm of acquired corrupt tendencies, ambitions and delusions that are called *chittavrittis*. Patanjali, known as the father of Yoga, had compiled the practices that the seekers of truth had been employing since times immemorial to eliminate the *chittavrittis* so that the *chitta* might regain its original state of tranquility, profundity without content and innocence. Regaining of this original state is inevitable for living a meaningful life, since it is only this original state of the *chitta* that can give the subtle feeling or sensation that timeless soul, alone, recognizes to be the indisputable proof of His existence. Like the laws of the physical universe that only the scientists discover, there are laws of the spiritual world that reveal themselves only to the true seekers of Truth. Without this subtle experience life turns into a rudderless ship, tossing on the dark waves of *chittavrittis*. How important the reversal of the *chitta* to its original state is can be gauged from the approach of Patanjali himself. In the opening line of his book, Patanjali says that this book only teaches the way to calm down *chittavrittis* (*chittavritti nirodhaye*).

It is yet not the direct union of the soul with God, a state of being in which the blossomed soul experiences the loving company of many blossomed souls like it, living in ecstatic union with God. The Sikh salvation grants total freedom to the liberated soul. It can come to this world of ours, the world of stocks and stones, to help souls struggling to get freed of the mire of suffering and frustration. It can also come to live in this world as a little known individual.

Haumey: *Haumey* is ego, the opposite of love, which captures all the faculties of the mind - the senses, the intellect, the I-ness and the *tanmatras*, i.e. the voice of the person, his scent, looks, his tastes and the feel of his touch - in its psychical net, like a fisherman. It can be likened to the ego and also the libido of Depth Pscychology. It is a blind force that catches consciousness, and all the mental and physical powers of the individual and imprisons them in a dark chamber that has no light. In that darkness, the mental powers captured unaware remain close to each other, almost blindly, throbbing helplessly and against their will. This behavior on the part of *haumey* breeds inner revolt inside each of these powers of the individual. They want to run away from each other, but the spider-web of *haumey* in which they are caught is too subtle and strong.

This distasteful and forced close proximity of an individual's powers, in a prison-house made of psychical forces, breeds wild passions. The encircling darkness born of *haumey* all around turns the individual against humanity. His faculties that were given to protect humanity start breeding pride, lust, violence, anger, greed and ignorant strife. The Gurus say that it is only love that can free the soul from this mad prison-house. If the soul in this unpleasant state practices love willfully, love imbues consciousness with its fragrance. The fragrance of love alone has the magical quality of setting this madhouse in order. Reason cannot restore order here, since many of the mental powers imprisoned by *haumey* do not respond to reason, and have little ability to grasp it.

The importance of love in Sikhism is due to its being the only ferry that can take across the madly raging waters of *Sansar* (Worldliness), and the clutches of *haumey,* straight to the home of the beloved *Waheguru.* No amount of wisdom charms the beloved Lord. It is only love, its simple yearning and pining, and its artless ache that the Lord finds irresistible, and that draw him to the loving soul.

Love is important in Sikhism for being the only panacea for man's immediate sickness - the sickness of being the prisoner of psychical darkness, due to the manipulations of *haumey.* Love is the only Pied Piper who can charm the maddening rats raised by the crafty *haumey* out of psychical darkness. Love charms the rats away and drowns them deep in the ocean of Nothing from which they had been raised by *haumey.*

The Sikh Gurus warn that either of the two - love or haumey - can live inside the heart and the mind. Both cannot. To love truly, is the condition of a sane life. Where love is not there haumey is. There insanity reigns. The life of such a being gets wasted as 'a native of the rocks' to use a phrase of Dr. Samuel Johnson.

Haumey is the ability to justify oneself, in spite of having a defective sense of justice and love. The Mogul rulers did not entirely lack the ideas of impartial justice and true love. Yet their ideals were tilted. They excused themselves for following the ideal of justice that was tilted in favor of their community. The Gurus differentiated between a king's inability to deliver absolute justice and his lack of will to deliver absolute justice. To give up the absolute ideal only because it was not practicable was not the path of the lovers of God. They said that even if the king lacked the intellectual and the spiritual honesty that were needed to comprehend absolute impartiality and justice, he should not make tilted justice the ideal of the State. The king should remain committed to attain alignment between his personal sense of justice and the divine sense of justice. This commitment, they thought, keeps the nation inspired by the right sense of justice. The Gurus said that if absolute justice was not practicable it was no excuse for the king to enshrine his personal, defective and tilted ideal as the ideal of the State. They were averse to a king's mixing the divine sense of absolute justice - which every ruler senses in spite of his inability to practice it - with his religious sense of justice. The Gurus thought that, in spite of being of divine origin, the religious sense of justice of a ruler was clouded and corrupted by the emotion of favoring the people of his own religion. The religious sense of justice is always muddled with emotions born of past history, and by bonds of a special fraternity with people of ones own religion. The courts - in the kingdom of a king who makes his religious sense of justice the State's ideal of justice - will be doing anything but justice. It will be an action similar to an astronomer's attempt to measure the distance of a star with a defective telescope - he would simply not be measuring the distance of that star. A king, who deviates from the absolute sense of justice in favor of his religious sense of justice, will be replacing love with *haumey* in the hearts of his people. He will be throwing their souls to the dogs of hell.

It explains the special significance the Gurus attached to the institution of "the *Sachche Badshah*" (the True King). Only that king had the right to rule whose sense of justice was aligned with the absolute sense of justice. A king whose sense of justice was aligned with his religious sense of justice will be, directly or indirectly, responsible for throwing away true lovers from all respectable, influential and powerful seats. He will be filling those seats with people who have *haumey*, not love in their souls. He will be filling even academic seats and seats that are meant for littérateurs, with people with tilted sense of Truth, Beauty and Good. The slight tilt of the king's ideal of justice is enough to corrupt the entire nation. Those who pursue *haumey* turn monstrous, in spite of being born human. In such times, the Gurus said, people should shift in their minds kingship to the True King, i.e. *Waheguru*. It would help them against the power of corruption that would grow from the person of the corrupt king and would corrupt the people due to its nationwide sweep. The most important thing in statecraft is not the ability to comprehend divine justice, but the will to comprehend and practice it. If the king has the will, Waheguru helps him to comprehend and practice it in many inexplicable ways.

Japji: *Japji* is a collection of hymns and devotional songs composed by the first Guru, Guru Nanak. It is the most sung book of the Sikhs. It is sung by the lay women and men, and the learned as well as those lost in searching their lover, *Nirankar*, the *Waheguru*.

Jina: Jina is another name of Tirthankaras.

Jivatma: Jivatma is the individual soul.

Karamkhand: The *Antahakaran* transcends the Gyan-Khanda after eliminating the chittavrittis and merging the psychological self in the *Waheguru*. It now ascends to *Karamkhand*. The *Karamkhand* is characterized by the growth of the inner eye that does not see the outer *Kudrat*, but sees *Kudrat* i.e. *Prakriti* i.e. Nature, at Her perfection. A new idyllic world opens in the heart of the seeker. He lives and acts in this very world that everybody calls the world, and yet he does not get disturbed by its daily sights of injustice, misery and suffering. It is not that he loses sympathy for the suffering people. Only he no longer experiences only grief and other negative aspects of the world. He does not get depressed by contemplating only suffering, cruelty and injustice in the world. His inner eye also sees the way to upturn the unjust and "the sorry scheme of things entire". He acquires the power to bring the world a little closer to truth and justice. The medieval world of India did not revert to its corrupt and fanatical form after the shock given to it by the ten Gurus.

The seeker whose heart rises to *Karamkhand* sees the outer world as it is, without adding any softening colors to it. His inner world of *Karamkhand*, which is full of sounding cataracts of joy, and floating, sparkling white clouds on an azure inner blue sky, is a dream world of perfection. It soothes his nerves. He neither sees illusions nor only the hard and ugly realities of life. This very world of worries and sorrows gets flooded for him with a new light that had never been on earth. The same old earth now fills him with tranquility and a soothing joy. He neither loses courage nor the will and energy to fill the lives of others with happiness and hope. It fires his spirit to bring his inner vision of the idyllic world to this world and to eliminate the corrupt spectacle and replace it with the idyllic world, as much as possible.

Kevalprem: *Kevalprem* is the emotional equivalent of the intellectual and spiritual ways of the flowering of the soul. It expresses total trust in the power of love, as fully as the phrase *Kevalgyan* expresses total trust in knowledge as the ultimate path of the soul to attain all that is attainable on earth and in heaven. *Kevalprem* brings happiness to earthly life and Nirvana to the life beyond. The Gurus were firm in their belief that mere knowledge was not enough to attain the ultimate bliss, i.e. Nirvana. Beyond knowledge lies the path of love, which transcends the distinction between knowledge and action. The tender emotion of love is the beginning of the spiritual life and also its end. The tender emotion of love has to be rekindled after the attainment of full knowledge, i.e. *Kevalgyan*. In the heart of one who has attained true knowledge, the tender emotion of love reappears spontaneously, after the attainment of knowledge. In its second appearance in the heart of a yogi it is no longer fragile, because it knows now that its tenderness is not weakness, but the source of both power and weakness. It is a tenderness that is beyond power. It is not devoid of power. It is rather the very source of power.

It is significant of Sikhism that it places a higher value on the moon, i.e. the symbol of love, as compared to the value it attaches to power whose symbol is the sun. In spite of using power to drive out the foreign rulers and to throw away the yoke of slavery, the Gurus were keen not to let the soul of the Sikhs get attached to power. They believed that attachment to power corrupted the soul. They asked the Sikhs to use power as free men without attaching their souls to it. It was possible to do this only for the soul that had realized *Kevalprem.* Love in all its original tenderness appears a second time in the soul only if it overcomes the lure of power.

The Sikh Gurus were not the only ones in emphasizing the need of rediscovering the tender emotion of love, after attaining knowledge. Ved Vyas, also, after attaining full flowering of his soul in knowledge, had devoted his life to the rediscovery of love. His soul attained bliss only after rediscovering love. His last work *"Srimad Bhagavatam"* testifies it. After writing seventeen *puranas* (the stores of India's ancient wisdom and mythology), the *Mahabharata* and the commentary on *Advaita Vedanta,* Vyas had found to his despair that knowledge had not illuminated his heart. It was only when his heart started pining for Krishna, like the innocent girls of *Vrindavan* that his heart blossomed like a lotus and got flooded with causeless joy. Only love could illumine the knowledge that he had already attained.

Khanda Di Pahul: *Khanda Di Pahul* was a sacrament that turned a saint into a soldier, without depriving him of his sainthood. It made him a fighter who fought, fired only by love, for the oppressed people. He did not need the negative emotion of hatred against the rulers to keep his spirits inflamed. This baptism by the sword was, simultaneously, a recollection in the soul of the infinite power of love, which was enough to meet any amount of fury, hatred and frenzy of the enemy-ruler. The Gurus and their fiery soldiers, like Banda Bairagi, proved in the battles that hatred was not needed to defeat the hatred nurtured by the enemy in his heart.

Kudarat: *Kudarat* is the creative power of *Waheguru* (God). It has also been called his body. *Kudarat* remains one with God, and gets separated from him only when he wills creation. She acts to fulfill the will for creation of the *Waheguru*. Apart from his wish she has no other wish. *Kudarat* in Sikhism is not Maya, which some Indian systems have confused with *Prakriti*. *Maya* is the trickster, i.e. the power that traps the individual soul and prevents its meeting with *Waheguru*.

Kudrat is not illusion. It is the material reality, which is as much real as the spiritual reality. It can be likened to the Thing-in-Itself of Kant.

Kudarat is not only the spirit that transforms into matter. It is also the beauty, sound and scent of nature that is all around us. It is the moonlight, the majestic Himalayas and the deep and cool deodar wood. The intellect cannot understand *Kudarat*. It is only the wondering eye that can have some intimations of *Kudarat*. "The intellect can only create mathematical models of reality, *Kudarat*, that need not represent her". This is what Stephen Hawking expects the intellect of the scientists and the mathematicians to do. He advises that they should not bother if their models do not agree with reality. From the Guru's point of view, a mathematical model that does not agree with reality is a clever and useful deviation that can never take the seeker of truth to Truth. *Kudarat* might be material and entirely different from Truth the *Waheguru* (the Wonderful Real), but the way to reach Truth and Reality lies in creating an intellectual model of *Kudarat* that agrees with *Kudarat*, i.e. the material reality, the universe. Deviation from *Kudarat* may bring scientific advancement, and enhance the ability to manipulate matter amazingly. But it will also produce side effects, like agitating the universe and creating disturbing ideas in the mind that force the scientists to abuse their ability and destroy both humanity and the universe. This abuse is no sign of excellence for which the scientist can congratulate himself. The scientist, no doubt, has the ability to abuse the universe, by applying his theory about a facet of it, out of greed, pride or anger, and causing catastrophic imbalances in it, like tsunami, heating of the earth, jungle fires, global dimming and global warming. This rampant abuse by science which prides in its ignorance of the nature of Nature, can turn the world warmer by 10^0 within a century. This abuse has been possible only because of God's will to grant total freedom to man in his dealings with God's creation. If man wants to destroy the universe, God does not interfere. He wants man to develop his sense of responsibility also along with rise in his knowledge. Pursuit of a scientific model of reality that does not represent the real universe is like forcing nature into a Procrustean bed. It results ultimately in deviation from Truth. The scientific truth can ill afford to ignore – what he would like to call – the imaginative Truth of the Rishi.

Langar: *Langar* is the kitchen attached to the Gurudwaras, i.e. the Sikh temples, created by the Gurus. It provides food to all the worshippers, as an immediate gift of God to his children. A parallel of this practice is the Christian practice of offering bread and wine to the devotee as a gift of Christ.

Mahat: *Mahat* is primordial matter. It is the subtlest form of matter, out of which all the subtle forms of matter (like the mind and the ego, beauty, scent, tastes, word etc.), and the gross forms of matter (like earth, water, fire, air and space) evolve. *Mahat* is the first material transformation of God's invisible power called Nature. Though material, *Mahat* is that form of matter which is subtler than both the subtle and the gross forms of matter.

Manmukh: *Manmukh* is the tendency to run after a wayward mind. It aims at pleasure, not truth. For the sake of a closer understanding, it can be identified with hedonism.

Masands: *Masands* were the police of the Gurus. The *Masands* were entrusted the duty to maintain law and order in the large gatherings of the Gurus, which children, women and laymen also attended. The *Masands* checked the outside elements too that might be on the look out to create disturbances in those gatherings.

Maya: Overstatement and understatement of truth both are *Maya*. *Maya* is not the universe and living beings created by God. They become *Maya* only when man with the help of his over-smart mental powers - like cunning, meanness, betrayal, exploitation and ungratefulness - manipulates his own character and the characters of others. A truth made more effective by isolating it from the whole of truth, and by dramatizing or sentimentalizing it, is also the work of *Maya*. Though *Maya* uses the creations of Nature (*Kudarat, Prakriti*), it drives truth out of them, and installs falsehood instead. *Maya* has the dexterity to create lies out of truth and sins out of virtues. Only he conquers *Maya* who exercises the discipline that reverses the cunning of *Maya*, and recreates Nature (*Kudarat/Prakriti*) out of *Maya*. It is not creating *Prakriti* literally, since *Prakriti* has already been created by God. It is in fact, liberating *Prakriti* from the glittering prisons of *Maya*. Nobody can realize God who does not know the art of separating *Maya* from *Prakriti*. It is only after achieving their separation that the seeker realizes that *Maya* was born of Nothingness, since on getting separated from *Prakriti*, *Maya* which looked formidable earlier, quietly disappears into Nothingness from which it had sprung.

Nad Anahad: *Nad Anahad* is the soundless word of *Waheguru* that is resonating in the universe, in every atom, in the veins and in the mind of man, and, in its most exquisite form, in the heart of man.

Nama-Yoga: *Nama-Yoga* is another name for *Sahaj*, i.e. the simple way to realize God. Literally it means getting united with the name of God. It helps since God's name is the ship that takes the devotee safely across the turbulent sea of life. Remembering the name of God in the heart regularly gives the seeker entry inside God's name. The word is the essence of creation, while God's name is the essence of the word. All creation, animate and inanimate, emanates from word. One who keeps remembering the name of God enters God's name. Several saints in India have reported the miracle that happened to them while remembering God and repeating His name during meditation, happiness and suffering, in short, under all conditions. They experienced as if they had entered God's name. Simply repeating God's name is their style of meditation. It is an established practice of the devotees of many sects. It is not the path of knowing and loving God intellectually – a path that many philosophers, like Spinoza and Kant followed. It is the path of experiencing God as immediacy, directly and immediately through the faculty of sensation. Devotees have experienced that sincere repetitions of God's name are born of the same rhythm – Om – that creates and pervades creation. Repetition of God's name unites through *Viniyoga* the rhythm of one's own individual existence with the rhythm of the universe. This union of inner and outer vibrations opens the inner eye, and the devotee starts sensing the infinite sweetness, compassion and wisdom of God. Such a lucky one has no use for intellectually knowing God, since intellect establishes the duality of the knower and the known, while repetition of his name makes him a feeling that dissolves all traces of duality. God becomes a feeling of the devotee that pervades his entire personality and makes his own being a part of this all pervasive feeling.

Sikhism believes that God is not indifferent to the quest of the seeker. Rather he walks towards the seeker several steps for one true step taken by the seeker towards God. The twenty-four variations of nature that unite almost magically to form one's body, and also the apparatus of sensing and knowing, are born of the Word, and are ever present in subtle forms in the Word. One who enters inside God's name experiences there such ecstasy and joy that he finds sexual pleasure a disturbance, not a pleasant diversion. Lust cannot tempt such a person. He/She has no use for the path of indulgence, pleasure and forgetfulness. The ship of the name of God, according to the Gurus, takes a lover of God to God faster than any other vehicle that the intellectual uses to reach him. The word is the subtlest tanmatra out of the five tanmatras. The right use of the word can take one to the zenith of heavens i.e. absolute freedom (*Moksha*). The word Rama is the smallest thing that is larger than the universe, according to the Gurus. One who enters this name has no use for any other discipline.

Nishkam Karma: *Nishkam Karma* is unmotivated action. It does not mean that it has no objective. The difference is that the objective is neither premeditated nor motivated. It is the action of the free soul that has attained synchronicity with Truth, the *Waheguru*, so that it spontaneously does only what is best to do in a given situation. It is the action born as naturally of a free soul as the bud is born of a twig.

Purusha, Nirankar Purusha, Akaal Purusha/ Purakh, Nirankar Alepa: These are the various names by which Sikhs remember God. Each of these names represents some special attribute of God. And yet the list is inexhaustible. It includes other names of God – Ram, Krishna, Govinda, Hari and still many others. The Sikh view of God can neither be confined to the tradition of devotees who see divine attributes in him nor can it be confined to the tradition of those who see him abstract and formless, beyond all attributes. A Sikh has full freedom to choose his God in accordance with the atmosphere of his heart. It is the atmosphere of the heart of the individual that creates his God in the form that gives it courage and joy. The *Waheguru* is the Absolute that includes all the divine attributes and is yet Wonderful, since the attributes do not define him. They do not touch even his fringes.

Pragya: *Pragya* is not a faculty of knowledge which is commonly available in people. It grows in the true seeker of truth, only after he/ she has sincerely and fully pursued the discipline of disinterested reason and prayer. The discipline does not consist only of learning the correct use of intellect. It also consists of overcoming the arrogance of the intellect, and of awakening the inherent ability in the intellect to recognize its limit. Only the seeker whose intellect has developed this ability can hope for the birth of *Pragya* in his mind, which satisfies all the three dimensions of man – reason, love and devotion.

Priya-Bhava: *Priya-Bhava* is a women's unconditional and exclusive love for her lover. She does not contemplate whether he is worthy of such love or not. Contemplation of the worthiness of the lover precedes love. It is done until love is born. To contemplate the character of the lover after the birth of love only corrupts love. The woman turns vengeful. The vengefulness turns her attention to other men. It is here that lust imprisons her love, and pollutes its purity. It is because love is blind to the qualities of manhood, only because it is awake to the qualities of the soul. It has no eye for the qualities of the mind and heart of a man, since true love, being born of the soul, can see only the qualities of the immortal thing in man, i.e. his soul. It is blind to the mortal qualities of the mind, the heart, or the manhood of her lover. Priya-Bhava is not confined to women. It is the discipline of true love. Every true lover, whether man or woman, has to develop it. Mixing love with intellectual comprehension is the fastest way of corrupting love.

It is essential to note that when the Gurus talk of the loving and pining woman, they are in fact, talking of the soul, not of woman or the female sex. In their terminology, all the souls, whether lodged in men's bodies or women's, are females, and the only male is the Soul, i.e. the *Waheguru*. They expect of every man too – not only woman – cultivation of *Priya-Bhava*. The Gurus call their own souls females, loving and pining for the only male, i.e. the *Waheguru*.

The Gurus' view of love's proverbial blindness is entirely different than what common people and sentimental poets make of it. It is in fact, no blindness but an enlightened sight. True love, according to them, opens the eyes of the soul, and shuts the wayward eyes of the body.

Another important distinction to be borne in mind, while discussing love and the *Priya-Bhava* of the Gurus, is that it has no undertones or overtones of sex. It has nothing of the mystery and holiness attached by modern psychologists to sex. Far from mixing sex with love as its inevitable part, the Gurus maintain that unless pining for love and pining for sex are treated as two entirely opposite emotions, love, instead of uniting with God, would be smoothing the passage to hell.

This view would become clearer if we pay attention to the fact that the Gurus specify that the *Priya-Bhava*, essential for uniting with the *Waheguru*, belongs only to the virgin who has no taste for lust. The soul has to cultivate this kind of love that does not stop pining even on attainment. The feeling of attainment in love in ignorant worldly couples, comes from duality and sexual gratification. However, fulfillment comes to the soul only after the individual soul and the Soul i.e. God become one through *Viniyoga*. This union of the imperfect and the perfect, the soul and God, is possible only through *Viniyoga* - the discipline of unity that unites opposites. *Viniyoga* unites opposites, while likes are united by Yoga. Opposites unite only when they make self-sacrifices unto each other and practice *Atmayagya*. It is *Viniyoga* alone that unites a warrior like Arjun or Guru Gobind Singh with God, the Merciful. The Sikh heaven is imagined as full of warriors pining for the love of God even in heaven, like the milkmaids of Virindavan pining for Krishna, in spite of meeting him every day. The pining is important since it is the only emotion that keeps the soul awake against satiation and heavenly sloth.

Rama-Nama: *Rama* is one of the names of God like many others such as *Waheguru, Akaal Purakh, Niranjan, and Nirankar Alepa*. A devotee who sincerely repeats the name of *Rama* in his heart enters the ship of God's name (discussed above) that takes through the high tides of this world straight to the Lord. *Rama-Nama* is, therefore, an aspect of *Nama-Yoga*.

Riddhis: *Riddhis* are divine graces that come to a true seeker of Truth or God. They could be spiritual beauty, charisma, irresistible charm, magnetism, the power to make a poor man rich even if his karma do not warrant it, the power to forecast, or the power to grant undeserved blessings to flatterers. The Ridelhis i.e. graces are devoid of spiritual pride or self-consciousness, and flow from the simple gestures or wish of the seeker of truth. All the Indian disciplines agree that only he/ she realizes God who does not get fascinated by the graces, the *Riddhis*. Humbleness, born of non-identification with such spiritual and supernatural graces that come spontaneously to a true seeker, is essential for realizing God or Truth. One cannot avoid *Riddhis*, but one can always avoid seeing them as one's own powers when grateful beneficiaries start revering him as the source of those graces. If he acknowledges their compliments, he gets corrupted. The soul of the true seeker sacrifices itself to the *Riddhis* and gets constantly reborn of them, and does not forget that, even though they flow from him spontaneously, they are God's powers, not his. Such a soul passes the final test, and qualifies to meet the beloved *Waheguru*.

Sachkhand: Even such a perfect inner world as the Karamkhand is not for the seeker to dwell for long. His inner world evolves further into *Sachkhand*, where only the blossomed, selected souls reside. Not even the uncaused spontaneous joy that springs from a hundred hidden brooks in his heart can hold him back. Now the fire in his heart is the fire of the pure virgin. The pining beloved, his soul, is now restless and impatient to meet her lover, the *Waheguru*. It can rest with nothing lesser now. There is no psychological self here, serving as the medium of union between the soul and the *Waheguru*. The soul is the virgin beloved here who needs no intermediary, and is bent on meeting the Beloved alone, come what may. The dark night and the raging storm and all the wild beasts of the jungle cannot frighten and prevent her from venturing alone on such a terrible journey.

Sadguru: *Sadguru* means the true teacher. A true teacher first awakens reverence and awe in the disciple for the teacher, with the specific motive to free him of *haumey* (his ego and libido), and then goes on to utilize his awe and reverence disinterestedly. He utilizes these highly sensitive and effective channels - awe and reverence - only to transmit true knowledge and love of God. He transmits through these intimate channels also the knowledge of the divine art practiced by God to do and yet to remain the non-doer. The disciple thus learns how to be a ferocious soldier who routes the enemy and yet the karma of killing does not taint his soul. It is the art of sacrificing all the karma, and their fruits too, to God. It is only detachment from fruits too, not only karma, that makes him the doer-non-doer, the ideal state of mind that Arjun had attained. Only a disinterested warrior of this extreme type can be called a soldier of God. He is not a soldier of God who kills those who do not believe in his concept of God, and who makes himself the decision as to who deserves to live and who does not, and yet deludes himself that he is a servant of God. He is a servant of his own will, and also of his pride that deludes him to call his own will the will of God.

The *Sadguru* passes on the most difficult knowledge to the disciple of attaining oneness with God through action/karma, utilizing the intimate psychological channels, newly opened by the aroused awe and reverence for the *Sadguru*. The true teacher (*Sadguru*) then diverts the awe and reverence of the disciple to God, and does not keep them attached to him (the Sadguru). A teacher who does not free the disciple after giving him the knowledge, and who does not divert the disciple's awe and reverence to God, ruins himself and the disciple both. Diverting the disciple's emotions of awe and reverence to God is crucial, because only this self-sacrifice makes the disciple aware that these channels are not meant to be used by anybody, however elevated, except God. It is only when the *Sadguru* diverts these channels to God that the disciple knows that, strictly speaking, the Sadguru had abused these channels. This abuse deserves forgiveness since it was done temporarily and that too only for the disciple's enlightenment. Unfortunately, many teachers in the times of Nanak would simply not give up the lure of the cozy elevation that they enjoyed by living permanently in these intimate channels of the souls of their disciples. They did not realize that this lure had blocked their own and their disciples' passage to enlightenment. Staying there longer than the immediate need only hastens the doom of the disciple and the teacher both. That was why

Nanak sanctified the word *Sadguru* to differentiate, for the benefit of the seekers, between the true and the false teacher.

The *Sadguru*, i.e. the true teacher, is always careful that the disciple treats God, the *Waheguru*, as his ultimate teacher. The true teacher is careful that the disciple treats his earthly Guru only as his intermediary Guru or the midwife. The true teacher has the disinterestedness of the Buddha, who had the freedom and courage to tell his disciple Ananda, who remained attached to the Buddha till the end: "You Ananda could not attain enlightenment because you remained attached to me".

Sahaj: *Sahaj* in Sikhism is not the same as Sahaj in Tantra. Sahaj in Tantra is a complex system of rituals and practices. In Sikhism it is the simple path of love and devotion to God and the Gurus. It does not involve rituals and could be as simple as remembering the name of God, serving humanity and fighting for the honor and safety of women, and children, or upholding the cause of the oppressed against the oppressor. One may not be learned or distinguished in any manner, if one has love and a simple heart, devoid of deception and cunning, he is sure to attain salvation. Devotion and submission to the path of the Gurus forbids condemnation of other faiths. The Gurus would call it religious indecency to call others, who follow some other faith, infidel. Those who characterize others as infidels, according to the Gurus, might reach hell earlier than an ordinary thief. Religious arrogance is the opposite of the path of love and service, since it rushes in where angels fear to tread.

Sangat: The word in Sikhism for a gathering of the lovers of *Waheguru* (God) is *Sangat*.

Sat: *Sat* means the existent while *Asat* means the non-existent, the illusory, the false and the fictitious. *Sat* includes God, liberation, *Kudarat* and the individual soul. True emotions like love, compassion, bravery, courage and kindness are also *Sat,* since they form part of God's virtues. Those who cultivate true emotions create strong ferries that can ferry through the deluge itself to take the devotee to God. At the same time those who cultivate negative emotions, like envy, hatred, greed, lechery, arrogance, bullying, violence and stupidity raise thorns in the field of their lives. They indeed create their journey through life difficult, and their journey after death disillusioning.

Satvik, Rajasik and Tamsik: Nature is seen by the Gurus as the interplay of three cosmic powers - *Satvik, Rajasik* and *Tamasik*. The English equivalents of these three words are: sublime, ameliorative and destructive. These three powers are present in every object of Nature. At any point of time one of them is generally active while the other two are hidden. They stay together. The other two may be present actually, virtually or in hiding, but all the three are always together. They are three friends that fight, try to oust each other, and yet love to stay close to one another. All the three are always in commotion. Darwin had seen the rampantly violent face of Nature that brooks no sentiment. To Darwin nature is the diversification of a single life-force - which is preponderantly dark - into several species. The species are running wild; some to eat up others, and, if possible, to wipe out them, while others are running to save themselves. Only those survive that have the cunning to change their shape or color, while running, so that they become indistinguishable from the stones or other uneatable objects. Quite contrarily, Tennyson had seen nature as an organized reality, in which 'the old order changeth giving place to new'. Wordsworth's view of nature was different from both Darwin and Tennysen. Wordsworth saw the third face of nature that was serene and sublime.

Kapil, the philosopher of Nature, and the Sikh Gurus would call Darwin's view of nature not the view of nature, but his view of one of the forces of nature. There are two more forces of nature, and all the three live simultaneously. One of the two remaining forces is entirely devoid of panic and violence. It is serene and sublime. Those who live in this force of nature do not indulge in the struggle for survival. Still they survive. They survive because they do not struggle for their own survival. They care only for the survival of others. They survive due to a spiritual law that is experienced only by those who can rise to live in this elevated life-force. This spiritual law says that they that live not for their own survival, but for the survival of the weaker ones, survive by the will of God, for God intervenes and protects them. Such noble men are very dear to God who do not fear death to save those humble and weak ones, who love to live no lesser, but are too humble and weak to protect themselves.

Darwin's theory has acquired the status of being scientific. But if science means dispassionate observation of facts, the remaining two theories of nature are no lesser scientific. Apart from the ruthless Darwinian killer-fighter life-force, there is the self-bestowing, sublime life-force that we find generally in the parents of all species. The Gurus say that the sun does not burn to enjoy itself. It burns to give light to others. The trees do not eat their fruits. They fruit for others. The rivers do not drink their water. They run from place to place to quench the thirst of others. Apart from these two forces in nature, one ruthless and the other tender, self-bestowing and sublime, there is one more life-force available in nature. This third life-force is the global life-force of civilization and culture. It is surviving along side of the Darwinian struggle for survival - a life-force, which has found its extreme manifestation in the religious extremists, who are men preying upon men.

Goethe saw Nature as the life-force that creates culture and civilization, and helps humanity to come out of darkness. Wordsworth saw Nature in the self-bestowing and other sublime virtues. Darwin saw Nature in the heartless and obscene struggle for selfish self-survival. The Sikh Gurus would say that none of these three views of the life-force is wrong. Yet each is only over-emphasizing one of the three forces of Nature, as if it were the whole.

The true Sikh brings these three forces of Nature in a state of equilibrium, and walks past them. He transcends Nature and stands before the *Nirankar Alepa*. The souls of the followers of the Sikh Gurus are asked to transcend all the three forces of nature. The soul can transcend nature only by sacrificing itself to all its three forces, and getting reborn of them. To live by any of the three is to invite, indirectly, the remaining two too. Those who live by nature reduce their lives to battlefields for all her three forms. This was the common message of the Sikh Gurus, and the ancient *rishis* and visionaries of India.

All these three forms of Nature are present inside human nature too. The Sikh does not get attached to any of them. He reveres these three forces in his nature equally as three mothers, and brings them to a state of equilibrium through *Atmayagya*. He thus transcends them to meet the Creator, who is beyond action and inaction. The God of Sikhism is the *Akarta-Karta*, who creates through *Kudarat*. He separates *Kudarat* from himself. He is *Nirankar* the Absolute, but *Alepa*, i.e. uninvolved. He creates the universe, and yet does not get directly involved in the act of creation.

Human life, according to Sikhism, is no whim or play of God. God does not make sport of man. Life is an opportunity to evolve and become like God. *Waheguru* gives this opportunity to every soul, not only once but again and again, in the form of repeated births. He wants the souls to develop all his virtues, like infinite and unconditioned love, wisdom and compassion. He wants the souls to get identified with him through the sweet pangs of love. It is the sweet pang of love that alone has the ability to come closer to *Waheguru* and know his nature. Waheguru's nature cannot be called nature in the sense in which the word 'nature' has been used hitherto.

Siddhis: The spiritual powers that come to a true seeker of God as temptations met on the road are called *Siddhis*. All Indian spiritual systems are unanimous on the point that the true seekers should shun the spiritual powers (*Siddhis*), because, in spite of being divine, they take the seeker away from God. They start coming to the seeker of God, unasked for. They are the spiritual temptations that lure away many seekers. The weak souls get fascinated by them and succumb to the power of creating miracles that the *Siddhis* grant.

Tanmatras: The five essences - smell, taste, looks, touch and word - are called *tanmatras*. They are the essences of the five elements, each residing inside its corresponding element, respectively, earth, water, fire, wind and space. The *tanmatras* assemble in different combinations to create all the attractive things on earth.

Tirthankaras: The twenty-four fully blossomed and enlightened Gurus of Jains are called Tirthankaras. They are distinguished for having liberated their souls of all negative emotions, like violence, anger, hatred, fear, envy, lust, pride and greed. The Jains believe that true knowledge is impossible to attain without freeing the soul of negative emotions. Apart from these 24 Tirthankaras, Jains believe that there are twenty Tirthankaras residing in some sort of Shangri-La (Videh Ksetra), accessible to souls living on earth that are unenlightened but are keen on enlightenment. The souls, thirsty for enlightenment but prisoners of doubts, can reach this Shangri-La to consult these illustrious twenty liberated and compassionate Gurus to get rid of their doubts. No Indian system gives the absolute status to skepticism as the only guarantor of true knowledge, unlike some Western philosophers, most of whom crowded only the twentieth century.

Vyavaharik and Parmarthik: The Indian philosophical thinking and living recognizes two meanings of the same "word" and "discipline", since in practice every idea or discipline loses some of its purity. Actions pull down every concept. It is inherent in human personality that the purity of its contemplation can never be translated wholly into practice. While turning the idea into action, much of its beauty and purity get lost.

The Gurus wanted their disciples not to get disheartened by this inevitability and not to take it for a defect of their character. Many *Siddhas* and learned men of India, in the times of the Gurus, had developed a dread of action, only because it did not translate into a deed the purity and perfection of an idea. They had started fearing this inability as a defect of their character. They feared that, since their rendering of an idea into action could not be as pure as the idea, if they translated their lofty ideas into action, it would add to their scroll of bad karma. This inhibition had taken them away from a life of action, and the people were getting deprived of their lofty way of practicing their noble ideas in their practical lives. The Gurus told their disciples that there was nothing to be ashamed of in the difference between an idea in the mind and the same idea in practice. They assured them that the comparative impurity in their deeds was not due to any defect in their character, but due to the inherent law of nature that the idea of a thing is purer than a rendering of it in action. They called its mental form, practised to attain Nirvana, *Paramarthik,* and its practical form, i.e. the rendering of the idea into action in society, to make it better, *Vyavaharik.*

The Gurus taught that an action or idea could have two objectives. If the objective was union of the soul with *Waheguru,* contemplation and action both were *Paramarthik.* If the motive was amelioration of the social and political life of the people, both contemplation and action were *Vyavaharik.*

Waheguru: *Waheguru* to the Sikh Gurus is what the Absolute is to Western Philosophy (Hegel, Bradley, Basanquet and others), and *Brahm* to Vedanta philosophy in India. *Waheguru* means "the wonderful God". The Sikh view of the Absolute as the Wonderful is aimed at reminding the seeker that the Absolute is beyond knowledge. Whatever the seeker knows about the Absolute/God falls always short of God. There are many of his attributes that remain outside the seeker's knowledge. Perfect knowledge, too, cannot comprehend him. Only artless love can. The catch in it is that while love can comprehend but cannot describe him, mere knowledge can neither comprehend nor describe him.

Waheguru includes and transcends every thing that comes within the range of human experience. Death of God, a suffering God, and the disappearance of God have been announced by certain prophets and intellectuals. These are only facets of God that men experience in extraordinary circumstances, according to Sikhism. But the facets of God, so experienced by highly evolved souls, do not belong to God. If Nietzsche experienced the death of God on seeing a mercilessly beaten horse on a street of Turin - a sight that aroused his pity and hopelessness beyond endurance – it was a true experience of his, but not the truth about God. His agonized wail 'God is dead' has no validity for a Sikh, since *Waheguru* (God) is beyond human experience, and is untouched by what man experiences about him. God cannot die, because God's death is a facet of God that man can experience, but a facet of God is not God. Death cannot contain God, since death is one of his facets, and all facets of God fail to contain him. All his facets disappear in the presence of God. He is *Nirankar*

Alepa, i.e. unrelated to his facets. He is the Wonderful *Waheguru*, and no facet can contain the Wonder that God is.

It is all right for a prophet, like Moses, to have experienced the disappearance of God more than 2000 years ago. But that does not mean that God has disappeared, since *Waheguru* appears in many forms and disappears, but resides in none. He cannot be contained in mystery or revelation either. He is ever new, over and above all his facets, and is the Wonder of wonders, even for mystery.

Waheguru is not wrathful. He does not send calamities to kill his sinful children. He is ever helpful to those who seek his help, and ever kind even to those who do not seek him. He is untouched by man's reverence or lack of it. Even the atheist cannot escape him for he is beyond being and non being.

Index